Improving Student Memory

D. Herrmann
National Center for Health Statistics, Hyattsville, MD
D. Raybeck
Hamilton College, Clinton, NY
D. Gutman
Cognitive Associates, Clinton, NY

Improving Student Memory

Hogrefe & Huber Publishers
Seattle · Toronto · Göttingen · Bern

Library of Congress Cataloging-in-Publication Data

Herrmann, Douglas J.
Improving student memory / by Douglas Herrmann, Douglas Raybeck, Dan Gutman
  p. cm.
  Includes bibliographical references and index.
  ISBN 0-88937-093-1
1. Mnemonics. 2. Study, Method of. I. Raybeck, Douglas.
II. Gutman, Dan. III. Title.
BF385.H447   1996   153.1'4—dc20   91-43049 CIP

Canadian Cataloguing in Publication Data

Herrmann, Douglas J.
  Improving student memory
Includes bibliographical references and index.
ISBN 0-88937-093-1
1. Memory. 2. Study, Method of. I. Raybeck, Douglas.
II. Gutman, Dan. III. Title.
BF385.H47   1996   153.1'4   C92-093252-5

First printing
Copyright © 1993 by Hogrefe & Huber Publishers
Second printing
Copyright © 1996 by Hogrefe & Huber Publishers

P. O. Box 2487, Kirkland, WA 98083-2487
12–14 Bruce Park Ave., Toronto, Ontario M4P 2S3

Printed in Germany

ISBN 0-88937-093-1
Hogrefe & Huber Publishers, Seattle • Toronto • Bern • Göttingen

Table of Contents

Preface

This book presents the latest and best approach to the improvement of memory and study skills. It is based in part on a popular-press book, SuperMemory (Rodale Press, 1990; written by Doug Herrmann with the assistance of Dan Gutman), and on innovations in teaching study skills developed by Herrmann and Doug Raybeck.

Improving Student Memory may be used like a textbook as part of a concerted effort to study and improve your memory, or it may be used like a dictionary to find ways to cope with particular memory problems. In either case, study skills are like any skill (athletic, mechanical, occupational, and so on) — they are improved only through study and practice. Thus, the usefulness of this book will be directly related to how much you learn initially and how often you subsequently apply and practice what you learn to problems as they arise.

Two assumptions are fundamental to the approach taken here. First, improvement of study skills requires consideration of all modes of psychological functioning. This assumption contrasts with that of the traditional approach, which relies primarily, if not exclusively, on improving skills through mental activities only.

Second, skill improvement requires extensive preparation that is specific to particular courses and tasks within courses. This assumption contrasts as well with the traditional approach, which recommends the acquisition of a few techniques that are supposedly applicable — like a miracle drug — to any and all courses.

The new approach recognizes that some techniques are broadly applicable, but it emphasizes task-specific methods as the best preparation for difficult course problems. Since the new approach is theoretically based, it explains how the methods of memory improvement may be tailored to those problems an individual most desires to address.

Educators will discover new methods here that have previously remained buried or merely implicit in the literature.

Preface for Teachers

We wrote this book to serve as a primary text for a course on study skills. However, it may also prove useful for courses in psychology of memory, psychology of cognition, educational psychology, and in courses designed to orient students to college life and its expectations.

One aspect of student psychology probably has endured over the years. Students generally prefer to enjoy life rather than to work hard. With few exceptions, they study only as much as necessary to achieve their academic goals, be they As, Bs or Cs. Today, however, the general nature of the study situation has changed. As is true for others in this society, the pace of student life has altered dramatically. Many students are engaged in extracurricular pursuits, social demands, and even employment that impinges upon their study time. Students who wish to be successful have no choice: they must become more efficient and, as their lives continue to change, they must be willing to learn new techniques to enhance their efficiency.

A great deal of the advice in current books devoted to study skills is similar to that offered decades ago. Nevertheless, there have been two fundamental changes in our understanding of study skills. Based on laboratory investigations, we now have a much better sense of the particular advantages of certain study practices, and we have a greater appreciation of the interrelationship between physical/emotional health and mental acuity. We can supply students with specific recommendations concerning their study habits and memory performance, and we can indicate the degree to which these specifics can improve their skills.

Science now possesses a significantly enhanced understanding of the interdependence of memory and the general operation of the mind. Memory performance is now seen as linked to a person's entire psychology. Knowledge of learning techniques and test taking skills is no longer sufficient. The brain is a biological entity and its functioning depends on both physiological and psychological factors. Successful students will appreciate the interrelationship between performance and physical/emotional well-being, and they will adopt habits that promote the former by addressing the latter.

This book explains the scientific reasons for the advice it advances. It describes the manner in which memory performance depends on one's entire psychology and on a better management of oneself, one's memory processes, and one's time. We have endeavored to ground each abstraction in concrete examples and, where appropriate, we have supplied evidence concerning our recommendations, as well as the reasoning behind them. We wanted our recommendations to be accessible, but we also wanted them to convey the import that derives from well founded research.

We believe students respond better to recommendations that they find credible, and that integrate with knowledge and perspectives that they already possess, or are in the process of acquiring. Thus, we believe you can further enhance the memory and study skills of your students by relating some of the specifics in this text to other findings and theories you may be discussing in class. Also, we would suggest that students already possess considerable experience with study situations and with examples of both successful and failed attempts at memory retrieval. In our years of teaching at Hamilton College and at the University of Maryland, we encouraged students to generate examples from their own lives to illustrate different aspects of memory processing. We found that students who did so were more likely to remember the material. Further, memory skills tend to become incorporated into student repertoires once:

– students come to their own realization that a certain practice works
– other students convince them that this is true
– they realize that their memory skills promote faster and more detailed learning of both academic and non-academic materials

– they realize that by improving memory skills they enhance their attractiveness to employers.

As you have probably observed in other contexts, students work more diligently when they appreciate the applicability of the material they are encountering. Many students are aware that they will change careers several times throughout their life and they should be able to appreciate the importance of being well equipped with basic, important and general skills. It is worth stressing that memory is one of the fundamental skills that enable people to cope with the new responsibilities and tasks of a rapidly changing world. Like other basic skills, such as reading, public speaking, and quantitative reasoning, memory skills will make students more effective in their private lives and in their careers.

Acknowledgements

We are grateful to our families for their encouragement and support while working on this project. In addition, we are grateful to students who used draft versions of the text in years past and, therefore, also played an important role in the text's development. Finally, thanks are due to Charlie Gerras, Michael Gruneberg, Michael Pressley, and Herb Weingartner whose encouragement helped considerably in the completion of this text.

Chapter 1
Scientific Background

The modern approach to memory and studying has evolved out of a variety of disciplines. As described at the outset of this chapter, systematic techniques for learning and remembering were first developed over two thousand years ago. Since then, these techniques were further refined by training people to improve their memory and study skills.

Around the turn of the century, scientific psychology began tackling the issue of how to learn and study. In the past few decades, this topic has been examined by a variety of scientists drawn from such areas as educational psychology, clinical psychology, psychiatry, neurology, gerontology, cognitive rehabilitation (brain damaged individuals with Alzheimer's disease, chronic alcoholism, auto-industrial accidents, wounded military), and human engineering (innovations in devices to assist impaired or normal cognition).

In some research, the knowledge about how to improve learning and remembering has come from observing clients or patients; in other investigations, our knowledge has been developed by painstaking, carefully controlled experimentation that focused on learning and remembering. These observational and experimental procedures will be explained at the beginning of the chapters that follow.

Psychological Theory and Studying

For more than 2000 years, students of all varieties and ages have sought to make the chore of studying easier. Consequently, various people have represented themselves as experts capable of changing anyone's memory performance for the better.

In 477 BC, the poet Simonides astounded his contemporaries with his memory. He attended a banquet where a catastrophe occurred. The roof of the banquet hall fell and killed many of those present. In order to notify the next of kin, it was necessary to identify all those who had attended. But it was not possible to do this with the mangled remains of the victims. Simonides solved this problem by recalling the name of every person at the dinner and where each sat. He claimed he was able to remember so easily because during the banquet he had imagined the people in their places at their tables.

Simonides' method came to be called the "method of loci" and was regarded in ancient Greece as *the* way to memorize something. If you lived back then and asked a memory scholar for help, you would have been told that to memorize some pieces of information, put each piece in a different location of a spatial image you have in your mind, such as a banquet table, the rooms of a house, etc. Later, when you want to remember the items, recall your image and it will lead you to them.

Over the years, other methods were derived from the loci procedure. For example, instead of memorizing items by putting them in an image of a place, you might place the items on mental "pegs", like a mental coat rack.

For example, one might memorize a rhymed list like "one is a bun, two is a shoe, three is a tree." This rhyme would then be used to commit to memory some information, such as three things to get at a store (milk, eggs, bread). One would imagine the milk sitting on a bun, some eggs in a shoe, and a loaf of bread hanging from a tree. When the rhyme is later recited, the images should help recall the original items.

The method of loci and other procedures derived from it have been passed down over the centuries as the key skills for studying. Today, as in ancient Greece, these methods are what you are advised to use when you seek to improve your memory skills through memory improvement books and courses.

Unfortunately, the loci-related methods are just about all you get from the numerous systems being offered even today. For various reasons, the memory improvement profession has not kept up with the times. Their memory training has incorporated little or nothing of the new methods of modern science. And to make matters worse, memory improvement books and courses have been given to making extravagant claims about the benefits of the training they offer (Herrmann & Searleman, 1992).

Psychologists, psychiatrists, physicians, and other specialists have sought to develop new methods of memory improvement for several reasons. First, the ancient methods — loci, peg, and others — have been found wanting. These methods are supposed to be generally applicable to any memory task that might confront you. However, research has shown that these techniques are not as general as their proponents might wish.

To begin with, they are not useful for all tasks. They are effective in learning lists, but are less readily applied for more complex material, such as learning a poem, document, or story. And in some situations, such as trying to mentally register someone's face, they are virtually useless.

Moreover, people who have been trained in the use of these methods frequently give them up a short time after learning them. Even psychologists who specialize in remedying memory problems rarely use them, despite having been trained in these techniques (Parks, Smith, & Cavanaugh, 1990; Herrmann, Rea, & Andrzejewski, 1987).

After finding that the ancient methods do not produce permanent memory abilities, many researchers in the past two decades have worked to develop new mental manipulations that are easier and more adaptable. Where ancient methods once monopolized the field, now many kinds of manipulations are being studied and advanced for improving memory performance. A growing knowledge of the different factors that affect memory has led scientists and health-care professionals to look beyond the ancient approaches. Memory can be improved by a variety of techniques which do not involve mental loci, pegs, and other related procedures. An interesting variety of techniques for facilitating a person's attitude, physical condition, mental state, conversational skills, and the use of physical memory aids has been found to reduce memory failures (Herrmann & Searleman, 1990, 1991; Herrmann, Weingartner, Searleman, & McEvoy, 1991; Poon, 1980; Yesavage, Lapp, & Sheikh, 1989).

The Scientific Approach

The scientific approach to study skill improvement requires a basic understanding of how memory techniques work. Rather than offering the single "pill" or a few all-purpose techniques, this book will help you assess the state of your memory, and then address your memory problems with specific activities, which will be called manipulations, that you select from inventories. The sheer number of manipulations you encounter here should suggest to you the importance of specific preparation in all aspects of the memory process.

Until the present, the new scientific approach to memory improvement has been practiced mainly in a small number of universities and colleges, where it has been developed. Virtually every book and commercial course available outside of these centers still relies primarily, if not exclusively, on the methods that originated 2000 years ago. This book provides you with the first account of the new scientific approach in a form available to the general public.

Our intent here is to present you with information and practical guidance for memory improvement based on current scientific knowledge in the field. Recent research has developed many more ways to improve memory ability than existed just a few years ago. While further investigation is needed to refine and balance the methods of the new approach, most scientists espouse a variety of skills and remedies to help your memory.

Our Plan for Improving Your Memory Performance

This book will assist you in improving your ability to study by thoroughly acquainting you with the different ways to manipulate your memory. Chapter 2 will give you an opportunity to evaluate your memory performance and to decide what memory tasks you especially would like to work on. Chapters 3, 4, and 5 will deal with manipulations that prepare you generally for memory tasks, i.e. manipulations of your attitude, condition, and social interactions. Chapters 5 and 6 will discuss environmental and mental manipulations that enhance memory processes directly. Chapter 7 will review how to develop your memory skills and how to use them with savvy. Chapter 8 directly addresses academic memory skills and contains specific practical suggestions for improving your study habits. Finally, Chapter 9 concludes with an explanation of how to prepare repertoires of manipulations that will be particularly suited to dealing with those tasks you find most annoying.

The Memory System

Where is Your Memory

Before you can choose the best way to improve your memory, you have to know how your memory works. The memory system is located in the brain and the brain stem, at the top of the spinal cord. As with other parts of the brain, the memory system receives information from the senses and sends signals that enable us to respond with speech or gestures (Squire & Butters, 1984; Squire, 1987).

It is well known that different portions of the brain perform different memory functions, and it turns out that a part of the brain stem is involved in registering information into long-term memory. The temporal lobes (the parts of the brain that lie alongside your ears) are also involved in registering memories.

Additionally, different types of memories are located in specific parts of the brain. People who have suffered brain damage in a certain area, as might result from an auto accident, may have great difficulty learning abstract concepts and yet be able to acquire motor skills.

Because the memory system is made of brain tissue, your memory performance is of course directly affected by the state of your brain. Poor health, fatigue, malnourishment, and substance abuse can all lead to lousy memory performance. Thus, one of the most obvious — but often neglected — ways to increase the efficiency of the your memory system is to improve your general physical condition.

Memory Processing

Although many memory functions have been located in the brain, many more functions have not yet been located. Nevertheless, even when it is unclear exactly where certain processes occur in the brain, there is still a good understanding of how memory processes may malfunction.

When memory fails us, it does so in one of three ways. It can fail to register something initially in memory; it can fail to retain over time that which was successfully registered; or it can fail to remember something, despite successful registration and retention (Talland, 1968).

The theory many psychologists advance (e. g. Atkinson & Shiffrin, 1968; Baddeley, 1986; Fodor, 1983; Loftus, 1980; Wilson, 1987) assumes that memory performance is due to a system of several components, each with its own specific job to do (Ellis & Hunt, 1989). Much like a stereo or computer system, each com-

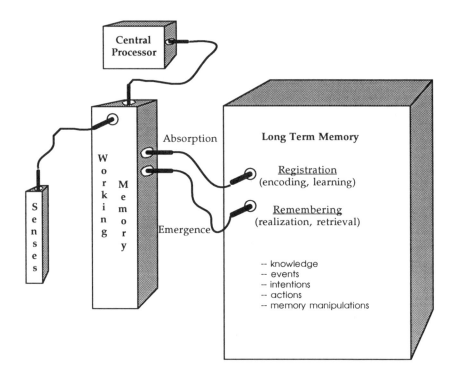

Figure 1.
A schematic of the human memory system.

ponent of the memory system contributes to the overall functioning of the system.

Figure 1 presents a simplified sketch of the functional components of the memory system and their connections. The system consists of four components: the senses, a working memory, a long-term memory, and a central processor. Working memory can contain any perceptions that are picked up by the senses or long-term memories that have just been remembered. The contents of working memory fade in about one minute, unless they are attended to. The central processor controls the amount of attention given to the contents of working memory (Anderson, 1983).

A memory trace is registered according to a basic sequence. Information in the world around us is picked up by the senses and then transferred to working memory. From working memory the information is absorbed into long-term memory.

The remembering of a trace also occurs according to a basic sequence. Once a trace has been registered, thoughts related to the trace information stimulate the trace in long-term memory. When the trace has been sufficiently stimulated, it emerges from long-term memory.

Attention

The single most important aspect of the memory system for improving memory performance is the process of attention. The likelihood that information in working memory will be absorbed or lead certain traces to emerge from long-term memory (Landauer, 1986) depends on how intensely we pay attention to the information in working memory.

Figure 2 illustrates this theoretical relationship. The horizontal axis of the figure pertains to the intensity of attention paid to information in working memory. The vertical axis shows the probability that the information will be absorbed into or emerge from long-term memory.

The figure indicates that the probability of absorption or emergence increases as the intensity of your attention increases. The probability of absorption or emergence is low when the intensity of attention is low.

A low intensity of attention limits the clarity of information that may be absorbed in long-term memory or that may stimulate the emergence of a desired memory from long-term memory. When better attention is paid to working memory, the information is clearer and facilitates absorption or emergence. More and clearer details will be registered in long-term memory, and the likelihood of remembering them later will increase.

Thus, by learning to raise the level of attention, we can enhance the quality of memory performance (Craik & Lockhart, 1972).

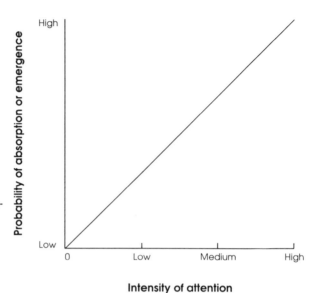

Figure 2.
The theoretical relationship between intensity of attention and the probability of absorption and emergence.

When we pay attention to the contents held in working memory, the level of intensity is not the only aspect that varies. Our attention also varies in relation to different details of the ideas, images, and perceptions being held in working memory. In other words, we pay more attention to some details than to others.

Naturally, those details paid the most attention are more likely to be registered than those we ignore. For example, moviegoers primarily watch the hero or heroine and pay much less attention to supporting actors or the set. When we reflect on the film afterwards, we again attend primarily to the "stars," even though we could focus to less compelling aspects of the film. We select which details of the film that we want to consider and remember more than others.

That is, we distribute our attention at will over the contents of working memory. Those details in working memory that we pay more attention to are more likely to be registered in, and to later emerge from, long-term memory.

The level and the distribution of attention combine to produce the overall amount of attention paid to each detail of a thought in working memory.

For example, your overall level of interest in a film will combine with your interest in certain details (perhaps a compelling performance, an exotic set, or a cute animal in the periphery of a scene).

The distinction between the level and distribution of attention is important to memory improvement because many of the manipulations that you can do to increase the level have no effect on the distribution of attention.

Conversely, many of the manipulations that alter the distribution of attention (by shifting your attention on to certain details in working memory) often have no effect on the overall level of intensity.

Thus, in order to maximize your memory performance, it is necessary for you to learn to use both kinds of manipulations of attention.

The techniques advanced in this book cover both aspects. A good memory requires an ability to set a high level of attention for all memory tasks and to control the distribution of attention. Your chances of registering and remembering information depend on learning ways to focus on the details that are most important and most likely to trigger recall.

The Nature of Memory Tasks

The accuracy and efficiency of your memory system — for both working memory and long-term memory — depends critically on how well your manipulations meet the attentional needs of particular memory tasks that your studying requires. Different tasks have different attentional needs because each task challenges you in different ways (Cohen, 1989).

There are three kinds of characteristics possessed by memory tasks that influence your attention to them and memory performance. These characteristics have to do with the components of memory tasks, the nature of information processed in the memory task, and the demand of the task to perform it intentionally or automatically (Hasher & Zacks, 1971; Shiffrin & Schnieder, 1977).

Components of a Memory Task. Many memory tasks appear to be similar to each other. Learning the name of an historical figure seems similar to learning the name of someone you have just met. But in some way, each memory task is different.

There are essentially five components present in a memory task (Cavanaugh, 1989; Herrmann, Rea, & Andrzejewski, 1988; Herrmann & Searleman, 1990; Herrmann, Weingartner, Searleman, & McEvoy, 1992; McEvoy, 1992; Perlmutter, 1988; Poon, 1980; Searleman & Herrmann, in press).

The first is your condition at the time of the task. Your physical and mental states are always fluctuating. Thus, your physical and mental condition differs from one memory task to another, although the tasks otherwise may seem similar. You may try to learn a name when in a cheerful state of mind and, subsequently, try to learn a name while tired and a bit down. You can see that the success at learning the name in the two situations will likely differ.

An important part of your mental condition is your attitude towards performance of a memory task. A positive or negative attitude about your performance for memory tasks in general and for the task that confronts you will affect your desire to perform the task. A positive or negative attitude will also affect how hard you try at a task. A positive attitude will lead you to attempt the project. A negative attitude may lead you to avoid it.

Your attitude will also affect the efficiency and accuracy of your performance of a memory task. A positive attitude will dispose you to perform quickly and correctly. A negative attitude may cause you to perform slowly and to make errors.

The second component has to do with whether you perform the task by yourself or in a social context. The presence of others often inspires us to try harder at memory tasks. Moreover, the presence of others often imposes memory tasks that simply do not arise when we are alone. For example, it is important to remember another's accomplishments and pet causes (as well as to remember not to mention another's failures).

The third component of a memory task pertains to the physical environment where the task occurs. Certain objects, signs, and visual patterns can activate memories far better than related ideas or thoughts. The same is true for certain sounds and odors.

Additionally, there are a large number of commercial products that are produced and sold explicitly as aids to memory. Alarms will remind you far better than you can remind yourself, for example, that you need to start studying for an upcoming exam.

The fourth component pertains to the mental requirements of a memory task. A memory task may require you to process a small amount of information or a great deal. The information may be unfamiliar or well known to you. It may be presented to you at a slow or a rapid rate. Thus, some tasks favor effective mental processes while other tasks make it likely that your memory presses will not be effective.

The last characteristic of memory tasks important to attention is intentionality. Memory performance depends on whether we perform a task intentionally or incidentally while pursuing other activities (Rock & Gutman, 1981).

When we perform memory tasks intentionally we deliberately direct our attention to that which we wish to register or remember. When we perform memory tasks incidentally, our attention is free to wander and we register or remember without conscious awareness of whatever we pay attention to, despite not intending to do so (Druckman & Swets, 1988).

During registration, our long-term memory continually absorbs some of whatever is in working memory (Landauer, 1986). In an incidental memory task, registration consists of absorption without any conscious influence. Registration in an incidental memory task is called encoding.

In an intentional memory task, registration consists of absorption that is deliberately influenced by directing attention to certain contents. Registration in an intentional task is called, universally, learning.

Learning may be conceived as encoding plus intentional manipulations. The distinction between learning and encoding is of considerable practical importance. Learning, on average, will result in a more detailed memory trace than encoding because we normally pay more attention to things we intend to learn than to things we only encode. Learning is more likely to result also in a useful memory than encoding because we are more likely to register what will be useful when we learn than when we encode.

During remembering, traces in our long-term memory are stimulated by the world around us to emerge into working memory (Harris & Wilkins, 1982). In an incidental memory task, remembering consists of emergence without any conscious influence. This type of remembering is called realizing. In an intentional memory task, remembering is deliberately influenced by directing attention to certain contents in the working memory. This type of remembering is called retrieval. Retrieval may be conceived as realizing plus emergence produced by intentional manipulations.

The distinction between retrieval and realizing is of practical importance as well. We are more likely to remember information, on average, when our recall is based on retrieval than when it based on realizing because we normally remember more when we intend to do so than when we do not. Retrieval is more likely to result in useful information than realizing since retrieval deliberately goes after certain memories whereas realizing occurs without a purpose.

Table 1–1 summarizes how the presence or absence of an intention to perform affects the kind of memory process used.

Table 1–1.
Registration and remembering processes as a function of intentionality
and memory function

Function	Incidental	Intentional
registration	encode	learn
remembering	realize	retrieve

A Theory of Study Skill Improvement

The theory of memory just reviewed suggests a path to study skill improvement much broader than traditional methods.

Since a memory task may differ in several ways, you cannot expect that a single manipulation or even several manipulations will prepare you for any and all tasks. The best formula for a substantial improvement requires you to acquire a large variety of techniques for enhancing attention to the mental contents encountered in unexpected tasks or in those specific tasks of greatest concern to you (Norman, 1982; Poon, 1980; Wilson & Moffat, 1984; Wilson, 1987; Yesavage, Lapp, & Sheik, 1989). Acquiring only a few manipulations — even if they are well-chosen — will leave you only partially prepared for improving at most memory tasks.

What are Memory Manipulations?

Manipulations improve your memory performance by optimizing the level and distribution of attention to memory tasks. However, they do not optimize attention directly. Instead, they act on one or more of the characteristics of memory tasks — the components of the task, the types of mental contents, and the intentionality behind task performance.

Manipulations can be divided into four kinds. Each type operates on one of the four task components.

The first type operates on your overall condition to ensure that you are fit physically and mentally for memory tasks. In social contexts, another type affects the flow of information in conversations and influence the ways others perceive and influence your memory performance. Manipulations of the physical environment enable it to stimulate your memory or even circumvent memory. Finally, manipulations of the mental contents of your consciousness systematically facilitate registration, retention, and remembering.

Applicability of Mental Manipulations to Study Tasks. When you decide on which mental manipulation to use in a certain task, you will have the many manipulations covered later in this book to choose among. Your choice will be among mental manipulations that are generally applicable to many tasks, or manipulations that are especially suited to the task you need to perform.

For example, intention tasks include the remembering of assignments and appointments. A general manipulation for these intention tasks is to rehearse the details of the task to oneself. A specific manipulation for the assignment could be to associate the date of the birthday with another event on that day or a day before. A specific manipulation for an appointment could be to form a similar association and also to imagine the person you are to meet alongside a clock set to the time of the appointment.

Current evidence indicates that manipulations which have been designed to be task specific improve memory more effectively than general manipulations.

Applicability of Manipulations and Intentionality. The manipulation you eventually choose to use depends on the nature of the task. Usually you are best off to use manipulations that appeal to you. If you use a manipulation that strikes you as uninteresting, chances are that you will have difficulty making it work well for you.

Your selection of a manipulation will also depend on whether the task you face is to be performed intentionally or incidentally. If the task is an intentional one, you can chose to work with any manipulation. If the task is an incidental one, you are restricted to manipulations that are carried out prior to the memory task, or ones which facilitate encoding or realizing during the task. These manipulations consist largely of those concerned with memory condition and memory attitude.

Forming Repertoires of Manipulations

Some memory tasks required of a student are very challenging (Flippo & Caverly, 1991; Weinstein, Goetz, & Alexander, 1988). There are many reasons why they challenge us. We may have difficulty with a task because of our condition, attitude, social context, environment, and/or the contents of working memory or long-term memory. We can attempt to rely on one manipulation to cope with a task but, when a task is especially annoying to us, it pays to use a variety of manipulations.

When you find a task troublesome, select a few manipulations that you can apply when the task arises. Such a task repertoire of manipulations will prepare you to respond quickly and accurately. Research shows that two or three manipulations lead to better memory performance than one. When a task is especially annoying, the extra effort in preparation will be worth even more to you.

The Need for a Complete Approach

The theory of memory improvement advanced here prescribes a comprehensive and specific approach to memory problems encountered while studying and facilitating memory processing

(Herrmann & Searleman, 1990; McEvoy, 1992; Poon, 1980; Yesavage, Lapp, Sheik, 1989). This approach is very much like the approaches that work best for developing other kinds of skills.

Suppose you wanted to improve your performance at a sport such as tennis, golf, or football. Depending on how serious you were, you would work on many different factors. You would seek better ways for getting into the best physical and mental condition to win. By adopting a more positive and realistic attitude about your ability to play, you could remove or overcome mental obstacles to succeeding at the game. By taking care to learn the customs of play and the tactics that suit specific arenas or opponents, you would be prepared to execute play appropriate to situations that arise. Through better knowledge and use of environmental details like the condition of the court or playing field, or special limits and advantages of certain kinds of equipment, you might make several specific adjustments that would benefit your play. The "mental game" of strategies and ploys could be studied to find more advantageous ways of playing specific situations or players.

And, of course, the more you learned about and practiced these manipulations, the better your performance would be. With practice, you would also develop your understanding of the game. Good players of all sports have an encyclopedic knowledge of manipulations that lead to a fit condition for the game, a proper attitude toward playing and players, a detailed knowledge of how to use the environment, an ability to deal with specific situations, and effective ways of practicing.

The next chapter will provide you with an opportunity to make an assessment of the memory problems on which you would most like to improve. Subsequent chapters explain how you can improve at each of the different kinds of manipulations that affect memory performance. Finally, the concluding chapter will describe how you combine the different kinds of manipulations into repertoires that will enable you to better deal with the memory tasks you find troublesome.

Summary

– Study skill improvement depends on changing several aspects of how you approach your course responsibilities and life in general.
– Improving your memory depends on raising your level of attention to the things you want to remember.
– The intensity and the distribution of your attention can be improved through intentional and incidental "manipulations" of the memory situation.
– No one manipulation — or study technique — will work for all courses or tasks within courses. Modern memory research shows that developing a repertoire of mental manipulations — made up of the right combinations of manipulations to fit specific memory tasks — gives the best results in improving academic performance.

• What passes for intelligence
is often just hard work
and a good memory.

Chapter 2
Scientific Background

Memory is evaluated today in a fashion that differs considerably from what would have been found in a memory improvement book just a few years back.

In the past, a person's memory was evaluated by having the person perform a small number of traditional tasks: recalling a list of digits, a list of words, a piece of prose, and some simple drawings. However, in the 1970s and 1980s research found that the performance of the traditional tasks does not generalize widely to other tasks.

For example, a deficit in digit recall was found to be unrelated to a person's ability to learn a list of words, or a prose passage, or even an everyday task like remembering phone numbers. It was this lack of generalizability in task performance that forced memory researchers to decide that an evaluation of a person's memory must include a wide variety of memory tasks.

Evaluation 2

Check Your Memory Abilities

How good is your memory? Really? Most people think they know the answer to this question, but research has shown that none of us have a very clear idea of how well our memory works. It is surprising how often people are completely wrong when they claim to be good at a certain memory task or bad at another.

There are various reasons why we perceive our abilities incorrectly. One is that our culture teaches, incorrectly, that memory ability is like a muscle — it's either strong or weak. Because we conceive of memory in this single-minded manner, we often fail to notice that people are good at some memory tasks and poor at others.

It is a fact that no one's memory is uniformly good or uniformly bad across all situations. Some people come to be known as having a "good memory," but this happens because they are good at valuable memory tasks — such as remembering names or important information. People come to be known as having a "bad memory" because they fail at conspicuous tasks, such as forgetting birthdays, anniversaries, and obligations in general.

Another reason we do not have a clear impression of our memory abilities is because we do not keep a systematic record of how often we succeed or fail at memory tasks. Our lives are often filled with events that at the time seem more important than how we fare at certain memory tasks. Because we pay little attention to how well our memory performs, we do not remember what our memory abilities are like (Herrmann, 1990a; Klatzky, 1984; Lachman, Steinberg, & Trotter, 1987; Morris, 1984).

Obviously, a realistic appraisal of your memory abilities is essential to setting worthwhile goals for memory improvement. Additionally, a remedy for a deficient ability can only be found if this ability is precisely identified in the first place. Thus, this chapter has the purpose of helping you identify which abilities need improving. Once you have acquired a realistic evaluation of your memory abilities, you will be in the right position to direct your efforts to improve your memory. Identification of those abilities which are strong will give you confidence to attempt tasks to which these abilities apply. Additionally, knowing which of your abilities are already strong will save you from wasting effort to improve abilities that need no improvement. Identification of memory abilities that are weak will allow you to develop ways to either avoid the tasks pertinent to these abilities or to improve these abilities. Thus, knowing your memory strengths and weaknesses enables you to hold reasonable expectations for yourself and to set attainable goals for improving your memory.

This chapter is intended to aid you in deciding how good your memory really is, especially as it is applied to studying and surviving in college. The chapter will begin by explaining how memory abilities are evaluated by professionals in psychology and by other books on memory improvement (Flippo & Caverly, 1990; Weinstein, Goetz, & Alexander, 1988; Forrest-Pressley, MacKinnon, & Waller, 1985). The chapter will then provide you with two procedures that you can use to make a partial evaluation of your memory. One procedure consists of extensive questionnaires which you may use to make a thorough inventory of impressions of your memory performance. A second procedure consists of carrying out a diary study of your memory performance over an interval of a few weeks.

Finally, you will examine your responses to the questionnaires and the diary, identify your memory strengths and weaknesses, and set goals for your memory-improvement efforts.

Standard Methods for Evaluating Study Skills

The evaluative methods recommended in this chapter do not measure memory performance as reliably as a memory-performance examination administered by a professional would (Grafman, 1984; Sternberg,1985; Wechsler, 1945; Wilding, & Valentine, 1988). But they are substantially better than self-administered memory tasks or tests administered to you by nonprofessionals, which have been recommended by previous memory-improvement books.

The method used here couples a sophisticated memory questionnaire with the keeping of a memory diary. The questionnaire is superior to those published in previous books because its design is based on more research and because it is considerably more extensive (Herrmann, 1990a; see also Dixon, Hertzog, & Hultsch, 1986; Hultsch, 1992). The memory diary provides a means of corroborating or challenging the observations recorded on the questionnaire. Memory diaries are generally regarded by professionals as yielding more accurate information about you than the questionnaire, because the diary record is made shortly after a memory task whereas a questionnaire is usually taken considerably later (Reason & MyCielska, 1983).

Memory Questionnaires

There are numerous memory tasks in our lives. The questionnaires below address many of these tasks. Four questionnaires are presented here to allow you to judge your performance in the four important categories of memory tasks: knowledge, events, intentions, and actions. Thus, when you have completed these questionnaires, you will be able to assess your overall performance in each of these memory-task categories as well as for each of many specific tasks within each category.

Knowledge

Primary, secondary, and higher education require us to learn a great deal of information. Depending on our interests, we have learned more about some subjects and less about others. Indeed, we may have avoided or lacked a chance to learn anything about some subjects. Similarly, our jobs and hobbies have led us to acquire quite a lot of knowledge. Our knowledge for information learned in and out of school is a separate matter from what we know about the events of our lives, the obligations we have to others, or our physical skills.

The questionnaire below requires you to imagine that you are asked questions (perhaps as part of a game, like "Trivial Pursuit") about some aspect of knowledge, and then to estimate how often you would be able to come up with the correct answer. In some cases, you may give yourself a low estimate because you never studied or did not do well at the topic. In other cases, you may give yourself a low estimate because, although you once learned and knew the topic fairly well, you now have forgotten it.

Below is a list of topics. For each one, indicate first whether you ever confronted and studied the topic — in your education, job, or as part of a hobby. If you are sure that you did study this topic, or if you just have a hunch that you learned about the topic at sometime, circle "yes"; otherwise circle "no." Next, for all topics to which you responded "yes," estimate how often you would be unable to remember the correct answer to a question about the topic. (Do not respond if you have never been exposed to the topic).

Your estimates for how often you would forget should be made on the seven point scale below. For example, if you think that you would almost never forget the answer to a question on the topic, circle 1 in the space provided, indicating that you feel your memory is excellent for the topic. If you were once exposed to the topic, but think that you would almost always forget, circle 7. If you think you would forget the answer for about half of the questions, circle 4. Circling 5 or 6 indicates you forget answers to more than half of the questions, but not all questions; a 2 or 3 indicates you forget answers less than half the time, but you do forget sometimes.

List of Topics

1 Never	2 Once in a While	3 Now and Then		4 About half the Time	5 Fairly Often		6 Very Often	7 Always
Agriculture	Yes	No	_____	Anthropology	Yes	No	
Art	Yes	No	_____	Biology	Yes	No	_____
Chemistry	Yes	No	_____	Cooking	Yes	No	_____
Drama	Yes	No	_____	Economics	Yes	No	_____
English	Yes	No	_____	Etiquette	Yes	No	_____
Foreign Lang.	Yes	No	_____	Geology	Yes	No	_____
Geography	Yes	No	_____	History	Yes	No	_____
Hygiene	Yes	No	_____	Law	Yes	No	_____
Literature	Yes	No	_____	Mathematics	Yes	No	_____
Music	Yes	No	_____	Philosophy	Yes	No	_____
Physics	Yes	No	_____	Politics	Yes	No	_____
Religion	Yes	No	_____	Social studies	Yes	No	_____
Sociology	Yes	No	_____	Sculpture	Yes	No	_____
Theater	Yes	No	_____	Books read	Yes	No	_____
Current news	Yes	No	_____	Past news	Yes	No	_____
Occupation	Yes	No	_____	Hobbies	Yes	No	_____
Home Repairs	Yes	No	_____	Jokes	Yes	No	_____
Spelling	Yes	No	_____	Often used phone			
Information learned				numbers	Yes	No	_____
in a job	Yes	No	_____				
How to get				Trivia	Yes	No	_____
around places				Sports	Yes	No	_____
you once lived	Yes	No	_____				
Stories	Yes	No	_____	Names of people			
Names of famous				known for a			
people	Yes	No	_____	long time	Yes	No	_____

Memory Diary

Questionnaires provide a good means for taking stock of what we believe our memory abilities to be. However, many of our successes and failures at remembering occur without us noticing them, making some of our questionnaire answers less accurate than we would like. Another way to learn about how our memory performs in everyday life is by keeping a diary. Indeed, a memory diary provides an especially good way to gain a more direct account of how your memory *actually* performs (Herrmann, 1990a; Reason & MyCielska, 1983).

If you forget an appointment, you record it in your memory diary. If you forget someone's name, you record that as well. By keeping a diary for one or more weeks, you can discover that some aspects of your memory performance are better and some are worse than you suspected.

Keeping a memory diary is relatively simple. You decide to pay attention to your failures at a selected set of memory tasks. In the diary, you make a note of each failure. To get an accurate impression of your typical performance, keep the diary for at least one week, but preferably for a month.

After keeping a diary for some interval, count how often you forgot for each task. The totals will indicate the tasks for which you might better prepare. Chances are you will find that you failed at some tasks much less often than you expected.

Table 2–1 below lists a set of memory tasks that are recommended for a first diary. These tasks are recommended because they are important to most people, and because they are fairly easy to observe. You may add other memory tasks to this set, and, of

Table 2–1
Recommended memory tasks for the first diary

Knowledge. You forgot some information you learned while in school, at work, or in some less formal situation.

Events
Recent Data. You need to remember a phone number or an address you just read out of the phone book moments before, but you find that you have forgotten some or all of what you wanted to remember and must check the book again.
Names You Know. You are unable to recall the names of a person you know.
Recent Events. You forget details of a movie, show, or some event while discussing it with other people who also observed the event.

Intentions
Forgot What To Do. You know that you were supposed to bring something to class but you forget what it is.
Forgot What To Bring. You discover, when you have just gone out, that you must return for something — a book perhaps — that you had intended to bring but accidentally left behind.

---

course, you may keep additional diaries in the future that deal with other memory tasks.

You can keep a memory diary in whatever form suits you best, whether on 3-by-5 cards or in a notebook. People usually find that a checklist facilitates keeping track of failures.

Table 2–2 below presents a list that you can use or modify to your liking. The table presents ten of the memory events described above and provides space for adding tasks of special interest to you. Photocopy this page 14 to 28 times and carry a copy with you for one to four weeks.

Each time you detect that your memory has failed in one of the ways listed, put a check mark alongside the relevant category. Also enter a few words that describe the failure so that you can later reflect on the event and on how you might better cope with similar situations in the future.

Sometimes, your memory failure will occur while you are with other people. If you feel shy or awkward about making your record at that time, wait until you are alone to enter a check on the diary checklist. However, the longer you wait to make a check, the greater the chances are that you will forget that you forgot — making your diary record less accurate than it could be.

Table 2–2
Your memory diary record

Memory Tasks	Day and Date _____

Dscription of Kind of Memory Failure

Knowledge _____

_____

Events — Recent Data _____

_____

Events — Names you know _____

_____

Events — Recent Events _____

_____

Intention — Forgot What To Do _____

_____

Intention — Take Away_____

_____

Scoring Your Diary Responses

Count the number of memory failures for each task over the period your diary was kept. Before you draw any conclusions from it, consider how often you confronted each memory task. You may have failed most often at a task you faced many times daily; yet, on the whole, your performance at that task may still have been good. For example, your impression of your ability to remember names will differ depending on whether you experienced only one introduction or thirty introductions in the diary period. Thus, it is necessary to change the diary records into a rating that you can later compare to your questionnaire answers.

For each of the tasks, rate your memory performance on a 7-point scale. A 7 indicates that your memory never or rarely failed during the diary period, relative to the number of opportunities for failure you encountered. Alternatively, a 1 indicates that your memory failed at almost every opportunity.

When you make your ratings, try to estimate how often you fail out of all opportunities you had. Research indicates that estimates made after the diary are sufficiently accurate. Thus, if you had 10 memory failures out of 20 chances at the task, your failure rate would be about half (a rating value of 4); if you had only 1 memory failure in 20 chances at the task, your failure rate would be "almost never" (a rating value of 7).

Record your ratings of your diary experiences in the right-hand margin alongside each kind of memory task listed on the Diary Record Summary sheet, shown in Table 2–2. Also transpose your answer on the questionnaire to the spot alongside of your diary rating in the table. These ratings will be used later for a comprehensive analysis of your memory performance.

Interpretation of Your Memory Questionnaire and Diary

The primary purpose of the various assessment tasks was to give you a clearer idea of how your memory actually performs in everyday life. As discussed earlier in this chapter, people are only partially aware of their success and failure at memory tasks, but their awareness of memory abilities increases after performing the assessment tasks employed here (Brennan, Winograd, Bridge, & Hiebert, 1986; Herrmann, 1990a).

A secondary purpose of these assessment tasks was to help you set goals for memory improvement. After completing the various assessment tasks, you are in an excellent position to choose those on which you would most like to concentrate. In this section, you will summarize the data you have gathered with the memory questionnaires and diary, interpret these data, and determine precise goals for your memory-improvement efforts.

Goalsetting for Study Skill Improvement

An accurate evaluation of your memory abilities is essential to improving memory performance, because different methods of improvement work best on different task categories and because the maximal improvement is usually obtained with methods that pertain to specific tasks. Thus, the questionnaire responses and diary responses provide you with concrete data which you can use to select the task categories and especially the specific tasks on which you would like to improve.

To begin with, you should consider which of the task categories are most important to your memory goals — knowledge, events, intentions, or actions. Which task categories matter the least to you? Recognition of the most and least important task categories will help you decide which specific tasks you want to devote your energy to improving as you proceed through this book.

In setting your goals at the task-specific level, you should review the tasks that you circled earlier on the memory questionnaire. Reconsider, in light of the diary experience and everything that you have thought about while working on this chapter, which specific tasks you want to work on later.

Once you are satisfied which tasks deserve to be improved, write the names of these in Table 2–3. In the next several chapters you will be learning information that will help you with all man-

Table 2–3
Specific study skill goals

1. _____
   _____
2. _____
   _____
3. _____
   _____
4. _____
   _____
5. _____
   _____
6. _____
   _____
7. _____
   _____
8. _____
   _____

ner of memory tasks generally. In the final chapter we will show how the knowledge of the intervening chapters can also be used to improve at the specific tasks you have listed in Table 2–3.

Summary

– You tackle or avoid courses depending on how you view your memory abilities. Unfortunately, most people are only partially aware of their study skills. Thus, they avoid courses and tasks within courses which they could succeed at, and take on tasks they should have skipped.
– A realistic knowledge of your study skills is necessary to work on your abilities that need improvement and to ignore your abilities that already are in good shape.
– You can achieve a realistic knowledge of your memory abilities by careful study of your answers on a comprehensive memory questionnaire and of your memory performance as recorded in a memory diary.

• Take extra care to remember
the things you do not
want to do.

Chapter 3
Scientific Background

Research began investigating the relationship between a person's memory performance and their physical and emotional state only recently. Such research typically tests a person's memory performance when he or she is in a particular emotional state (e.g., angry) or physical state (e.g., sleepy) at different times in different states (e.g., very angry, irritated, calm).

In some studies, the researcher has attempted to put the subject in a particular state, such as doing something to irritate the subject or to have the subject go without sleep. In other studies, researchers have simply asked subjects how they felt, and then examined how they performed memory tasks.

Since it would be unethical to induce physical or emotional stress against the will of subjects, investigations which attempt to put people in a certain state must obtain permission prior to begin. However, obtaining permission to do something stressful to a subject makes the results difficult to generalize since people do not usually give permission to others to treat them poorly. To circumvent such problems, a lot or research has asked people to imagine they were in a certain state, e.g. anger, and then tested their memory once they felt they had achieved that state.

Presently, we are unsure how well research on imagined states mimics the effects of real states. Nevertheless, even with the problems that this kind of research faces, we have a far better appreciation of the role of physical and emotional states in memory performance that just a generation ago.

Memory
Condition

Did you know that your mental and physical condition — like whether you get enough vitamins, and whether you're getting enough sleep — can have a major impact on whether you remember someone's name or a fact on an exam?

When people are asked how to improve memory performance, they almost never mention taking care of their health, reducing stress, or adopting a better attitude towards memory tasks. Nevertheless, there is ample research to show that the overall memory performance of students can range from good to poor simply because of their physical and/or mental condition (Davies & Thompson, 1988; Herrmann & Searleman, 1990; Risko, Alvarez, & Fairbanks, 1991). An increase in physical fitness, general health, sleep, relaxation, and realistic attitudes improves memory performance. Also, certain times in the day are better for registering and remembering information. Changes in your routine can interfere with your memory unless you take steps to recover from such changes.

Your condition is the single most important factor in how you perform incidental memory tasks — when you are not aware that you are doing a memory task. Your condition is also a major factor in your performance of intentional memory tasks, because your use of mental manipulations is dulled if your condition is poor. If you foresee periods in which you want to be at your intellectual best — taking a test, for instance — take better care of your condition, if only for several days preceding the event. It can work to your advantage.

The recommendations in this chapter aren't quick fixes, but they will help you lay the groundwork for better memory performance. They do involve more of a commitment than taking a pill that promises you a better memory, or memorizing supposedly miraculous memory strategies. In fact, they can even involve major lifestyle changes. But, if you really want to change your memory performance, they'll be worth it.

The Influence of Condition on Memory Mechanisms

As we've discussed, attention is one key to memory performance. Poor condition lessens memory performance because it robs us of our ability to pay attention. A deal settled over a "two-martini" lunch will seem hazy a day later. A late night spent studying often results in fatigue that interferes with the remembering of whatever was learned.

Because deficiencies in either physical or mental condition lessen attention, the rate of absorption of information into long-term memory decreases, and the rate at which traces emerge from long-term memory into working memory decreases as well. Some deficiencies may interfere with attention to mental efforts at registration or remembering, leading to omissions and errors in performance. If your condition is poor when good memory performance is desired, the entire memory system clearly will not function well. In terms of the memory model presented in Chapter 1, poor condition may impair memory processes in several ways. The upper panel of Figure 3 presents the memory model of the first chapter, a model of a system in good condition. The lower panel presents a model of the memory system in poor condition.

As you can clearly see, poor condition impairs the system in several ways. First, it lessens the ability of the central processor to attend to the contents of working memory. Thus, no idea or image in working memory is likely to be attended to strongly. Conse-

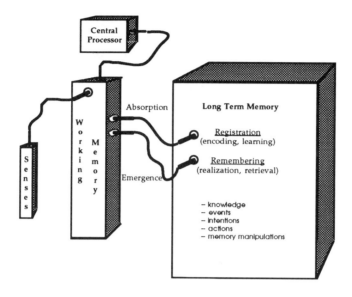

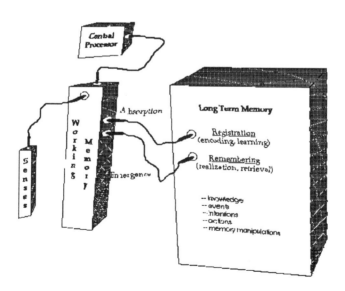

Figure 3.
The memory system in good and poor condition.

quently, no idea or image will produce a salient trace in long-term memory or will forcefully prod desired memories to emerge from long-term memory. Second, long-term memory's physiological receptivity to absorption or its physiological readiness for emergence may be reduced by poor condition. What's the solution? When poor condition has impaired the memory system, manipulations of physical and mental condition are needed to restore the system to proper functioning (Herrmann & Searleman, 1990, 1992).

Manipulations of condition are applicable to a wide range of memory tasks. You can use these manipulations to do better at memory tasks of considerable personal importance:

– giving a speech
– making an oral report
– participating in a lab practicum
– questioning your professor about what will be on an upcoming exam.

You can also use these manipulations to do better at all manner of memory tasks — often ones you cannot anticipate — which may or may not arise at certain occasions:

– tasks that must be carried out at a high school reunion, such as remembering names or recalling where you put your coat
– tasks that must be carried out during a job interview, such as answering questions about your qualifications or remembering to return the interviewer's pen.

Physical Condition

Aspects of your physical condition can critically influence your memory performance (see Table 3–1). In addressing these aspects, the question is not so much how to manipulate your physical condition to favor memory, as it is how to avoid the failures to take care of yourself that impair memory. In some cases, a deficiency is beyond correction. However, the prescriptions that follow mainly address physical concerns most adults encounter and can

Table 3–1
Physical states that impair memory performance

Poor Health
minor
major
Poor Nutrition
Overeating
Adverse Substances
Fatigue from Work or Play
Lack of Sleep

---

correct. A hearty dose of common sense combined with a few innovative manipulations can rectify most conditioning problems enough to substantially improve your memory performance.

Fitness

Exercise helps you maintain your strength and your cardiovascular condition, and thereby keeps you physically ready for memory tasks. It also helps relieve you of the "blues," lessens stress, improves sleep, and enhances digestion — all of which help memory. Some researchers suspect exercise may be especially effective for facilitating short-term memory performance, but this claim has not yet been fully investigated.

The exercise you engage in to improve memory need not be excessive. A 20-minute walk each day is probably sufficient to improve memory performance if you have not been exercising previously.

Your Energy Cycles

Your strength for memory tasks is cyclical. There are certain times in the day and across days of the week when memory functions best. For most people, the best time to perform memory tasks is between 11 a. m. and 4 p. m. This peak in memory performance probably occurs for several reasons: people get more involved with their activities by mid-day; they gradually lose their sharpness later in the day as general fatigue sets in; and their attentiveness varies with daily biological cycles (such as body temperature, respiration rate, pulse rate; Wyon, Andersen, & Lundqvist, 1979). Memory ability also tends to be at its best on Fridays and Saturdays. A peak in memory performance occurs on these days, probably because the anticipation of the weekend picks up a person's mood (Folkard & Monk, 1978).

Although the typical peak times for memory performance occur in the middle of the day and at the end of the week, some people will have different peak times. You can judge what times are peak for you simply by paying attention to when you are most alert and most able to think clearly. Obviously if you work the night shift or on weekends, your peak times will be different from those of people who work 9 to 5, Monday to Friday.

There is also evidence that your routine time for waking and sleeping affects your daily peaks for memory tasks. If you are a "morning" person, who goes to bed early and rises early, you learn more readily earlier in the day. If you are an "evening" person, you will probably learn more readily later in the day.

Because of our natural cycles, the times we choose to schedule events will affect our success or failure at memory tasks. You can make the best use of your reserves of strength by performing memory tasks when these reserves are at their peak. For example, if you are a typical person, take on memory tasks in the middle of the day and toward the end of the week. If you have control over the scheduling of an important meeting, schedule it around 10:30 a. m. (a little earlier if you are a morning person, a little later if you are an evening person) on a Thursday or a Friday. Try to minimize or at least decrease the number of memory tasks you must carry out when you anticipate disruptions in your daily and weekly cycles. When life does not allow you to schedule an event at an optimal time, you can at least attempt to be more alert when the event does occur.

Disruptions to your cycle diminish your cognitive capacity. Interruptions to your sleep can wear you down considerably. Shifts in your cycle, which may be caused by a radical change in your schedule such as occurs in shiftwork, or by travel that induces "jet lag," interfere with your ability to pay attention and do memory tasks (Idzikowski, 1984). Such changes make it harder to pick up new information and remember old information.

If your cycle is disrupted by traveling, you may find it hard to remember directions on how to get to your hotel, or what room the desk clerk just gave you in the hotel, or where you put your bag just before you asked the desk clerk about your room. Thus, when there is a shift in your cycle, allow extra time to recuperate before taking on major tasks that rely on your intellect and your memory.

Sleep and Sleep Learning

Proper sleep obviously makes a person strong and alert for memory tasks. Getting sufficient sleep before an exam or an interview is essential in order for you to remember quickly and accurately. We all can recall occasions when we were forced to stay awake much longer than usual and fumbled for our words and struggled to remember answers the next day that normally we would have remembered easily.

You can ensure getting a good night's sleep if you avoid eating and drinking in the evening, avoid thinking about your troubles prior to bedtime, and if you go to bed at approximately the same time every night. Also, avoid using sleeping pills. The sleep they induce is usually not as refreshing as natural sleep. Sleeping pills often have a carry-over effect the next day, making you less able to register new memories and less susceptible to stimulation that will help you remember.

There is some evidence to show that going to sleep immediately after learning leads you to remember what you learned better than putting off going to bed after learning. Apparently, playing cards or going out to eat after a study session does not help your memory as much as going to bed directly after the study session. Thus, if you can arrange it, study until lights out, dive in bed, and go to sleep!

It has often been claimed that a person can learn while asleep, and that "sleep-learning" makes a deeper impression than learning while awake. A great deal of research has been done on this topic, and the conclusion is very clear: people do not learn while asleep. If you play a record or tape during the night and learn some of what is played, you are remembering what you heard while actually awake. When you are truly asleep, you learn nothing. If you need to learn something, get a good night's sleep and use your waking hours to study it.

Eating Habits

Diet has been suspected of affecting memory performance for centuries. In the 15th century, for example, roasted fowls and young hares, as well as apples, nuts, and red wine were recommended for improving one's memory (see A. E. Middleton's Memory Systems published by G. S. Fellows in 1888).

Similarly, today's nutrition experts say that poor nutrition places limits on memory performance. Some experts maintain that a normal diet supplies sufficient vitamin levels to guard against deficiencies that produce memory deficits. Others claim that certain foods must be included in everyone's diet or that vitamins must be supplemented to prevent memory-related deficiencies. The rationale usually offered for why vitamins may help memory is that they enhance brain chemistry. This remains to be proven, largely because too little research has been done on the effects of vitamins on the chemistry of the normal brain.

The foods that experts recommend as "memory nutritious" include beef, pork, kidneys, liver, fish, shellfish, milk, eggs, cheese, vegetables, kelp, and onions. Recently, it has been reported that drinking lemonade right after studying facilitates later recall, apparently because sugar aids the absorption of information into long-term memory (Gold, 1987). Whatever you eat, moderate amounts are recommended before you perform memory tasks. Large amounts of food make you sleepy and unable to pay attention during registration and remembering.

"Memory nutritious" vitamins and minerals include choline, B-complex vitamins (especially Bl, B6, and B12), iodine, manganese, folic acid, and L-tyrosine. At least one vitamin pill is sold explicitly as a facilitator of memory ("Memory Booster," produced by Puritan Pride). However, vitamin supplements probably won't improve the memory performance of most people.

If you feel that your diet or eating habits are so irregular that you might have a mild vitamin deficiency, try a supplement. But don't expect it to work like a magic pill, and be careful not to take too much: vitamin overdoses can be dangerous.

If you suspect you have a nutritional disorder, you obviously should consult a physician. But you should also recognize that how much you eat can be as important to memory performance as what you eat. Specifically, you should be careful not to eat a great deal before an exam or a special academic challenge, such as a speech in class. Overeating will diminish your ability to concentrate and remember (Smith, 1988).

Sensory Difficulties

Poor eyesight or hearing can prevent a person from performing memory tasks well because such difficulties slow the initial registration of information and make it harder to notice cues that can help remembering. These sensory difficulties may also lead others to conclude that a person has memory deficiencies. People draw this erroneous conclusion because they assume that unsatisfactory memory performance occurs only because of memory problems. Since many people try to conceal sight or hearing problems, it is not surprising when others attribute an unsatisfactory memory performance to memory alone rather than to the sensory problem.

Unfortunately, when a person with a sensory deficiency explains frankly that a memory failure was due to such a deficiency, the explanation may be regarded as an excuse rather than the truth.

If you believe that one of your senses needs help, do not hesitate to get yourself examined by a physician. If your loss is sufficient, you will probably be advised to use either an occasional corrective device such as magnifying glasses or phone-loudness boosters or a permanent corrective device such as eyeglasses, or a hearing aid. Either kind of device may impose some inconvenience, but your improved performance will be ample compensation.

Illness

We all get sick from time to time. When we do, we perform mental tasks less well, including memory tasks. Illnesses, major and minor, interfere with memory performance because discomfort diminishes attention. When our ability to pay attention is lessened, we do not register or remember as well as when we are healthy.

Even a minor illness can impair memory performance. Did you ever come down with a bad cold the day you had to give a speech from memory? Chances are that you had difficulty remembering much of what you had to say.

Taking steps to reduce discomfort and control symptoms will improve memory performance during an illness. If you have a big exam when you're sick, ask for a deferral or postponement — there's no way you'll be at your best. If you can't get excused, make sure that you're as well-rested as possible.

If your illness is chronic, there are other things you can do to minimize the distractions to memory performance caused by your illness. Be sure to check whether the side-effects of your treatment or medication influence memory. Medicines are rarely identified explicitly as interfering with memory per se. But if a medicine diminishes your capacity to pay attention, it is routinely pointed out on the box and label.

Any medicine that lowers your attentive powers will reduce how much you register and remember. If a prescription medicine lessens your ability to pay attention, you should discuss with your physician whether you should take it.

Memory Illnesses

Certain illnesses impair memory so severely that they are known as "memory illnesses." These include Alzheimer's disease, Korsakoff's (alcoholic) syndrome, major strokes and mini-strokes, and low blood pressure (Kahn, 1986; Mayes, 1988; Wilson, 1987).

Alzheimer's disease (1907) is the most widely known memory illness. Articles on this disease occur frequently in newsmagazines and on TV because it has a devastating effect on the memory abilities of its victims.

Korsakoff's syndrome involves a progressive and eventually severe loss of the ability to register new memories (Birnbaum & Parker, 1977). The victim recalls knowledge and events of the past prior to the onset of memory difficulties. The cause of Korsakoff's syndrome is excessive drinking of alcohol over a prolonged period.

A stroke is produced by a blood clot that enters the brain and causes some cells to die. Mini-strokes involve many tiny clots that are dispersed throughout the brain. They render a person confused and less able to focus attention.

Unless you are a senior citizen who has returned to school, students will almost never have to worry about their memory ability being impaired a a major memory illness. There are, however, other serious conditions to which everyone is potentially vulnerable.

For example, very low blood pressure, a life threatening condition, reduces ability to register and remember. Apparently, low blood pressure impairs memory because it lessens a person's ability to pay attention. Fortunately, the medicines that are used to treat low blood pressure restore attentive powers and alleviate the memory problems that go along with the condition.

All of these illnesses require a physician's care. If you believe that you or someone close to you has developed a serious memory problem, you should consult a physician.

Adverse Substances

Several substances impair memory performance. Perhaps the best known is alcohol, sometimes called the "amnesia food." Drink can mask sorrows and diminish memory for events that occur under its influence. Conversely, frequent and extensive memory loss from drink foretells the onset of a severe drinking problem.

Extensive memory loss from drink may come about because a drinking bout impairs brain chemistry or because drinking itself provides an excuse to "forget" antisocial acts performed during the bout. As mentioned under the memory illness section above, prolonged use of alcohol causes permanent and obvious damage to a person's memory system (Birnbaum & Parker, 1977).

Marijuana has effects on memory that are similar to those produced by alcohol. Research has examined the effect of a pill form of marijuana that induces a high comparable to several drinks. People who take this pill learn a list of words more slowly than sober people. When asked to recognize whether a digit was in a digit series presented moments before, people under the influence of marijuana recognize the test digit more slowly than people not under the influence (Block & Wittenborn, 1984; Darley, Tinklenberg, Hollister, & Atkinson, 1973). Because of such research, our government advises the public that marijuana impairs memory.

It is sometimes held that mind-altering substances and stimulants have a state-dependent effect on memory (Swanson & Kinsbourne, 1979). According to this theory, a memory registered when sober can be more accurately recalled when sober, and events observed when under the influence of a drug or alcohol can be more accurately recalled later when under the influence again. Conversely, this theory predicts poorer performance when a memory is remembered in a state different from the one in which it was registered.

This theory underlies some claims that people make about the effects of alcohol or marijuana on memory. For example, some people say, "When I'm sober I can't remember things I did at a party the night before, but if I have a drink or a joint I recall the party better."

Despite such claims, research has not provided clear support for the state dependency of any mind-altering substance or stimulant. Research on alcohol has suggested a small effect of state dependency. Some research has suggested that memories formed under the influence of marijuana might be state dependent, but again the effect is very small.

Thus, remembering still appears to be best accomplished when in a state of sobriety. Some students study while under the influence and some people in business plan strategy over several drinks. Usually the justification is that learning is more effective when relaxed.

However, the student later will often complain that an exam was scored unfairly low and the business person will lament that certain aspects of a project were poorly presented at the meeting. In fact, the exam was probably scored fairly and the presentation at the meeting was clear and complete. The real basis of these complaints is that the memory task was performed under the influence.

If you are serious about performing a certain memory task well, the research is clear: alcohol and marijuana will impair your memory performance.

Stimulants

Who hasn't used a cup of coffee to help themselves stay alert while studying? Mild stimulants commonly found in tea, coffee, sodas, or tobacco supposedly make you more attentive and, thus, better able to register and remember. However, you should know that stimulants are as likely to have adverse effects on memory as they are to be beneficial. Even if they could enhance performance at some level, the ideal doses are currently unknown.

If you are wide awake and well rested, mild stimulation from caffeine or nicotine can do little to further enhance your memory performance. Indeed, if you have too much of a stimulant, you will become jittery, find it difficult to sleep, and your memory performance will suffer. Additionally, if you are a habitual or addicted user, having to go without a stimulant will also make you jittery and affect your memory performance. However, if you are likely to fall asleep and you must learn information by a certain deadline, a mild stimulant may help you stay awake and pay attention at least somewhat.

Surprisingly, little research has been done with humans to explore the effects of stimulants on memory. Some studies have found that coffee had a facilitative effect on memory but other studies found a detrimental effect. No studies have examined the effect on memory of nonprescription stimulant products, based on caffeine, such as NoDoz and Vivarin.

It has sometimes been assumed that nicotine facilitates memory, presumably because it may make a person alert while performing a memory task (Peeke & Peeke, 1984; Wittenborn, 1988). However, recent research indicates very clearly that nicotine can impair memory performance considerably, as much as occurs from a couple alcoholic drinks (Spillich, 1987). This research has shown, for example, that nonsmokers were quicker than smokers at performing a task requiring temporary remembering of a list of digits. Moreover, nonsmokers scored higher on the five tests that make up the Wechsler Memory Scale (described in Chapter 2): memory for a written passage, digit span, reproduction of a visual pattern, and learning pairs of words. The research indicates that if you smoke, do not do so during a memory task. And if you worry about your memory performance in general, you might consider quitting.

Some people believe that amphetamines enhance memory. These drugs will keep someone awake for a memory task. However, they are highly addictive and dangerous. Avoid them. Any short-term gain they offer can quickly turn to tragedy.

In general, you're better off not using stimulants or, at least, using them moderately. Stimulants may come in handy fighting fatigue, but they almost always exact a cost. While keeping you awake, they also make you more distractible — putting you at a disadvantage for memory tasks. If you need to stay awake, some relatively safe stimulants like coffee and tea may be useful. But what might help you the most is a dose of motivation.

Finally, a word of caution about so called "memory medicines." Presently, no such substances exist. All of the medicines reputed to facilitate memory actually facilitate attention. Perhaps an "attention medicine" may be regarded as good enough because attention is so important to memory. These medicines are, among others, magnesium pemoline (Cylert), Piracetam (not sold in the U.S.), vasopressin, and naloxone. All these medicines require a prescription and would not be prescribed to you unless you have one of the serious memory illnesses described earlier in this chapter. If you do not have one of the memory illnesses, you really do not want one of these medicines. The effect they have on performance is negligible. People who have taken one of these drugs typically recall one more word out of a list of 30 words than they would have without the drug. Additionally, these drugs induce various side effects, such as increased tension. For some of these medicines, the side effects can even be fatal. Memory medicines are like the fountain of youth. They promise something that we know can never be delivered.

But even if a miraculous medicine could be developed to give you a perfect memory, would you truly desire it? I think not. A fully effective memory medicine would make you remember everything.

Suppose you took a memory tablet before studying for an exam. You would register the material perfectly, but you would also register every time you picked up your pencil, every cup of coffee, every belch, and so on. When taking the exam, not only would the relevant material emerge into memory, but so also would everything else registered.

In short, your recall would be distracted by an endless stream of petty details irrelevant to a memory task. Maybe a memory drug will be developed that could overcome such a problem. But science is a long way from developing such a drug.

Physical Condition Checklist

Clearly, good physical condition is one of the necessary ingredients for good memory performance. As discussed above, your ability to pay attention is affected by your strength which in turn depends on your physical condition (see Figure 4). To avoid lowering the level of your memory performance, you should follow some common sense guidelines:

1. Promptly treat or seek treatment of major and minor illnesses. Discomfort distracts.

2. Avoid the use of adverse substances. They impair your ability to pay attention.

3. Eat a well-balanced diet, and do not overeat before memory tasks. A well-balanced diet ensures strength and optimal brain chemistry for when you attempt memory tasks. Moderate eating avoids the sleepiness that comes with overeating.

4. Get enough sleep and keep to your natural cycles of wakefulness and sleep. Sufficient sleep and consistent cycles keep you strong and alert to register and remember.

5. Take account of your peaks — whether you are a morning or an evening person — when you schedule important or demand-

ing memory tasks. If you can arrange it, perform memory tasks when you are strongest and most attentive.

6. Everyone gets tired. Rest when time allows during the day so that you will be up to your memory commitments.

7. Stay in shape. Physical vigor is necessary for mental vigor. Physical weariness is always coupled with mental weariness. If you are physically fit, you will also be fit for memory tasks.

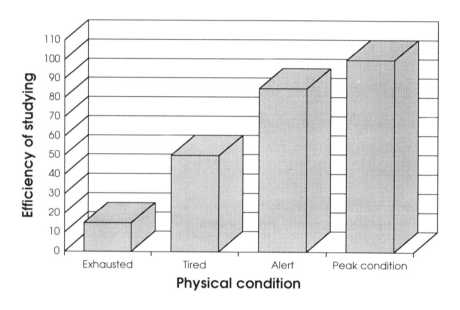

Figure 4.
The effect of physical condition on the efficacy of a person's studying (hypothetical data based on the research literature).

Mental Condition

Sometimes our concentration or clarity of thought is less than optimal. We are unable to focus on what we are reading, what others are saying, or even on what we just said. At other times, our emotions are stirred up. We are upset by a snide remark or by being told to do something by our boss.

Since disrupted concentration and disturbed emotions impair attention, either state will affect how much information we register and remember. Additionally, because mental states affect the physical state of the brain, they may reduce the absorbing and emerging powers of long-term memory (see Figure 5).

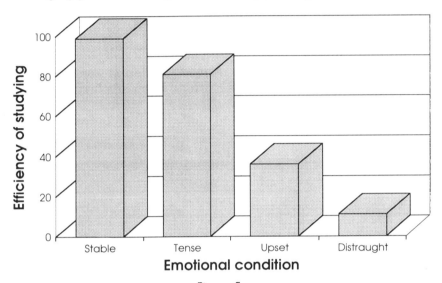

Figure 5.
The effect of emotional condition on the efficacy of a person's studying (hypothetical data based on the research literature).

The manipulations used to restore normal mental states have a more general effect than the manipulations of physical states. For example, manipulations that act to improve concentration will also tend to help emotional states as well. Table 3–2 lists some of the mental states that affect your efficiency at studying.

Table 3–2
Mental states that impair memory performance

Confusion
Being in a Rut
Anxiety
Excessive Ups
Downs
Preoccupation
Excessive Relaxation

Diminished Concentration

A hectic and harried lifestyle can leave otherwise fit people occasionally disoriented. Whatever its origin, confusion hampers performance. It lowers the level of attention to our immediate surroundings, and it lowers our ability to focus attention.

Sometimes the things we do when we do not concentrate are comical as well as annoying. Who hasn't, with some embarrassment, done something like stepping in the shower with socks on or saying thank you to a Coke machine when it delivers a can of soda?

Alternatively, a very predictable and routinized lifestyle can also lower attention and ability to concentrate. Sometimes we become so relaxed and adept at our tasks that we can do two tasks at once — for instance, preparing a meal while thinking about some problem at work.

Proficiency is usually admirable and rewarding. However, proficiency sometimes backfires. Research has shown that a great deal of experience and practice at a task leads performance to become automatic, sometimes so automatic that we cease to pay full attention to the task at hand. As our attention wanes or wanders, errors increase and these errors can have drastic consequences. Some airplane accidents have been found to be caused by very (perhaps overly) experienced pilots having inadvertently thrown a switch in the wrong direction (Reason & MyCielska, 1983).

Your ability to concentrate is affected by how well your environment allows you to pay attention to what you are doing. Research has found that there are optimum levels of noise and physical comfort for performing memory tasks. Total silence and maximum comfort are probably not the best conditions for your memory. Neither are tight-fitting clothes, uncomfortable furniture, or extremely loud noises.

Whether a situation provides you too little or too much comfort is a matter of personal taste. Some people enjoy tight clothes. If a person truly functions best with rock-'n-roll blasting in the background, then it should blast on; it would be a mistake to put on Bach or to turn the stereo off altogether.

In general, slight discomfort will make a person more alert than will coziness. Slight discomfort ensures that you will not be drowsy. Coziness gives a feeling of safety, but it may lead you to fall asleep. Slight discomfort will make you ready to pay attention. Thus, to ensure that you will pay better attention to memory tasks, choose environments and modes of dress that are not too comfortable.

Stress

Memory is disturbed by stress. Nurses who work in high-stress situations, such as an intensive care ward, manifest more memory failures than those who work on routine wards (Broadbent, Cooper, Fitzgerald, & Parks, 1982). Women scheduled to have mastectomies manifest a greater number of memory and absent mindedness errors than usual in the period just prior to surgery (Reason & Lucas, 1984; Reason, 1988, 1989).

Although stress can be debilitating, we need an optimal level of it to survive (Spielberger, Gonzales, & Fletcher, 1979). Too little or too much stress makes us vulnerable to illness. A proper level of stress keeps us alert and active as we cope with the problems of everyday life.

Likewise, too little or too much stress lessens memory performance. Stage fright can cause one to forget lines in a play. Conversely, total complacency will lead an actor to fail to recognize a cue. Some stress will at least keep an actor alert.

Test anxiety will distract you and stifle your ability to recall information. On the other hand, indifference to the importance of a test will make you try too little to remember and to overlook clues to appropriate answers. Again, some anxiety will ensure you are alert during a test.

Moods

Normal ups and downs affect memory performance. When things are going our way, we feel positive about life. Positive moods dispose us to pay attention to whatever happens and, thus, to perform memory tasks more efficiently (Matlin & Stang, 1978).

However, extremely positive feelings may interfere with memory performance. When we are deliriously happy, such as when deeply in love, we may pay more attention inwardly to our deliciously positive feelings and less attention to other important things in our life.

Negative moods, whatever their intensity, impair memory performance. A slightly negative mood, such as the down we feel after someone insults us, diminishes our ability to pay attention. Normal depression weakens memory performance because a preoccupation with unhappy thoughts lowers our level of attention and reduces our capacity to focus attention (Erdelyi & Goldberg, 1979; Hertel, 1992; Yesavage, Sheikh, & Lapp,1990). Attentive powers may also be lowered by depression because it can alter brain chemistry in a way that slows absorption and emergence.

An intensely negative mood, such as might occur after a big argument with someone we care about, will impair memory performance (Zarit, Gallagher, & Kramer,1981). If the intense mood is an active — one such as anger or rage — it energizes us too much and makes us too distractible to perform memory tasks well.

If the intense mood involves depression, it may render us extremely withdrawn. Severe ("clinical") depression weakens memory so much that some doctors regard memory failure as a major indicator of clinical depression — even when patients themselves do not complain of depression. Treatments that relieve depression (such as antidepressant drugs or psychotherapy) also restore memory abilities (Watts, 1988).

It has been proposed that our success at remembering depends on our mood during remembering being comparable with our mood when the memory was registered (Bower, 1980). This proposal is the "state dependency" issue discussed earlier in this chapter with respect to certain substances (alcohol, marijuana). As with substance use, research suggests that remembering may be enhanced sometimes by striving for mood comparability. However, it is not yet clear just how to create the comparable mood that might facilitate remembering.

Relaxation

Relaxation relieves stress and decreases the distractibility that interferes with memory performance. You know, of course, a variety of ways to relax: a snooze on your sofa, reminiscing with a friend, listening to music, watching TV. Exercise, as discussed earlier in the chapter, reduces stress and improves your mood.

Perhaps the form of relaxation best known to facilitate memory is yoga. Hatha yoga teaches a series of exercises or body postures separate from yoga philosophy that can be conducive to memory. The movements involved are similar to those in traditional calisthenics, but they are executed in slower and more graceful ways. Yoga's effectiveness for producing physiological states of relaxation — states that are beneficial to memory in general — is widely accepted.

by Amanda Herrmann (at age 9)

Figure 6.
The yoga position called the "candle," claimed by yoga masters
to improve memory.

Yoga masters regard certain body postures as particularly beneficial to memory performance. One group of such postures places the head lower than the rest of the body. This group includes the head stand, the "candle" where you prop up your back and feet with your hands as shown in Figure 6, or simply hanging one's head down over the edge while lying on a bed. The rationale for the supposed effect of these postures is that by driving more blood to the brain than usual, they facilitate memory performance both immediately following the exercise and for an indefinite period beyond, because the exercise presumably helps brain functioning in general. One study found that the head inversion technique did help the memory performance of older subjects.

Another group of yoga postures that may help memory concern the spine. These postures gently twist the spine, as you would when locking your knees while touching your toes with the opposite hand. Spinal exercises, supposedly, make a person feel better overall, and hence more ready for memory tasks.

The yoga procedure for muscle relaxation is also held to facilitate memory. In this posture, you lie on a firm surface and gradually relax the muscles of the body. Considerable research has shown that regular muscle relaxation diminishes your susceptibility to stress-related illnesses. Yoga masters suggest the posture aids memory itself. They advise engaging in muscle relaxation until the body is extremely flaccid. Once in the relaxation state, you may study (often with a tape recorder, because lifting a book or notes would disrupt the relaxation of the arm involved), or you can attempt to remember something you found hard to recall in a normal or less relaxed state.

The rationale seems plausible. If you have been anxious about a memory task, muscle relaxation may facilitate your performance. Relaxation techniques have generally been found to facilitate the memory of the elderly (Yesavage, Rose, & Spiegel, 1982; Yesavage & Sikah, 1990). More research is needed to explore and validate all the various claims of Hatha Yoga for improving memory. To the extent that the exercises help you relax, they can certainly provide some benefit.

In the past two decades there have been numerous systems of relaxation developed that may also facilitate memory performance. Perhaps the best known is Transcendental Meditation (TM). TM teaches a person to engage in the yoga method of muscle relaxation, just described, while repeating a word or sound (called a "mantra"). The repetition also helps to induce a relaxed state and reinforces the effects of muscle relaxation.

Other relaxation systems include methods for creating and dwelling on comforting imagery (sometimes called "positive imaging" or "creative visualization"), for experiencing sensory deprivation (the Lily tank), for learning to control your brain waves (Alpha wave control), for learning to control your blood pressure and pulse rate (Biofeedback), for controlling what you say to yourself (neurolinguistic programming), and still others.

Indeed, relaxation systems are presently being developed faster than researchers have been able to evaluate their effectiveness. Properly used, these techniques can reduce stress and thereby facilitate your memory performance in at least the short-term. However, you should know that some people have claimed these systems had a negative effect on them, including nervous breakdowns. Until the effects of these systems are better researched, I cannot endorse any one of them as effective or safe. If you decide to undertake training in one of these systems, I advise that you do the following. Talk carefully with a few people you know who have gone through the training. Do not take the training if you have been going through a rough emotional period. If your nature is that you occasionally get very upset over life's problems, check with a psychologist or psychiatrist about whether the system might have a bad effect on you.

Many psychologists will tell you that you need not pay a lot of money for a system to relax. Stretching out on your sofa, listening to music, playing ball, visiting with friends — any of these will relax you sufficiently to achieve better memory performance.

Attention Training

Condition manipulations improve memory performance because they remedy deficiencies that lower attention. All condition manipulations improve our capacity to pay attention. Unfortunately, however, the improvements are essentially temporary. They will disappear when we begin to neglect our condition. It would be very helpful if there were manipulations that produce permanent increases in our capacity to attend (Plude, 1992). There have been, in fact, a number of proposals for training people to have greater powers of attention.

Four kinds of attention training have been proposed.

- One kind attempts to increase your ability to sustain attention. It is commonly known among sentries in the military, police officers on stakeout, and security guards that experience is necessary to maintain sensitivity to detecting intruders and potentially dangerous people. Some researchers believe you can develop such experience through practice at listening for faint, unpredictable sounds or looking for dim, unpredictable lights. For example, you may practice by watching and listening for planes in the sky or for squad cars with radar on the highway.
- A second kind of attention training attempts to increase your ability to divide your attention. Research indicates that practice at doing two things at once can improve your ability to pay attention to two things simultaneously. For example, you may practice watching TV while maintaining a conversation.
- A third kind of attention training attempts to increase your ability to notice details. Research shows that practice at picking out a detail in a scene or a sound in a mix of sounds results in improved performance.
- A fourth kind of attention training attempts to increase your ability to resist distraction. Research has found that practice can improve your ability to pay attention to something despite distractions.

Most research that demonstrates an effect of attention training has been done with brain-damaged patients. This research requires a patient to perform one or more of the kinds of training just mentioned. Often the training is done with a desktop computer which presents the patient with a perceptual task requiring some kind of attentive process (Wilson & Moffat, 1984; Wilson, 1987). For example, a patient might attempt to detect a spot on a screen, keep track of the position of two or more moving spots, pick out details from a complex pattern, or keep track of a single spot while the background changes randomly.

Patients often show improved performance on tasks such as these, and this seems to help in performing everyday memory tasks. However, it is not clear that these practice tasks improve a patient's general attentive capacity. Rather, they increase their confidence in being able to cope with challenging tasks. Once a patient recognizes that performance at a computer task has improved, he or she feels more able to tackle some routine memory tasks.

Research with normal adults indicates that ability to pay attention in general cannot be improved by training with the procedures just described for desktop computers. But research does indicate that the ability of normal adults to pay attention can be improved for particular tasks.

If you desire to improve your attentive powers, you are advised to practice at paying attention in the situation you want your memory to succeed.

For example, suppose you want to improve your ability to pay attention to what a speaker says during a meeting. You can improve this ability by attending as many talks as possible and attempting to pay attention to what the speaker says. Please note that for practice to work, you have to engage in a lot of it, perhaps over a month or two. Attention training is no simple proposition, and you may wish to influence your attentive powers by manipulating your condition in the other ways described in this chapter.

Attitudes

Whenever a memory task arises, you have an attitude towards it. The attitude may address the *content* of the task — what you have to register or remember. For example, the attitude may have to do with your views on studying French or Greek. The attitude may also address the *kind* of memory task. For example, the attitude may reflect your views on the studying of foreign-language vocabulary or grammar.

Your attitude may facilitate or impair your performance because it affects your inclination to try to perform the task and your ability to sustain attention while performing the task (Forrest-Pressley, MacKinnon, & Waller, 1985). Since memory performance is affected by your attitudes, one way that you can improve your memory performance is by improving these attitudes.

Attitudes about one's memory abilities for different tasks are typically deeply rooted. The origin of your attitudes comes from your upbringing and how you have observed yourself perform memory tasks. Hence, we cannot change them easily. But they can be changed (Herrmann, 1990a).

An attitude has three characteristics which may or may not be appropriate. First, an attitude conveys a belief about something, such as "foreign languages are easy to learn" or "foreign languages are almost impossible to learn."

Second, the belief is valued positively or negatively. We are attracted to the study of foreign languages or we are repelled by it.

And third, we value a belief with a certain strength. We are attracted or repelled by the study of foreign languages weakly, moderately, or strongly. If you decide that certain attitudes are damaging to your memory performance, you can change them by changing the belief, its value, and/or its strength.

Changing Attitudes About Task Content

Your attitudes about the content of a memory task may be inappropriate. It might be that, with your background, the content would be more interesting and easier to learn than you think. If this is the case, your performance of a task will be inefficient and possibly in error.

Certain kinds of task content are especially difficult to register and remember. Each kind of task requires a special approach so that the attitude can be altered to facilitate memory performance. These problematic kinds of task content are as follows:

– *Uninteresting Information.* Boring information is obviously hard to register and remember. Unfortunately, we often are unaware of how uninteresting something is to us until it is too late. We will often forget something that someone said or something that we were to do because we were uninterested.

To avoid such difficulties, you need to decide ahead of time whether it is important that you remember something. Then, if you recognize that something is uninteresting to you, beware. Take extra the steps described in the chapters to follow this one to ensure that you will remember it.

– *Negative Information.* Memories connected with strong negative emotion are usually easy to remember. In fact, they are often so easily remembered that they intrude into consciousness when you would rather forget them.

But memories connected with only moderately negative emotion may be more difficult to recall. The emotion can lead us to suppress the memory. Suppression is a common reaction to negative feelings. As Scarlett O'Hara preferred to say, "I'll think about it tomorrow." Unfortunately, suppression often leads to forgetting other obligations, like meetings or chores, and gets us into trouble.

There are two ways to protect yourself against suppression. The first way is to convince yourself that the content of the memory should really be viewed positively. Obviously, this is not always possible or appropriate. If the boss fires you, positive feelings will be hard to come by. Also, when using this manipulation bear in mind that, even if you can convince yourself of some of the good aspects of a memory's content, negative feelings will still remain with the memory. Thus, while adopting a positive view may diminish the likelihood of suppression, it will still be possible.

A second way to protect a memory against suppression is to develop plans to force yourself to think about the memory when necessary. For example, to enable yourself to remember to attend a meeting that you would dearly like to miss but should not, set two alarms and ask someone to give you a timely reminder to go. Or if you know that you will be asked to discuss some unpleasant topic at a meeting, such as a bungled project for which you were responsible, review the details before you attend. Make a special effort to look knowledgeable about the incompetence. If you take deliberate prior steps to face up to the negative memory, suppression will be less likely to occur.

– *Personally Upsetting Information.* Some negative memories are so threatening that they are repressed (Erdelyi & Goldberg,

1979). While suppressed memories can be remembered with effort, repressed memories cannot be remembered at will. Repression removes any awareness of the information, blocking it from our normal means of remembering.

The classic example of repression is the soap opera character who, after some traumatic experience, becomes unable to remember it at all. Some psychologists believe that everyone represses some memories; others believe that repression occurs less commonly and that it may indicate a serious adjustment problem.

Access to repressed memories comes only after recalling many related memories (a process Freud called "psychoanalysis" and made central to psychotherapy). If you suspect yourself of repressing part or all of an important memory (or memories), consult a clinical psychologist about the problem. The recovery of a repressed memory is something we cannot expect to do alone.

Disturbing information that is not suppressed or repressed may be distorted instead. The distortion may occur either during registration or later during retention, to make it consistent with our self-image and goals (Greenwald, 1980). Distortions are difficult to detect because they protect our view of ourselves. Some distortion in memory is normal, but an excessive amount can lead to maladjustment. When a memory has become distorted, others are often first to recognize and point out the distortion to us. By being open to the possibility, we are more likely to discover and correct distorted memories.

Changing Attitudes about the Kind of Memory Task

Most people think their attitudes about which tasks they excel at are correct. They feel as confident about their notion of how well they register and remember as they do about other abilities, such as vision or hearing.

However, as discussed in Chapter 2, the truth is that most of us have only a partially accurate view of how well we perform different memory tasks (Herrmann, 1990a; Morris, 1984). When people are asked how well they perform memory tasks in everyday life and in the laboratory, their answers agree only somewhat with how well they actually perform these tasks.

Sometimes people hold an incorrect attitude because they believe they have observed their memory to succeed when it failed or to fail when it succeeded. Sometimes they hold an incorrect attitude because they have been given an incorrect report about their memory. "Knowing thy memory" is neither easy nor common (Klatzky, 1984).

Since attitudes about the difficulty of memory tasks are often flawed, your decisions about which tasks you should tackle or avoid are often wrong. Thus, you can improve your handling of memory tasks by correcting inappropriate attitudes about the processing requirements of memory tasks.

Note that a correction does not necessarily mean that these attitudes should be made positive. Positive attitudes that are untrue will only lead us astray, making us try tasks we should avoid or not trying hard enough at tasks we incorrectly suppose we are good at. What you need are attitudes that are correct, so you do the tasks you are good at and avoid the tasks you find difficult, or that you work at becoming better at performing difficult tasks. To ensure that your beliefs about memory tasks are correct, you need an assessment of what tasks you are actually good and bad at, an assessment such as was discussed in Chapter 2.

Ironically, people may have a negative attitude about having to perform certain memory tasks that they know they are good at. For example, some good students report disliking the process of studying. Unfortunately, negative task-attitudes have negative consequences. These attitudes will lead you to pay less attention during studying and to respond less quickly and efficiently while taking exams. The obvious manipulation needed here is to develop reasons for believing that the task is worth performing. Often it is difficult to think of positive reasons, whereupon you should ask someone else for help.

It also happens that people value positively having to perform tasks that they are poor at. For example, some poor students report they regard studying as important and wish they were better at it. Fortunately, positive task-attitudes will facilitate paying attention while studying.

Mental Condition Checklist

The information reviewed above on mental condition and memory performance makes it clear that a good mental condition is necessary for good memory performance. Thus, to avoid lowering the level of your memory performance, you should — as Mom and Dad would advise generally — do the following:

1. Maintain an optimum level of activity — that is, avoid a hectic lifestyle, and avoid getting in a rut. Too little or too much to do lessens your capacity to pay attention.

2. Try to keep stress at a manageable level. A little stress keeps you alive and alert to perform memory tasks, but too much of it makes you distractible.

3. Engage in recreational activities such as hobbies, sports, and socializing. They relieve the stress that may hinder your memory performance.

4. Relax daily, on weekends, and on annual vacations. It will also reduce stress and renew your strength.

5. Rest, by taking catnaps. It will also renew periodically just before having to do a memory task.

6. Exercise. You will be less stressed, stronger, and have a more positive viewpoint when you perform memory tasks.

7. Try innovative ways of relaxing, such as yoga exercise and yoga meditation.

8. Talk out your problems. Alleviation of depression and a more positive outlook will make you more able to register and remember.

9. Choose harmonious environments for studying, ones that set the right noise level and do not contain overly comfortable furniture, and wear comfortable clothing. Discomfort decreases your concentration for studying.

10. Maintain appropriate attitudes towards memory tasks, prioritize information to motivate yourself and establish the level of effort that will be required.

Conclusion

This chapter has described a variety of ways to manipulate your physical and mental condition to enhance your performance of memory tasks.

Condition manipulations are an important part of your memory knowledge because they are often the only way to ensure improved performance of memory tasks that you either "can't see coming" or do not recognize until they have "come and gone."

If you know you have an important memory task coming up, do one or more of the several manipulations discussed here to enhance your condition.

If you wish to improve your memory widely across all manner of tasks, consistent care of your condition will give you much of the improvement you desire.

The next four chapters present other manipulations to facilitate your memory. Like condition manipulations, these manipulations focus your attention in a manner that helps you acquire and retrieve information. However, the manipulations you will learn about next involve doing things with the environment or with your thoughts.

Summary

- Manipulations that alleviate inadequate physical and mental states can have marked influence on your ability to study.
- Your condition can make you more ready to pay attention to memory tasks and make your long-term memory more ready to absorb new traces or to have old traces emerge.

Chapter 4
Scientific Background

Research regarding the influence of social factors on memory processing is quite new, with most of this work carried out only in the past decade. Researchers have used different kinds of tasks to examine the roles of various types of social information on memory performance. Several investigators have examined the effects of social stereotypes on memory performance. Thus, they have asked people to whom a stereotype might apply, to perform a task relevant to the stereotype characteristics. For example, the stereotypes that suggest women are good at remembering such domestic things as a grocery list, while men are good at remembering matters of business could be exmployed in such research.

Another kind of investigation has examined the effects of the dynamics of social interaction on memory performance, such as the pace of conversation, or the use of intimidation in conversation. The *dynamics of social interactions* have been shown to affect memory through conversational manipulations and conformity pressures influencing what information a person retains.

Finally, research on social cognition has investigated how *attitudes* held by oneself and others towards a certain topic, the *roles* that we and others are playing at the time, and the kind of *impression* we want to make can affect memory performance. Such research has shown that a person's success at learning is dependent on his or her ability to work cooperatively with the teacher.

Social Context

4

Now that we've established the importance of condition — both physical and mental — it's time to look at another major influence on your intellectual performance: social factors.

Every social situation requires you to demonstrate that you know who others are and what they do. You must make and meet appointments, repay favors, do chores that others depend on you to do. Your performance of such tasks helps determine how others judge and treat you.

Failure to perform these memory tasks can lead your family, friends, and acquaintances to make negative judgments about your caring, sensitivity, manners, or even intelligence. Alternatively, successful performance can lead others to make correspondingly positive judgments about you. Because your relationships with others can be seriously affected by your performance of various memory tasks, successful memory performance becomes especially important in social contexts (Best, 1992; Wyer & Srull, 1989).

Ironically, your memory is more likely to fail when you are with others than when you are alone. This failure usually occurs in social contexts in one of three ways. You fail sometimes because you simply do not realize that a person expects you to remember something, or to remember it to a certain degree. You fail other times because social situations are too distracting to use your memory effectively. Finally, even if you have successfully performed the memory task expected of you, you may still fail to communicate adequately that you have learned or remembered something.

This chapter will explain how various aspects of social situations affect your memory performance. You will examine the memory performance that others expect of you: which tasks you should perform and how well you should perform them. Sometimes there are symbols that remind us to do some social memory task (see Figure 7). But more often, we have to listen to what others tell us about their needs. Your increased awareness of these expectations will demonstrate to your family members, friends, and acquaintances that you can remember the information important to your relationship with them.

Figure 7.
Internationally recognized symbols that direct a person to "not forget" certain information: to carry out actions, a string around a finger; to remember the past, an elephant; to remember a loved one, "forget-me-not" flowers and cupid.

You will examine how interacting with others distracts you and robs from your ability to concentrate on memory tasks. You will learn how to control the flow of conversations so as to have more mental time to perform memory tasks. You will examine the communication factors that render a person's recall less than convincing despite possessing an underlying memory that is accurate and complete. Your greater appreciation of these factors will enable you to recall what you remember in a more plausible fashion.

Recognizing the Memory Performance Expected of You

Level of Performance of a Memory Task. Often, others may feel you have failed at a memory task even though you believe you have succeeded. For example, you may recall what took place at a certain party or meeting, whereupon someone else tells you that your recall is wrong or incomplete. This discrepancy occurs because other people often have different expectations than you for what constitutes good memory performance.

It is not enough that you know your memory is correct. If someone else erroneously thinks their memory is richer and more accurate, they are not likely to believe yours. Even if they realize they do not have an inkling of the answer, they still will have criteria as to how well they think you should perform a particular memory task. Several sources influence their criteria.

Your Memory Reputation. Perhaps of greatest importance to the way others judge your memory performance is your memory reputation. In any circle of acquaintances or co-workers you have known for awhile, you have a reputation for how you succeed or fail at memory tasks. Like reputations for other characteristics such as loyalty, diligence, or discretion, memory reputations are based generally on our past behavior patterns.

Most people would regard a reputation for a good memory as desirable. If your memory reputation is excellent and you forget some fact or something you were to do, others will say you were tired or that even the best will falter sometime. However, a "good" reputation is also likely to bring extra responsibilities. If you are known for "always remembering details," people may ask you to remember more than your share of chores or projects.

On the other hand, a bad memory reputation is usually regarded as an undesirable emblem of weakness or incompetence. When your reputation is terrible, others may hold it against you. If you succeed in remembering some obscure fact or actually do as you promised, others will say it was a fluke. However, a bad memory reputation can free one from excessive impositions. If you are known to be "absentminded," people will be reluctant to burden you with memory tasks, giving you extra free time.

Memory Stereotypes. All of us recognize the dangers of stereotypes. However, people are often surprised to find that stereotypes can govern how others judge our memory performance.

Some examples of some memory stereotypes are listed in Table 4–1 (Herrmann, 1990c). This table presents the average ratings made by a dozen college students at Hamilton College. They were asked to estimate four kinds of memory ability as a function of a person's age, occupation, and marital roles.

Table 4-1.

Family					
Young Adult	4.4	4.8	4.5	4.5	4.6
Wife	4.6	5.1	4.7	4.0	4.6
Husband	4.8	4.8	4.0	4.4	4.5
Middle-aged person	5.1	4.7	4.1	4.2	4.5
Senior citizen	4.6	4.2	3.4	3.5	3.9
Child	2.5	3.4	3.5	3.5	3.2
Occupation					
Airline pilot	6.0	5.1	5.8	6.4	5.8
Lawyer	6.6	5.4	5.1	5.1	5.6
Professor	6.9	5.2	4.8	4.5	5.4
Mechanic	5.2	4.0	5.0	6.4	5.2
Reporter	5.4	5.8	4.9	4.7	5.2
Receptionist	4.9	4.9	5.3	5.0	5.0
Politician	5.9	5.3	4.8	4.1	5.0
Police officer	4.9	4.5	5.0	5.7	5.0
Plumber	4.7	3.8	5.0	5.8	4.8
Company spokesperson	5.5	4.5	4.7	4.1	4.7
Salesperson	5.3	4.4	4.4	4.3	4.6

The table shows expectations in memory performance are a function of the specific kind of task and the person's role. Notice how the ratings are lowest for a child, highest for young and middle-aged adults, and lower again for the senior citizen. Among the occupations, pilots are judged to have the best memory overall, although lawyers and professors are judged higher than pilots regarding knowledge. Memory stereotypes have also been established also for sex (Crawford, Herrmann, Holdsworth, Randall & Robbins, 1986; Herrmann, Crawford, & Holdsworth, 1992; Loftus, Banaji, Schooler, & Foster, 1987; Raybeck, 1986) and age (Best, 1991; Hamlett, Best, & Davis,1991).

If stereotypes can affect the way ratings are made regarding memory performance, then it is likely that stereotypes affect the way we are judged by others in daily life. Thus, when someone's reaction to your memory performance is unrealistically high or low, consider whether it may be because of stereotypical beliefs associated with your age, occupation, gender, or other characteristics. In such a case, you cannot expect to change their stereotype, because it has been established with years of learning. However, you can take steps to alter your memory performance to alter their judgement.

If they view your performance as unrealistically high, you may want to relax when performing memory tasks around them because you are already doing very well. If they view your performance as unrealistically low and you cannot avoid having to deal with them, you may want to make a greater effort at preparing for tasks around them so as to correct for the unfair negative bias in their stereotype. You should know that there are committees and college officials on your campus who can help you if you feel that prejudicial attitudes about your memory ability, or any other characteristic, are interfering with your academic performance or a professor's evaluation of your performance.

Feedback. Sometimes people comment about how well or how poorly you performed a memory task. However, this "memory feedback" cannot be taken at face value (Best, 1992). People often deliberately contrive to make memory performance appear better or worse than it really is. They do so in order to achieve certain social goals (Gentry & Herrmann, 1990). Their comments about your memory may be intended to flatter or insult you, or they may be intended to show you kindness or anger indirectly.

Regardless of the intention behind a contrivance, it is important to distinguish contrived feedback from accurate and deserved feedback. As discussed in Chapter 2 and 3, you are best off if your attitudes about your memory abilities are accurate. If you believe a negative contrivance about your memory, it will lower your confidence and lead you to perform the memory task poorly. Believing positive contrivances will only hamper your performance because they will give you an unrealistic sense of your memory ability.

Six kinds of memory contrivances are especially common, as described below.

Contrivances of Others About Your Memory

1. *Memory Insult:* A person points out a memory failure of yours that otherwise might have been overlooked and claims that the failure is indicative of a "bad memory."
   For example, you forget that Columbus' third ship was the Santa Maria and a companion lambastes you for your idiocy. Chances are that the person who says this is angry with you for something unrelated to their love of history.

2. *Memory Praise:* A person praises your success at a memory task far beyond what it deserves and claims your success is indicative of a "good memory."
   For example, you remember the Nina, Pinta, and Santa Maria and a colleague declares you are brilliant! Enjoy the praise but beware that the other person wants something.

3. *Memory Alibi:* A person makes excuses for a memory failure you have.
   You forgot to pick up a quart of milk on the way home from work. Someone present forgives this mistake, noting that after a long day you have a right to be tired. This may be genuine forgiveness, or the comment may be based on a desire to get a favor from you later.

4. *Memory Responsibility Charge:* A person claims that performing a memory task was your responsibility and not someone else's, such as the person making the claim.
   You arrive home without the milk, thinking that someone else was to pick it up, only to be accused of being irresponsible.

5. *Memory Non-Cooperation:* A person fails to help you at a
   memory task, although he or she is capable of doing so.
   In response to a query, you say "Nina, Pinta, and Santa ..."
   (but you just can't get it), and a friend, who surely knows
   Columbus' saga, volunteers nothing. Such an obvious decision
   not to help when help could be offered shows your friend has
   some concern about your friendship.

6. *Memory Fraud:* A person claims your memory is in error on some
   point, although you both know that this claim is untrue.
   Such a refutation of you bodes ill for your relationship with this
   person. Of course, people will also contrive about their own memory performance as well as yours.

If someone seems to forget more than you do, it may be that
they have feigned forgetting to let you feel better about your memory ability and enhance your attitude towards this person. If someone attempts to gloss over a particular instance of forgetting, it
may be that this person does not want you to be able to hold something against him or her.

Be alert to recognize when someone's memory performance is
not what it seems to be and to the social motives behind another's
contrivance about his or her own memory. Generally, you should
be very careful about using another person as the standard for
judging your memory ability.

Using Others as Memory Aids

Sometimes we do not feel like making an effort at a memory task
that arises in conversation. Instead, we may try to use someone
present as a memory aid. We may ask them to answer a question
that we could have answered if we really tried. Or we ask them
to register and retain some information and to tell us about it later.
Or we may ask them to remind us later when we are supposed to
do something.

Unfortunately, there are definite disadvantages to using a friend
or an acquaintance as a memory aid. First, the person you regard
as an authority for remembering facts may provide you with in-

accuracies (Goldsmith & Pillemer, 1988). Using others as a "re-minder service" can get you into trouble if the person aiding you has a faulty memory.

Second, even if the person has a good memory and can be counted on to remember or register memories for you, there is no such thing as a free lunch. People who are willing to remember for you will eventually expect to be paid back. They know you have imposed on them. The use of others as memory aids is a last-ditch manipulation.

Social Pressures

Influence of People Present on What we Remember. Sometimes people assert confidently that our recall is inadequate. Because of their doubt, we are often inclined to doubt ourselves.

This doubt can arise even if we are initially sure of our recol-lection. Most people will disbelieve their own eyes and accept the account of several other people. People find it especially difficult

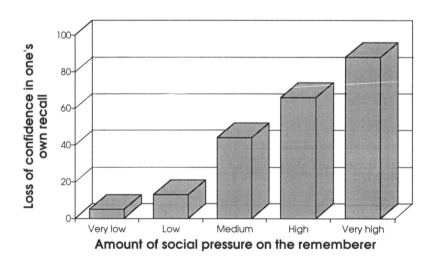

Figure 8.
The effect of social pressure on a person's confidence in what he or she recalls (hypothetical data based on the research literature).

to hold a lone dissenting view among well-respected friends or authorities (Asch, 1956). For example, if while reminiscing about a previous good time you recall events differently from several of your friends, you will tend to doubt your recall and revise your memory according to their version. The effect of social pressure on your confidence in what you recall is summarized in Figure 8.

It is not possible to suggest an easy way to insulate your memory from the influence of all group pressures (Raybeck, 1986). But bear in mind that your memory may be right when others say it is wrong. Because you could be right, you should guard against revising your memories simply to lessen the social pressures disagreement can trigger. If others attack your recall, check later for corroborating evidence. Don't alter your memory just because others challenge it.

Influences of Groups We Identify with on What We Remember

The accuracy of your recall for information can be affected by the influences of groups to which you belong — even when the members of a group are not present.

We learn and retain more about matters that are consistent with our religious, political, and social beliefs. Considerable evidence shows that we edit our memories, so they record our actions or words in a socially more favorable light (Greenwald, 1980).

We also tend to better retain ideas that are consistent with our socially relevant interests. For example, after reading a balanced passage that discusses the pros and cons of a political issue, most people retain more accurately the facts about the side they favor, and less accurately facts from the position they oppose.

To avoid having biased memories, spend extra time studying the facts that stand contrary to your position, especially when it is important that you remember an event or information accurately.

For example, when you overhear an argument, pay special attention to the points you disliked because they are the ones you are likely to forget. This extra care will lead your memory to be more accurate. An especially valuable by-product of this balanced rehearsal is that people disinclined to your point of view will give you additional credit for being open-minded because you possess an unusually accurate memory for the other point of view.

Communicating about Your Memory in a Convincing Manner

Assuming you have successfully recalled something in a social context, you may still have a problem convincing others that your recall is correct.

There are three ways you can increase the likelihood that others will believe in what you recall. You can express your recall with an appropriate degree of confidence, you can strive to make the contents of your recall include the most essential details, and you can couch your recall in language that best describes your memory performance.

1. *Expression.* Overstatement or understatement of the confidence in your recall will likely hurt your credibility. Considerable research has demonstrated that witnesses in court will be regarded as remembering the truth if they sit up and speak confidently.

   John Dean, of Watergate fame, was regarded as having an excellent memory because he conveyed his recall of the events of Nixon's presidency in a convincing fashion, despite later investigation having shown Dean's recall was full of inaccuracies (Neisser, 1982).

2. *Content.* To be convincing, your memory claim should be internally consistent. Although inconsistencies appear in even highly accurate reports from memory, major contradictions between facts make a report appear illogical and indicate the memory underlying the report is distorted.

   The people you interact with will invariably discount what you recall if it contains obvious inconsistencies. Your recall will tend to be better accepted if you have corroborating sources, such as newspapers, books, or memos. Or your source can be someone whose memory is trusted who can "back up" what you say.

3. *Memory Language.* Your recall will be more credible if you couch it in appropriate memory vocabulary — the terms and catch phrases we use to describe our memory states.

Consider for example, the range of common verbs used to express varying degrees of certainty. You may indicate that you suspect, believe, think, know, guarantee, or even swear that something you remember is true (Searle, 1969). These different memory terms have subtly different meanings. As you become more sensitive to memory terminology, you can express yourself better. For example, after having forgotten to do something for a friend, you may choose to excuse yourself by saying your memory "overloaded." The success of this claim will depend on whether you can demonstrate why your memory was overloaded. Or you may excuse yourself by saying you have a memory "like a sieve." The success of this claim will depend on whether your friend knows or can be convinced that your memory fails with unintentional and unusual frequency.

Besides appropriate use of memory language, you can improve your communication of memory performance even more by effective use of nonverbal signals.

Many nonverbal signals concerning memory are virtually universal. When we recognize someone on the street, a smile or a widened gaze can be sufficient to signal our recognition. If you fail to remember something, you may groan or shake your head. If you want a moment longer to come up with something that you are sure you can remember, you may repeatedly mutter "oh" or shake your hand in the air.

Combining appropriate nonverbal signals with verbal claims can make for an even more persuasive case that your memory is accurate.

The Current Status of Your Relationship with a Person

This obvious point cannot be left unsaid: people will be inclined to judge your memory favorably or unfavorably depending on how you are getting along with them. The status of your relationships with others will depend on how you have treated them regarding many matters, including their performance of memory tasks. The sympathy or harshness with which others view your memory will in part be a function of how you have treated their own memory performance.

As shown in Table 4–2, there is an unwritten social code of memory etiquette, and your adherence or rejection of it will usually come back to haunt you.

Table 4–2
Some rules of memory etiquette

1. Do not comment on another's lack of memory ability. If someone in a discussion continually forgets items just mentioned, do not point this out or else you will appear rude.
2. If you must correct a memory error, do so politely. When a friend recalls some information incorrectly and you must correct lest someone else be set wrong, do so in a considerate manner ("you meant XXX, didn't you?")
3. Ignore unimportant memory errors, especially if the person is a loved one.
4. Do not point out unintentional repeated recalls, especially if the person is elderly. If grandpa is going to tell you the battle of Bull Run for the two hundredth time, consider that you'll be doing the same before too long.
5. Remember what another person was talking about prior to an interruption in a conversation. Failure to remember what someone was just talking about may make you seem, however wrongly, uninterested and insincere.
6. Remember the successes of others, and forget their failures.

Summary

Social situations require us to perform many memory tasks. This chapter has shown that there are several things you can do to make your memory perform better in social contexts. Recognize what memory tasks others expect you to perform. Recognize how factors such as your reputation and stereotypes that might apply to you affect the level of memory performance others expect of you. Use conversational manipulations to keep from being distracted, to buy time, and to gather information that will enable you to better perform memory tasks in class.

Resist social pressures to recall facts and events as others might want you to. Recall plausibly by remembering logically consistent information and by expressing yourself with appropriate memory language and nonverbal signals.

Chapter 5
Scientific Background

Modern research into mental manipulations began at the turn of the century, but it is important to bear in mind that this research has built upon a 2000 year history of efforts to devise better methods to learn and remember. Considerable scientific progress has refined anecdotal knowledge of mental manipulations and developed new techniques. This research employs one of two very reliable and effective procedures.

One procedure simply asked people what kind of mental manipulations they use when performing a certain learning task, such as whether they use imagery in learning a list and, if so, whether the imagery is bizarre or not. However, the reports of manipulation use can be attributed to the notion that people with different degrees of memory ability tend to choose different learning techniques. Consequently, reports of mental manipulation use may reflect differences in the abilities of the people reporting, rather than the effectiveness of various manipulations.

Because reports of manipulation use are not definitive, additional investigation is done into the actual use of experimental procedures. For example, research may direct one group of people to use one kind of mental manipulation, such as imagery in learning a list, while another group uses another kind of manipulation, such as bizarre imagery in learning the same list. If there are differences in performance, they may then be attributed to whether a person used bizarreness in imagery during learning. Issues such as this are currently under investigation.

Mental Manipulations

5

Ever since the time of the ancient Greeks, memory experts have tried to find simple mental tricks that would help them overcome the limits and inconsistencies of memory (Herrmann & Searleman, 1990, 1992). The techniques they developed go by a number of different names: mnemonics, mnemotechnics (both words deriving from Mnemonsyne, the Greek goddess of memory), memory strategies, or "artificial memories." In this book, we refer to these techniques as "mental manipulations."

Almost everyone has tried to use a mental pattern, outline, or key to help them memorize information. Some of the more popular techniques include repeating lists to ourselves, quizzing ourselves on material we need to memorize, organizing information so it will be more meaningful and memorable, restating fundamental ideas to be remembered, relating key ideas to a familiar pattern that will help us retrieve them, and visualizing the scenario in which our memory will have to perform. Over time, these mental manipulations have become almost the sole focus of memory training courses and books. As a result, most people think of them as the only way to improve their memory.

Unfortunately, memory isn't that easy to control. Research shows that learning a single mental technique helps your memory only for a specific situation — and that you can't substantially improve your overall memory without mastering a broad assortment of techniques (Herrmann, Rea, & Andrzejewski, 1987; Herrmann, 1990b). As discussed earlier, mental manipulations aren't the only factor determining your memory performance. Your condition, attitude, environment, and the social context all strongly influence your performance, and their effects must be addressed in any conscientious effort to improve your memory.

Still, mental manipulations can play an important part in a program of memory improvement. They all have a common goal — to help you learn, retain, and retrieve information. If you use the right technique in the right way, you can improve from 100 to 200 percent. For example, suppose you had to attempt to learn as many items as possible on a 30 item list but were not given much time to do so. You might only be able to remember 10 items. If you had used certain mnemonics, in the same amount of time, you might have learned 20 items, a 100% increase. And if you had used yet another kind of mnemonic, you might have learned all 30 items, 300% of unaided recall.

What's in This Chapter

Unlike most books on memory improvement, we won't claim to show you a few general procedures that will work for all readers and all situations. As you'll see, the sheer number and diversity of mental manipulations are strong evidence that a single, foolproof, all-purpose technique doesn't exist.

This chapter will introduce you to a wide variety of mental manipulations. Some of them were devised as long as two thousand years ago, and some were developed through research during the past two decades. Most of us will have used one or more at some time, but it's likely that we did so without much forethought or consistency.

These manipulations are designed to help you learn, retain, and retrieve information. Out of the many techniques that I'll present, you're sure to find several that you can adapt to your own needs and abilities.

The chapter will also explain how mental manipulations differ in kind. Some manipulations emphasize rehearsal, others embellishing information, and others associating what is to be learned or remembered. Knowledge of of these different kinds of manipulations will enable you to choose the right manipulation for the task confronting you and to customize mental manipulations to serve you better.

The manipulations covered here are intended to prepare you for a wide variety of situations, especially for unexpected memory tasks. Chapter Seven will propose additional manipulations designed to serve specific tasks and will propose modifications of manipulations advanced in this chapter so they can apply to certain tasks. But often you will not know in advance that a certain memory task will arise, in which case you will need to know at least four or five of the broad, non-specific manipulations taught in this chapter.

Below you will be acquainted with a little more theory of how we learn, and you will be presented with a range of learning manipulations. Then you will read about the factors that lead us to forget and the manipulations we can use to ensure we retain information we need. Finally, you will be presented with explanations of how remembering occurs and manipulations to retrieve information when it is not forthcoming.

How Do Mental Manipulations Work?

First, mental manipulations are relevant only to intentional memory tasks, in which you are conscious of the information you must learn or retrieve (Ericsson, 1985; Morris, 1977; Pressley & Levin, 1983). When your boss asks you to remember something, you are aware of what is asked of you and you intend to do it.

Incidental tasks, in which information is automatically encoded into or emerges from long-term memory, cannot be handled with mental manipulations. Often we are asked to recall something that happened when we were present but not paying attention. When this occurs, all we can do is to try to remember what we registered incidentally. At that point, it is too late for us to have intentionally learned what is asked of us.

Second, mental manipulations work by intensifying your attention to information during the learning, retention, and retrieval phases of the memory process. A manipulation causes you to process — in some way — that information, and your increased attention leads to either or both of two mental processes that affect the memory traces in your long-term memory. In one process, new information can be absorbed from working memory into long-term memory. In the other process, your attention can activate existing traces in long-term memory that have similar informational content.

Once an existing trace is activated, its activation can spread to other associated traces. When a trace has received enough activation — either directly or indirectly — its contents will emerge into consciousness. Therefore, when you want to learn, you should use mental manipulations that make you pay enough attention to the information you want to remember to form traces to constitute an adequate record of the information.

Once the trace has been formed, the memory system retains it. Unfortunately, this system has its shortcomings much like other systems of retaining information and experiences (film, newsprint). As the retention period increases, it becomes harder to find what you want in storage. Its hidden amidst everything else, and the physical record is disintegrating. Because memory traces become less accessible with time, it is necessary to refresh memory in order to be sure you have retained it.

When you want to retrieve information, you should use mental manipulations that make you pay enough attention to the informational "clues" you've been given to activate secondary traces. Once these traces are sufficiently activated, this activation spreads and converges on the desired trace, causing it to emerge from long-term memory into consciousness. (See Chapter 1 or the glossary for definitions of many of these technical terms.)

When Should You *Not* Use the Mental Manipulations Taught in This Chapter?

The boost in memory performance that mental manipulations can give comes with a price tag — it takes both time and effort to use a mental manipulation. If you have time to execute the manipulation, and/or the task deserves the effort, a mental manipulation can be your best way to deal with a particular memory task. In many cases, you may not have the time, or you'll decide that the particular memory task just isn't worth the effort.

As useful as the mental manipulations taught in this chapter *may* be, they are not as powerful as mental manipulations *can* be. Mental manipulations that have been modified to be used for a specific memory task are usually more efficient and more effective than the non-specific manipulations discussed here. Consequently, if you want to prepare yourself to respond better to a particular memory task, you will need to acquire manipulations designed specifically to deal with this task. However, task specific mental manipulations require extra preparation before the task arises and there are far too many tasks for which it would be possible to prepare task-specific manipulations. Thus, as a foundation — as insurance — it is wise to know several of the mental manipulations discussed in this chapter. Additionally, knowing about these non-specific mental manipulations will help you appreciate and develop the task-specific manipulations.

Your intellectual style and tastes will also be important in your choice of mental manipulations. There is no sense in trying to learn a manipulation that seems foreign, weird, or stupid to you. So choose manipulations that suit you.

Ultimately, the best way to be sure that a manipulation will help you remember is to try using it. Compare the effort and effectiveness of different manipulations. Generally the best manipulation is one that both meets your goals for effectiveness and fits your intellectual style.

The remainder of this chapter presents with manipulations for each phase of memory: learning, retention, and retrieval. Take note of which manipulations appeal to you as you read through the chapter. By its end, try to have identified three or four manipulations for each phase of memory. Knowledge of several non-specific manipulations will prepare you to cope better with a wide variety of memory tasks, especially ones that occur unexpectedly or infrequently.

How We Learn

Learning occurs when you intentionally pay attention to the contents of working memory, leading them to be absorbed into long-term memory. Mental manipulations influence what is absorbed into long-term memory in one or more of four distinct ways.

- First, a mental manipulation can increase the *strength* of an item's trace. Repeating an item, for example, will keep it in your working memory longer, possibly increasing the intensity of your attention. As a result, a stronger trace will be absorbed into your long-term memory.

The way an increase in attention can increase the strength of a memory trace can be compared to how much clearer a photograph will be if it's taken in bright light than if it's taken in dimmer light. The stronger the trace, the more familiar we are with an item. Consider when you attempt to register a person's phone number in memory, at least long enough to dial it. Rehearsing the number by repeating it to yourself or out loud boosts the strength of the number in memory.

- Second, a mental manipulation can foster the encoding of *attributes* of the information that would otherwise probably not be included in the memory trace. Examples of the attributes of information would include whether the idea is an object, an action, or a quality. Examples of the attributes of an object would include its size, shape, and color.

You can make a memory trace easier to retrieve by incorporating surprising or interesting attributes. For example, you can improve your ability to remember the name of a person you've just been introduced to by analyzing the national origin of their name, or by determining the number of vowels and consonants in the name. In both cases, your analysis of the name increases your attention to the name. Most people don't pay much attention to attributes like this, but the additional attention will definitely help you register the information in your memory.

- Third, we can use mental manipulations to establish an *association* between two or more items we wish to learn, or between items we need to learn and more familiar items already in our memory. Sometimes the associations are conventional; other times they are idiosyncratic. In attempting to learn someone's name, we can associate it with someone else we know with a similar name or we may associate it with the town, county, or state they are from.

Associations are established by any manipulation that makes you attend jointly to items that are separate in consciousness. Paying attention separately to two items will not result in their being associated. For example, suppose you are studying vocabulary to a foreign language. You will not know learn which foreign terms go with certain English terms simply by reading through the list of foreign words and then the list of English words. Joint attention to the corresponding foreign and English items is necessary to produce an association of the appropriate translations.

Associations differ from each other (Bellezza, 1981, 1983). An association can be bidirectional — if item A reminds you of item B, item B will also remind you of A. Or they can be unidirectional — A reminds you of B, but not vice versa.

For example, if people are asked to "free associate" — that is, to say what word comes to mind when they hear another word — what they say reveals the directionality of associations. If they hear the word "smart," they often think of the word "intelligent"; and if they hear the word "intelligent", many think of "smart." Thus, "intelligent" and "smart" share bi-directional associations. On the other hand, if people free associate to the word "hot," many will say "dog," but when asked to give a word association for "dog," almost no one will say "hot."

As the number of associations between an item and other items in memory increases, its trace is said to become "more meaningful." The more associations, the easier the trace is to retain and retrieve from memory. Additionally, associative patterns may occur when an item's associations number more than one (Anderson, 1983). Patterns are important because they affect retrieval.

For example, we may not be able to remember a poem, prayer, or song if we start with one of the middle lines — because our associations form a line-to-line pattern starting from the first line of the text. Try singing the Star Spangled Banner from the middle. Or try recalling the Pledge of Allegiance from the word "indivisible." My bet is that in either case you will have difficulty unless you start at the beginning.

- Fourth, a mental manipulation can establish a framework that facilitates the retrieval of the memorized items. By exploiting certain characteristics of each item, we can devise a *retrieval structure* for finding all of the items in memory (Ericcson, 1985; Chase & Ericsson, 1982).

One such manipulation is the "first letter mnemonic" for learning a short list. To remember a list of grocery items — milk, eggs, bread, and Alka-Seltzer — you could arrange the first letter of each item to form the word "beam." When you go to the store, you could recall one item for each letter of the word until you retrieved the entire list.

Figure 9 shows that a list learned using a retrieval structure has twice as many avenues for retrieval from long-term memory as a list learned without a structure.

The top panel shows a memory trace for a shopping list that was learned without a retrieval structure. The trace is remembered in two steps. The physical situation — the setting you are in, the people you are with, what others say — elicits your memory for this situation when you originally learned the list. Your memory for the situation elicits, in turn, your memory of the information — in this case, the shopping list.

The lower panel shows a memory trace for a shopping list that was learned by forming a retrieval structure. This trace can be remembered by the physical situation eliciting your memory of the learning situation and therefore the shopping list. In addition, the memory of the learning situation can *separately* elicit the retrieval structure, which can also elicit the desired information.

For some people, and for some tasks, retrieval structures may seem like excess baggage — too much work for too little reward. In fact, retrieval structures are eventually forgotten. The structures fade in memory because the direct association between the situation and the trace increases sufficiently with use, making the retrieval structure unnecessary. However, until the association is well-established, the retrieval structure is invaluable. Besides giving you a second path to successfully retrieving the memory, retrieval structures augment the learning process itself. The added

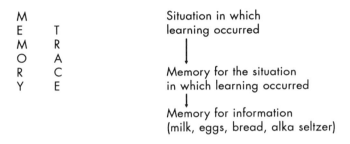

Without a Retrieval Structure

```
M                    Situation in which
E       T            learning occurred
M       R
O       A                    |
R       C            Memory for the situation
Y       E            in which learning occurred
                             |
                     Memory for information
                     (milk, eggs, bread, alka seltzer)
```

With a Retrieval Structure

```
M                    Situation in which
E       T            learning occurred
M       R                    |
O       A            Memory for the situation ———→ Memory for
R       C            in which learning occurred  — Retrieval
Y       E                    |              ←       Structure
                     Memory for information          (BEAM)
                     (milk, eggs, bread, alka seltzer)
```

Figure 9.
Memory learned with and without a retrieval structure.
The top panel shows how situational cues elicit the information that was
learned without a retrieval structure. The bottom panel shows how this
process works for information that was learned with a retrieval structure.
Note that in the bottom panel, the retrieval structure provides an extra link
to situational cues.

process of forming a retrieval structure causes you to pay more
attention to the trace, making it stronger, embellishing it with
more attributes, and activating its associations with other traces.

Figure 10 illustrates the importance of these four effects. To
simplify the illustration, the figure depicts a simple memory trace,
without showing the association with the situation in which the
learning occurred.

Panel A shows the trace as it would be registered in long-term
memory when the trace information has not been subjected to a
mental manipulation. Panel B shows the trace after it has received
a strength-building manipulation. Stronger traces will emerge

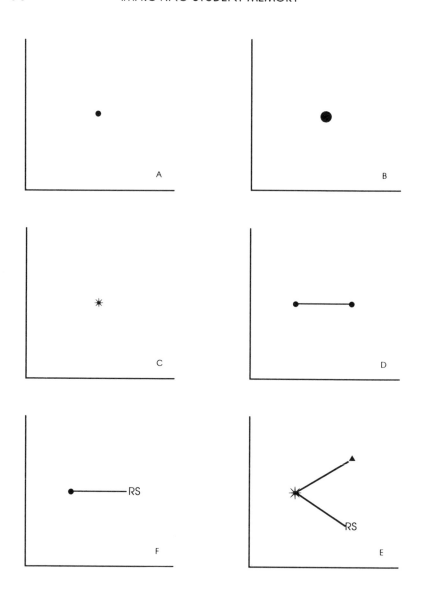

Figure 10.
Illustrations of the different effects of mental manipulations on a trace.
Panel A: registered trace before a manipulation. Panel B: a trace after a
strength manipulation. Panel C: a trace after an attribute manipulation.
Panel D: a trace associated with another trace. Panel E: a trace associated
with a retrieval structure. Panel F: a trace after all four manipulations.

from long-term memory into consciousness more readily than weak traces.

Panel C shows the trace after it has been subjected to an attribute manipulation. Thinking about an attribute tends to activate a trace bearing it, and leads the trace to emerge into consciousness.

For example, the attribute "white" may activate "milk," and "stomach remedy" may activate "Alka-Seltzer." Thus, a trace with many attributes is easier to remember than one with few attributes.

Panel D shows the trace after association with another trace. There are two kinds of possible associations: one kind involves pre-existing associations, like the one between "milk" and "shake." The other involves new associations, like the one formed here between "milk" and "Alka-Seltzer." In either case, the information associated with the target trace affects the trace in the same way as attributes do: the associated information tends to activate the desired trace and leads it to emerge into consciousness.

Panel E shows the trace associated with a retrieval structure, as described above.

Finally, Panel F shows a trace that has been subjected to all four effects of mental manipulations — strength, attribute, association, and a retrieval structure.

Most of the mental manipulations covered in this chapter will improve your ability to register information in memory in more than one way — usually in some combination of the four categories I've discussed. The more effects that a manipulation produces, the better it will work. Retrieval of the memory in Panel F is considerably more likely than in any of the other panels. In this final case, the trace is more familiar to memory, due to added strength, as well as more likely to be activated and emerge, due to the presence of relevant attributes, associated information, and the activation of the retrieval structure.

Most importantly, the relationship between categories tends to be hierarchical, with the manipulations in each category also producing the effects typical of the categories that come before it in the strength-attributes-associations-structures hierarchy.

Thus, while strength manipulations affect only strength, attribute manipulations also increase the strength of the trace; association manipulations also increase both strength and the number of attributes; and retrieval structures also provide greater strength, more attributes, and more associations.

If you desire that you remember some information briefly, strength manipulations are what you need. For example, an idea may occur to you during a conversation that you want to bring up before the conversation is over. You want a manipulation that will enable you to remember the idea long enough to bring it up, but not necessarily to remember the idea forever.

However, as the need for durability of a memory increases, you should use increasingly more powerful manipulations in the hierarchy of attributes, associations, and retrieval structures. If you want to remember something critical that someone said at a meeting so you can relate it to your boss later, you are going to want to use one or more of the more powerful manipulations.

An Inventory of Learning Manipulations

The inventory that follows presents you with a variety of learning manipulations organized according to the manipulations' dominant effect — that is, whether it operates primarily through building the strength, attributes or associations with the trace, or retrieval structures designed for the trace. Within each category of effect, the different kinds of manipulations are generally presented in alphabetical order.

In order to illustrate for you how these manipulations are used, we will make use of a story — told below — that involves many routine memory tasks. The story and examples have been concocted solely to illustrate the use of the manipulations. Don't worry about having to remember the details of this story, and please realize that the examples of mental manipulations given below don't reflect the range of complexity of the actual memory tasks to which you could apply or adapt them. Even so, they should give you a pretty good idea of how the manipulations are used.

Strength Manipulations

Manipulations that augment the strength of a trace are of two kinds: those that foster paying attention and those that involve rehearsal. If used with unusual intensity, both attention and rehearsal manipulations can also lead to registration of attributes and associations with secondary traces. However, as normally used, the principal effect of these manipulations is to increase trace strength.

Attention

These manipulations focus your attention on the details that should be registered. They are important in situations where remembering only the gist of information will not be sufficient.

- *Mental Snapshot.* When attempting to remember a scene, scan it systematically, then close your eyes and question yourself about the scene; open your eyes and note what you missed. Repeat the cycle until you are satisfied that you have registered the scene in memory. — To etch in memory the time your bowling team won a trophy, take a mental snapshot.
- *Multimodal.* Perceive or imagine what you must register in memory with as many of your senses, or "sensory modes," as possible: how does it look, how is it said, how does it feel. — In order to remember what happened at a conference you attended with Bill, register the various events there multimodally.
- *Reflection.* Think back on information just noticed or understood. Many recommend a daily practice if your work makes it important to remember routine details or if you place great importance on reminiscing. — You will remember better the things you do with daily reflection.

Rehearsal

Rehearsal is particularly useful for two kinds of situations: when you want to keep information in consciousness, but are not concerned about establishing a long-term memory; or when you are not motivated to use a more challenging or elaborate manipulation to establish a long-term memory.

- *Acting Out.* Act out the information you want to register. — For example, when studying history with George and Arlene, you can imagine key events you should know and then, like an actor, overtly act out the interactions as you imagine them.
- *Simple Rehearsal.* Repeat the items to be learned to yourself over and over. — For example, on being introduced to Bill, say to yourself "Bill, Bill, Bill, Bill, ..."
- *Articulatory Rehearsal.* Repeat the items while carefully enunciating each syllable and noting the placement of the tongue in your mouth as you pronounce the words. — On learning someone's name, rehearsing the articulation of the name will stamp it into memory. Such as, "B, B, B, ih, ih, l, l, l."
- *Cumulative Rehearsal.* Repeat the items in successively larger groups. — For example, in learning several names, say to yourself "Bill; Bill, Sarah; Bill, Sarah, George; Bill, Sarah, George, and Arlene."
- *Rhythmic Rehearsal.* Repeat the items in a rhythmic pattern, either in syllables or with a certain beat. — For example in learning a name, say to yourself "Bill — Bill, Bill, Bill — Bill, Bill."
- *Spaced Rehearsal.* Repeat the items to yourself at increasing intervals in which each successive interval is twice as long as the preceding one. — For example, after having been introduced to someone, such as Bill, say his name to yourself once, wait a second, say it again, wait two seconds, say it again, wait four seconds, say it again, and so on (Landauer & Bjork, 1978).

Attribute Manipulations

Anything that may be learned in memory can be characterized by a set of attributes. People, for example, can be characterized as large or small, rich or poor, bright or dull, and so on. Objects can similarly be described as large or small, rounded or angular, light or dark. Ideas can be analyzed as interesting or uninteresting, simple or complex, and positive or negative. Attribute manipulations are designed to foster your registration of more attributes than you would otherwise register.

The more attributes you include in a memory trace, the better. Each additional attribute provides one more way to retrieve the trace. There are several learning manipulations that are designed to increase the number of attributes you would normally incorporate in a trace. Registering more attributes leads you to deepen your comprehension of the details and implications of the information to be learned. These manipulations also increase trace strength. They are useful for learning information that is initially difficult or uninteresting, or that must be remembered in particular detail.

- *Affect elicitation.* Attend to your feelings concerning what is to be learned, or dredge up such feelings as you rehearse. — If when you first meet George or Sarah, you find something pleasing or repugnant about them, dwell on this.
- *Attribute judgments.* Make judgments related to the nature of the items. — For example, judge how "rich" each name to be learned sounds (as "Abercrombie" sounds more affluent than, say "Smith").
- *Description.* Verbally describe to yourself what you plan to learn, and study your description. — For example, to learn someone's face, describe for yourself the shape of the eyes, nose, mouth, etc. Notice that George has greyed beard, blue eyes, and slender build.
- *Meaning analysis (semantic).* Consider the meaning of the information and subtle variations of that meaning. — For example, to remember that Bill is a mechanic, analyze the meaning of the word "mechanic:" one who repairs mechanisms, usually automotive, but also other machines.
- *Phonetic analysis.* Consider the sounds that make up the stimulus. — To remember that Bill is a mechanic, sound out the syllables of the word me-can-ik, rather than just repeat them.
- *Prioritize.* Judge the importance, i.e. the priority, of information to be learned. — If going bowling with the gang is more important than returning your neighbor's cake tin, realize and remain aware of this.
- *Question.* Ask whatever can be asked about the information: if? who? what? where? when? whose? whether? why? to what

purpose? under what conditions? how? in what manner? how much? how many? how often? for how long? by? of? in? — If you want to be able to remember what Bill and Arlene tell you about their jobs at the chemical firm, ask them a lot of questions about their jobs. Both the asking and the answers build up a durable memory.

- *Self-referencing*. Judge how an item to be learned might relate to you as a person or to some aspect of your past. — For example, in learning about Sarah and George's jobs, you might decide how you regard the newspaper they work for: how well it is laid out, whether you feel it gives fair and balanced coverage of the news. Doing so makes it "your" newspaper and thereby ties in what Sarah and George tell you.

- *Temporal ordering*. Describe, or even imitate, to yourself the relative intervals between successive things to be learned. — For example, in learning the names of some people you just met, take note of how much time intervened between each meeting, such as two minutes between meeting Bill and Sarah, and five minutes between meeting Sarah and Arlene.

- *Understanding*. To learn information, come to know it from several perspectives. — Thus, if you need to make a presentation at work, you will recall your ideas most easily if you concentrate on understanding rather than memorizing only key phrases (Raybeck, 1992a).

- *Visual analysis*. Consider the visual characteristics of what is to be learned. — To remember that Bill is a mechanic, visualize the printed structure of the word "mechanic," m — two upside-down "V's" joined; e — a pattern similar to pacman; c — an "o" with a bite out of it; etc.

Association Manipulations

Association manipulations enable you to relate different traces with each other. Both traces may be new or may have already been established in memory. Association manipulations are called for when it will be necessary to remember that a trace is related to certain information, or when the material taken by itself is difficult to learn.

Associations are often necessary to successfully carry out certain tasks. For example, suppose that while traveling you stop and ask someone for directions. For the directions to lead you to the right place, the steps must be registered — thus, associated — in a proper order.

The process of forming associations can also enhance the strength of the items you associate and foster registration of the attributes of the items. Even if the association between items is unnecessary, the process of associating makes your registration of the items themselves easier. Finally, associations with old information may function as a casual retrieval structure for the new trace.

Simple Associative Manipulations

The simplest associative pattern involves just two traces. The manipulations below apply to this kind of association. These manipulations are helpful for situations in which a desired trace can or must be activated by a very restricted piece of information.

- *Verbal.* Determine whether one item to be learned possesses direct or indirect verbal associations with another item to be learned. Then rehearse both the items and the associations between them. For example, suppose you had to buy some items at the store before getting together with George. In trying to remember milk, eggs, bread and Alka Seltzer, you may recall that milk and eggs are associated, as are eggs and bread. Alka seltzer seems to be on its own here.
- *Present With Past Events.* Determine similarities between a current and a past event. For example, you may attempt to remember a certain story you have read by likening it to a different story you read previously. You may better register in memory a conference you attended with Bill and Arlene if you identify how the conference resembles others you have attended.
- *Relations (meaningful).* Judge whether there are meaningful relations between two items to be learned. You might look for similarity, contrasts, or a common category. For example, to

register in memory that a certain country was mentioned in a newspaper as being in a state of war, note the other countries in the conflict.

- *Relations (phonetic).* Judge the ways that two or more items to be learned sound similar to each other. To remember the names of obscure countries mentioned in a textbook, you might note that the sound of one is similar to the sound of the other country.
- *Relations (visual).* Judge the ways that items to be learned may or may not be visually similar. To learn the names of obscure countries reported in a textbook, you can also judge whether the letters in one country look like the letters in another country.

Organization

Organization manipulations increase the strength of items in a trace and the associations between these items. They are used when the information you must learn conforms to a specific structure.

The varieties of animals and plants, for example, are organized according to a system of subspecies, which you would learn separately in order to associate particular animals or plants. These manipulations are also extremely useful when you must acquire a great number of items or pieces of information. Extensive research has shown that organized information is learned as much as four times faster than the same information devoid of organization.

- *Clustering (meaningful).* Organize items into clusters, so that each cluster contains items with similar meanings. For example, group the names on a list by gender: (Bill, George) (Sarah, Arlene).
- *Clustering (phonetic).* Organize items into clusters, so that each cluster contains items with similar sounds. For example, group names by their similarity in sound: Sarah, George, and Arlene all have an "r" sound.
- *Diagram.* Sketch the relationship of items to be learned. For example, if you know certain people are friends, note and review this link on paper: Bill-Sarah, Arlene-George.

- *Sequence*. Arrange stimuli mentally in the sequence of presentation or in the sequence that you feel is most natural. For example, to learn the names of several people you just met, take note of the order in which you met them: first Bill, then Sarah, then George, and finally Arlene.
- *Spatial arrangement*. Notice the spatial arrangement of stimuli. When learning the names of several people you just met, take note of where they were standing or sitting. Bill, for example, was standing next to Sarah, and George next to Arlene.

Retrieval Structure Manipulations

Retrieval structures are most useful for important information that you need to remember perfectly or almost perfectly (Bellezza, 1981; Ericsson, 1985; Higbee, 1988). The manipulations that create retrieval structures fall into one of four categories: elaboration, reduction, transformation, and technical.

- Elaboration manipulations create a retrieval structure that builds on the information to be remembered.
- Reduction manipulations create a structure that relies on part of the trace information.
- Transformation manipulations change the information to be learned into secondary information which is different in form but related in a meaningful way to the primary material.
- Technical manipulations manipulate information according to a scheme that you must memorize ahead of time. (Schemes memorized to facilitate learning are sometimes called "mnemonics" or, less often, "mnemotechny.")

The easiest manipulations to learn and use fall in the elaboration and reduction categories. Transformation manipulations are somewhat more difficult to learn and use, and the technical manipulations require the most effort.

There is also, presently, no evidence that one category of retrieval-structure manipulations is more effective than another — although, generally retrieval-structure manipulations have been shown to register more effectively than strength, attribute, and association manipulations. It is perfectly sensible for you to apply more than one manipulation to the same task, because remembering is enhanced by each manipulation used. The multiple manipulations applied to a given task may come from the same category or from different categories.

Each of the four retrieval-structure categories is discussed in separate sections below. These sections are ordered from the least to most challenging categories.

Elaborations

Elaboration manipulations build a retrieval structure that combines the information to be learned with additional information. The elaboration of the information provides you a code that leads to retrieval of the desired information because the code incorporates the information.

People who learn to read music are often advised to remember the notes on the upper part of sheet music by learning this elaborative structure: "Every Good Boy Does Fine." This structure indicates the notes on the lines of sheet music with the first letter of each word in the structure: E, G, B, D, and F. If you decide to use a retrieval structure, you must learn it well because a forgotten or partially remembered elaboration is useless.

- *Acrostic.* Form a poem or free verse in which each line describes something of what is to be remembered and the first letter of each word beginning a line forms a word. For example, to remember Bill's name, elaborate by saying that "Bill" is a Brave Intrepid Lovable Lug or Bumbling Idiotic Lumbering Lug.
- *Ad hoc.* Cast information to be learned in the form of a limerick. For example, to learn the name of four people on a bowling team (Bill, George, Sarah, and Arlene), you might form the limerick, "There once was the greatest of all bowling teams, made up of Bill, Sarah, George, and Arlene." There are dictionaries of customary ad hoc mnemonics for learning certain information (Pugh, 1970) (see Figure 11).
- *Image (color).* Imagine that the item to be learned appears in one color against a different colored background. Use colors that catch your attention. For example, to remember the name of a product sold by Bill and Arlene's company, imagine it in bright purple against a violet background, if you prefer har-

Thirty days have September, April, June, and November
When short February comes, all the rest have 31 except
February which has 28, 'til leap year makes it 29.

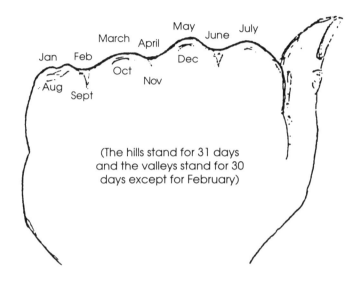

March April May June July
Jan Feb Dec
Oct Nov
Aug Sept

(The hills stand for 31 days
and the valleys stand for 30
days except for February)

Figure 11.
Ad hoc mnemonics for remembering the number of days in the months.

monious colors; or purple against a bright green background,
if you prefer clashing colors. The same process could be used
to register a person's face or an object you wanted to remember.

– *Image (color with affect).* Imagine that what is to be learned
appears in a color that is symbolic of how you feel about it. For
example, suppose Bill introduces you to an acquaintance of his.
If you like this person, register his facial features in silver or
gold; if this person annoys you, use red paint; if you dislike this
person, use paint with a muddy color.

– *Image (graphic).* Form an image of the letters of a word in print
or of the way they were spoken to you. On being introduced to
Arlene, visualize the letters of her name.

– Integrate the items to be learned into a visual image. For example, to register that the name of the newspaper Sarah and

George work for is the Sentinel, imagine a one "cent" coin was mailed to someone name Nel — "cent-ta-nel."

- *Mediation (verbal).* Associate items to be learned with a word that has established associations with the item. For example, to register that Bill pitches a baseball with a curve, you might discover a mediator such as "baseball-round-curve."
- *Number elaboration.* If you have to learn a number, state it to yourself in the form of money (or in minutes, years, phone numbers, zip codes, dates). For example, suppose you decided to learn Sarah's phone number, 733–3121. This number might be coded as the price of a meal: one for your dish, $7.33; and one for the total bill, $31.21.
- *Principle stating.* Describe a pattern or regularity that is apparent in the material to be learned. For example, after attending a play, state to yourself whether the story was a tragedy or a comedy.
- *Ridicule.* Turn the item to be learned into an amusing or ridiculous name or pun. For example, when you first meet Sarah and learn that her last name is "Smith," change it to "Smithiewithy" or to "Smoothie Smith" or any combination that strikes you as funny.
- *Sentence generation.* Generate a sentence that contains the items to be learned. For example, to learn Sarah's last name, embed the name in a sentence, such as, "I just met Sarah Smith, a resident of Des Moines." The sentence need not be true to serve as a retrieval structure, but a true sentence has the advantage of supplementing the targeted information with other useful information. Also, if the generated sentence is false, try to make it blatantly so, or else over time you may be inclined to remember it as a fact!
- *Story generation.* Generate a story that contains the items to be learned. For example, "Once upon a time, Bill lived in the city. To make his living, he worked as a mechanic." You may choose to make a story on the same bases given above for the sentence generation manipulation.

Reductions

Reduction manipulations extract and apply part of the information in the trace to form a retrieval structure. You may prefer them to elaboration manipulations because reductions are shorter and usually easier to remember.

The reductions yield a structure that relates to the information to be learned much like shorthand does to dictation. However, reductions tend to point more ambiguously than elaborations to the information you want to remember. Nevertheless, if the reduction is naturally memorable to you, it will be more manageable.

- *Abbreviation.* Form a smaller word by using a few letters from a larger word. For example, to remember the name Bill, form the smaller nonsense word. In many cases, a ready-made abbreviation can be found in standard sources. (White, 1971).
- *Bleaching.* Imagine the item to be learned in black and white. For example, to remember Arlene's face, an object, or a scene, imagine it devoid of color.
- *First Letter Coding.* Arrange the initials in a list of items into a word (often by adding other letters). For example, to learn three names (George, Bill, and Arlene), form the word GAB. (First letter coding results in an acronym and may be viewed as a form of an acrostic).
- *Sentence reduction.* Form a word or words from the first letters of some of the words in a sentence. For example, suppose you wanted to quote Lincoln in a presentation you had to make at work. To learn "Four score and seven years ago," form the word combination of "fasasyago."
- *Summary stating.* Identify key words in a passage or story that will stand for the overall issue or theme.

Transformations

These manipulations generate a retrieval structure by transforming or translating the primary information of the trace into secondary information. The secondary information bears a conventional relationship with the primary information you wish to register. The resulting retrieval structure tends to be about the same length as the trace word(s), and so it avoids the excessive length of elaboration manipulations, as well as the ambiguity of reduction manipulations. Furthermore, by exploiting conventional relationships of meaning, transformations remain closer to the meaning of the trace than do elaborations or reductions. This more direct significance may make them more effective for you.

You may especially prefer transformations for situations that require an enhanced understanding of the meaning of the information you registered. Transformations were made the cornerstone of one of the most popular memory systems in the last century (Loisette, 1896) because these transformations lead to a meaningful trace. Indeed, it may be argued that transformations provide one of the best ways of helping yourself to comprehend information, as well as to register it.

– *Synonym Generation*. Determine the best synonym for the word to be learned. For example, to register that a certain country mentioned in the Sentinel is a democracy, rehearse also that it is a "free state."
– *Contrast Generation*. Determine the best contrast for the word to be learned. For example, to register that a certain country mentioned in the Sentinel is a democracy, rehearse that it is "not a totalitarian state."
– *Class-Member Generation*. Determine the words that are in the same class as the word to be learned. To register that a certain country is a democracy, rehearse that its people enjoy the same freedoms as, say, Canada, Great Britain, and the United States.
– *Homophonic Generation*. Determine the word(s) that most sounds like the word to be learned. For example, to register that a certain country is a dictatorship, rehearse that this form of government sounds something like "dictate or ship."
– *Comprehensive Generation*. Determine the set of terms that reflect all the possible relations of sound and meaning with the word to be learned. This judgment combines the previous relation generations of synonym, contrast, class, and homophonic determinations, applying each manipulation to the trace.

Technical Schemes

These manipulations are called "technical" because their use requires more involved instructions and preparation (Bellezza, 1981, 1983). To use them, you need to memorize an encoding scheme before you attempt to register new information. Technical manipulations depart from the preceding retrieval-structure manipulations, which make use of knowledge implicit in the information to be learned. Instead, technical schemes relate the information to special material that you have learned previously.

The technical manipulations have a long history. The method of loci, discussed below, was devised over 2000 years ago. The other methods presented here were devised somewhere between the Renaissance and the 18th century (Feinaigle, 1812). Because the technical manipulations have been around for so long, they are the kind of mental manipulations most often equated with memory improvement.

Nevertheless, a word of warning must be given concerning these manipulations. Although technical mnemonics are known to be highly effective, a great deal of effort is necessary to learn and use them well. Many people find they do not want to invest the effort. And those who do learn these manipulations tend to stop using them, apparently because of the continuing effort needed to apply them (Bellezza, 1983; Higbee, 1981; Lapp, 1983; Park, Smith & Cavanaugh 1990). Indeed, research has found that most memory experts do not choose to use these mnemonics.

Nevertheless, if you feel highly motivated to make the effort these methods require, you should consult one of the many books that concentrate on them to supplement the brief account given here. A thorough and clear account of the technical mnemonics may be found in *How to Develop an Exceptional Memory* by Young and Gibson (1962) or in *Improving Your Memory Skills* by Bellezza (1982).

- *Link*. When learning a list of ordered or unordered items, form an image involving the first and second terms, then an image of the second and third terms, and so on. For example, to learn the bowling team's names, form an image of Bill handing a bowling ball to Sarah, Sarah throwing the ball at the pins set up by George, and George giving the score sheet to Arlene.

– *Loci.* When learning a list of items, imagine a familiar building (such as your home), and then imagine placing each item in a different room. For the bowling team example, leave Bill in the foyer, Sarah in the living room, George in the kitchen, and Arlene in the dining room. It is sometimes recommended that a person have several loci in mind: buildings, churches, golf courses, car, town, or terrain. Figure 12 presents an example of the use of the method of loci by a student in preparation for an exam. It is not necessary to sketch the loci as this student did; a mental image of the loci is sufficient.

House of Memory Floor Plan

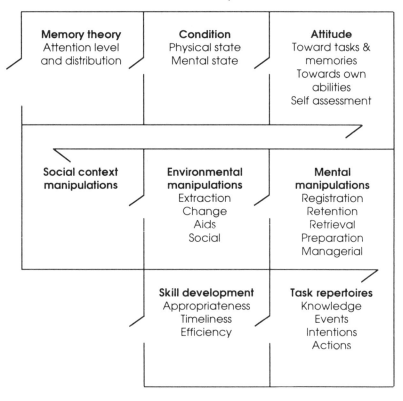

Figure 12.
An example of the method of loci as a student applied it to studying the principles of memory involvement advanced in this book.

- *Number/letter Conversion.* Translate digits to be learned into letters by this scheme: 1 = t, d, or th; 2 = n; 3= m; 4 = r; 5 =l; 6 = g, j, ch, sh; 7= c, k, hard g, q; 8 = f, ph, or v; 9 is p, b; and 0 = z,s, or soft c. Vowels are not assigned a number. To register the date Columbus discovered America (1492), code the number 1 as t, 4 as r, 9 as b, and 2 as n; this conversion yields "trbn" as equivalent to 1492. Since "trbn" is meaningless, a couple of vowels can be added to these letters to yield the word "turban." Now, if you forget the exact data of Columbus' discovery, you can still remember the converted structure, "turban," and, by re-converting it, retrieve the date. This conversion scheme can also be used to register words. If you wanted to register that someone's name is Bill, code it as 955, where B is represented by 9, each l as a 5, and i is ignored because it is a vowel.

- *Peg (alphabet).* You must first learn a system of letter-to-word peg pairs in which each pair represents one letter of the alphabet. For example, you might assign the following words to the first four letters: a = ace, b = bee, c = sea, and d = deed. To use this system to learn names, you mentally "peg" the person to the word. For example, you might imagine Bill holding an ace, Sarah being pursued by a bee, George standing in the sea, and Arlene performing some good deed.

- *Peg (image).* You must first learn a peg system consisting of number/word pairs that may be used for memorization on many occasions. In memorization, each word to be learned is associated with each peg word by constructing an image that contains both, as shown in the mediation image above.

There are several different ways that pegs may be constructed, although you need only one system for memorization. The most common kind of peg system is composed of numbers and peg words that rhyme. For example, you might construct the following rhyme system: "One is a bun, two is a shoe, three is a tree, and four is a door." Suppose you had four chores to do: go to the library, grocery, gas station, and meet George. First, you might imagine the library coming out of a bun, then imagine a shoe in the window of the grocery, a gas station up in a tree, and George's picture plastered over a door. The rhyme peg manipulation is useful for learning lists. (See Bellezza, 1982, or Young and Gibson, 1962, for a complete set of rhyme pegs.)

Another way that image-pegs are constructed involves peg words whose first letter visually resembles the number. For example, you might assign this system: "1 is Ice, 2 is Zoo, 3 is Beer, and 4 is Ant." In yet another variation, the "rotten peg" system uses displeasing or offensive peg words: "1 = Limburger cheese, 2 = dog feces, and 3 = sour milk." As you have probably guessed, you could devise an alternate peg system around any topic that pleases or fascinates you, such as food, movies, or rock stars.

- *Peg (verbal).* This peg system is also learned beforehand for use on many occasions. The pegs are adjectives that provide additional meaning in a fashion analogous to how image pegs provide an imaginary visual context for information to be learned. The adjectives should be ones that intrigue you. For example, a person might learn a system in which one is smart, two is exciting, three is cunning, and four is cocky. This system may be used to learn a list of items by conceptually linking the peg word and the word to be learned just as is done using the Mediation manipulation (Verbal).
- *Elaboration technique described above.* For example, to register chores to be done at the library, gas station, grocery, and involving George, you might form the following sentences: The library is for the smart. The gas station sign was exciting. The grocer sets out the specials in a cunning manner. And George is very cocky when things have gone well.

An Inventory of Retention Manipulations

After memory records are registered in long-term memory, they almost always become harder and harder to remember as time passes. With a great deal of time, we remember them only faintly and often we cannot remember them at all. It is true that some of our memories are easy to remember throughout our lifetimes, especially ones that carry personal significance. But memories that are always accessible are not of concern to us here. Our concern is the memory that becomes harder to remember with time, despite our wishing to remember it whenever we want.

The Causes of Forgetting

Forgetting information already registered in long-term memory comes about by brain processes that have one of two effects. Some processes destroy part or all of memories and, thereby, make the original information no longer available in memory. Other processes allow traces to remain intact in memory but make them less accessible to retrieval processes.

– *Loss of Availability.* There are several ways that memories become unavailable or inaccessible. Several processes are believed to be involved in the loss of information from memory. The best known such process is that of decay — in which the trace erodes physiologically. Brain cells are known to die from the effects of drinking alcohol and from the high temperatures that come with illness. The loss of such cells can be expected to hinder memory.

However, it is not necessary that a trace disappear for it to become unavailable in memory. A trace may become selectively altered by several processes. For example, by one process, traces may be intentionally revised to change the original memory for personal reasons. Our renditions of our recent triumphs (at work, in sports, in social relationships) are usually presented by us in a way that casts our behavior in the best light. Similarly, traumatic events may be retold to ourselves in a way the protects us from the full pain a complete account would elicit.

By another process, traces may be unconsciously distorted. The information we hold about ourselves, others, and issues is rendered more consistent and favorable (as described in Chapter Four on social context). Because these processes occur unconsciously, the alterations are not usually detected by us.

Finally, some new experiences may write over the traces of related past experiences and lead us to unlearn the past experiences. In a process similar to how tape recorders erase a prior recording as a new recording is made, unlearning destroys prior traces. It is doubtful that the mind works just like a tape recorder, but there is considerable evidence that we do occasionally unlearn past information and skills.

– *Loss of Accessibility.* There are several processes that lessen accessibility of traces that remain available in memory. This may come about through willful inattention to the memory trace — that is, not rehearsing the trace when possible. Willful inattention is useful in avoiding the later remembering of trivial information or mundane events.

Lessened accessibility may also occur because a memory trace, already well rehearsed and encoded in memory, has been deliberately suppressed. Suppression is a normal process that is often necessary to survival in an information packed world. For example, as you start up a new project, it is natural to put out of mind the activities you have just been concerned with. Similarly, because of this natural suppression, some people believe that your tendency to forget will increase if you are in the habit of acquiring trivia.

Finally, accessibility to emotionally threatening memories may be unconsciously lessened to almost zero by repression. This loss in accessibility is often normal as well because it may be adaptive for us not to dwell on such memories. However, engaging in repression to an unrealistic extent may be sign of adjustment difficulties.

Often only part of a memory trace becomes inaccessible. When part of a trace is lost, retrieval may become error prone. The loss of trace information, if sufficient, interferes with our ability to remember accurately. In some cases, we may be aware that our memory is inadequate to the task, such as when we are uncertain whether to give credit for an idea to ourselves or someone else. In other cases, we are not aware that part of the trace is inaccessible. In such "cases of mistaken identity," we accidentally recognize a fact as relevant to another topic, like confusing the properties of chemical elements or attributing some historic act to the wrong historic figure.

Accessibility may also be thwarted simply because testing conditions do not provide enough cues for successful retrieval. A desired trace may not be retrieved because the cues present when remembering is attempted are inadequate for the job. According to this view, if the cues that were present during learning are present at some later point, the memory will emerge, even if we do not intend to retrieve it. But if the situation provides too few of the cues present at learning, we will forget what the cues are calling for.

– *Pseudoforgetting*. It is important to note that what seems like forgetting is not always the case. Neither a loss of availability or accessibility is involved. For example, you may appear to have forgotten something requested of you because you never properly registered the information in the first place.

You probably have had experiences when someone has asserted that you must remember a certain meeting or social engagement whereupon, on reflection, you realize that you never attended the event. You may also appear to have forgotten because you did not understand a request for you to remember something or did not grasp the cues that might elicit the desired memory. This situation was mentioned in Chapter 3 when it was noted that people may appear to forget some information or past experience because poor eyesight or hearing prevented them from noticing relevant cues.

Manipulations that Forestall Unavailability and Inaccessibility

There are only a few manipulations that focus just on retention. Each of these manipulations act on one or more of the different causes of forgetting described above. The manipulations currently known come largely from common knowledge about memory and a small body of research on retention.

Different kinds of tasks have different rates of forgetting. Skilled actions are remembered indefinitely (you never forget how to ride a bicycle, as they say), as are some forms of knowledge acquired in school. Events may or may not be remembered for reasons that researchers are just beginning to investigate. Intentions appear to be retained poorly, but they too have only recently been subjected to investigation. Figure 13 shows the retention rates for three kinds of information encountered in school.

Unfortunately, research has yet to systematically compare retention rates for different kinds of information and to develop manipulations of retention that are sensitive to the kind of information involved. Instead, the retention manipulations now known address four general retention situations that cut across many memory tasks. Using these manipulations requires discipline.

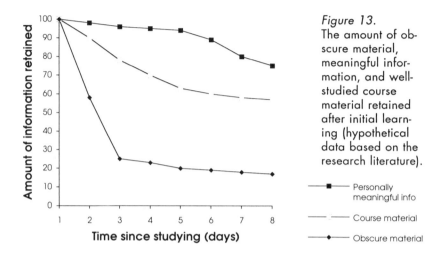

Figure 13.
The amount of obscure material, meaningful information, and well-studied course material retained after initial learning (hypothetical data based on the research literature).

Once registration has been carried out, most people are happy to trust a memory to retention until retrieval is required. But when the task is sufficiently important to you, and you lack confidence in your eventual ability to remember, one or more of the manipulations will prove well worth the effort. The following inventory first describes situations in which you might expect retention problems, then lists potential safeguards.

If you fear that the information will not 'stick' because it is uninteresting or foreign to you:

– *Review Periodically.* Retention begins anew each time a memory is fully re-registered. Review often until you recall at the level of accuracy required; subsequently, you may review less frequently as long as you continue to recall adequately. It is wise if your review involves some of your original registration manipulations, such as strength, attribute, association, and retrieval structure. — Prevents loss from decay, distortion, interference, suppression, and unlearning.

If you sense that information just learned may be confused with other similar information that you might encounter:

– *Avoid similar information.* If possible, avoid having to learn material that is similar in content to the material you wish to retain. For example, if you can avoid it, do not attempt to learn

simultaneously, or in succession, two foreign languages or the details of two highly related projects at work. — Prevents loss from interference, suppression, and unlearning.
- *Sleep or rest.* If the retention interval is brief (say, one or two days), sleep as much as possible during the retention interval. Sleep allows you to avoid encountering new information that could interfere with what you learned or could lead you to suppress what you have learned in order to consider the newly encountered information. — Delays decay and prevents forgetting due to interference, suppression, and unlearning.

If you worry that you might not be able to retrieve the desired information when you need it, or will not retrieve it fast enough:

- *Anticipate Remembering Situations.* Try to imagine situations in which you might be called on to remember. Doing so will help to prepare you to recognize, when in the remembering task, the cues that were present during learning, and thereby stimulate the memory to emerge when it is needed. — Prevents forgetting due to not noticing retrieval cues.

If you recognize that you may forget something because you find the topic unpleasant to think about long enough for registration to occur:
- *Make Moderately Unpleasant Memories Salient.* If you have an unpleasant memory task that you do not want to forget (for example, writing a thank-you note to an obnoxious person with whom you must remain on good terms), take steps that will lead you to not suppress thinking about the memory. Such steps might include thinking of reasons why you want to remember the unpleasant information or consequences that will ensue if you fail to remember. For a discussion of such steps, see the section on mood in Chapter 2. — Prevents repression, revision, intentional forgetting, and suppression.

When Forgetting is What You Want

In some cases, you might prefer a memory loss to perfect retention. At one extreme, spies, members of organized crime, and some politicians often wish they did not know or could forget certain information. At a more common level, the rest of us occasionally have bad days that we would like to forget.

Like retention manipulations, manipulations for intentional forgetting have yet to receive much scientific attention. Thus, these manipulations are few in number, unsophisticated, and obvious, including taking one's mind off the undesired memory by distraction, changes of scene and time, and mind-altering substances — whose effects are more onerous than the offending memories.

An Inventory of Retrieval Manipulations

Sometimes we are certain that we could recall everything about some topic or event if only we were presented with the right cues. Other times we doubt that we could recall some information or some event, even if we spent the rest of our lives trying.

In order to remember information that eludes us, it is necessary to try one or more manipulations to retrieve information from memory. The more retrieval manipulations we try, the better our chances for success. There is no guarantee that even a prolonged interrogation of memory with retrieval manipulations will dig up the desired memory. Nevertheless, the use of retrieval manipulations will generally come up with more information than if no effort is made at all to retrieve (Adams, 1985).

The Inventory below describes several potentially effective retrieval manipulations. These manipulations make the desired trace emerge from long-term memory into consciousness by stimulating either surrounding traces or part of the trace itself.

A trace or part of a trace is stimulated in long-term memory whenever information that makes up the trace is attended to in consciousness, Thus, retrieval manipulations involve attending to information in consciousness that is related in some manner to the four effects of learning manipulations on traces: strength, attributes, associations, and retrieval structures.

Retrieval Based on Strength

Strength is the weakest retrieval manipulation. When you cannot retrieve a trace on the basis of attributes, associations, or retrieval structures, you must carry out a strength search as a last resort. For this search, you examine the trace strength of potentially appropriate memories. The trace that possesses the level of strength you expect the memory to have is regarded as the trace required. The fact that a trace possesses the requisite level of strength does not necessarily prove that you have remembered fully or correctly. Occasionally, the strength search has the side effect of activating specific trace information and thereby providing access to the trace itself.

Retrieval Based on Attributes

Most of the known retrieval manipulations access a trace through one of its attributes. These manipulations assume that traces usually emerge fully into consciousness once a person is aware of one or a few of its attributes (Herrmann, 1990b). This assumption proves correct often enough to make attribute manipulations the best and most likely to retrieve a trace.

There are two kinds of attribute manipulations. One kind attempts to gain access by dwelling on an attribute of the trace you already *know* to be true. The other kind of manipulation gains access by dwelling on an attribute that you suspect is probably true of the trace. The likelihood that an attribute manipulation will be effective depends upon the number of attributes you generate and on the importance or relevance of a given attribute to the memory.

These manipulations attempt to retrieve the entire trace from a part — that is, from an attribute — of the trace. Examples of partial trace information are numerous: remembering when an historic event took place but not where; recognizing that you have met a person previously but failing to recall when or where; recalling how you felt about an issue while being unable to remember all of the reasons why you felt the way you did.

Whenever you know you are remembering less than all of a trace, you can assume that just a few of the trace's attributes are available to you as well. Once you do retrieve a known attribute of a trace, focus attention on the attribute until the full trace emerges. This attention serves to activate the attribute in long-term memory. The attribute's activation then spreads to the desired trace, causing it to emerge into consciousness.

A critical process in using known attributes to retrieve a trace is reconstruction (Neisser & Winograd, 1988; Schank, 1982). When considered separately, the attributes you do know are often insufficient to make the trace emerge. In such cases, it is useful to reconstruct or "piece" attributes together into a plausible, albeit incomplete, account of the event or information desired. Often the reconstructed memory, or the pattern of known attributes, leads to educated guesses of other attributes. For example, knowing when you met someone can often allow you to guess likely places where the meeting took place. Sometimes, a reconstruction, such as both when and where the meeting took place leads the full trace to emerge from memory. There are four different ways that attributes may be manipulated for reconstruction.

- *Associate Attribute.* Recall as best you can the key attributes you know of the memory trace. Then, reconstruct. This manipulation is the first one to attempt when dealing with known attributes. If it is unsuccessful in making the trace emerge, then try one or both of the following manipulations.
- *Part Reconstruction.* Recall as best you can the key attributes that pertain to the part of the memory you do know. For example, in recalling an event, concentrate on remembering where the event occurred. Then attempt to recall the whole memory. Continue alternating between attempting to recall the parts of the memory trace and attempting to recall the trace entirely.
- *Sequential Reconstruction.* Recall attributes according to the time of occurrence or time of registration. For example, try to recall recent information, then initial information, and finally the information in between.
- *Probable-Attribute Manipulations.* Often, we vaguely sense which memory trace we want to recall, but still are unable to recall enough attributes to stimulate it to emerge. In such cases, we have no chance of retrieving the desired memory except through guessing an attribute of the memory. If you are lucky enough to guess an actual attribute of the trace, the attribute

may cause the rest of the trace to emerge. Of course, a guess that comes up with an attribute that is irrelevant to the trace will not facilitate retrieval and may diminish your chances of a successful retrieval even further.

The manipulations below constitute different guessing schemes. They provide ways of guessing the attributes that probably make up a trace. As last-ditch maneuvers, they are tried when surer manipulations have failed and you are desperate to achieve retrieval.

- *Alphabet search.* Ask yourself, does the information you wish to remember began with an A? a B? a C? and so on. For example, you may attempt to remember the name of a person by generating names beginning with A, then with B, and on through Z. If you are lucky, you will generate the appropriate name and recognize it as the correct one.
- *Free generation of attributes.* Recall everything you can that is in some way associated with the information you are trying to remember, and then try to recognize any actual attributes of the memory trace among the indirect association you generated. For example, in trying to remember directions, you might freely associate the names of streets, or of stores or landmarks, and then see if you recognize any of the streets, stores, or landmarks as being on the route you are trying to recall.
- *Question.* Ask as many relevant questions you can about the information to be retrieved: if? of? by? in? who? what? when? where? whose? whether? why? whence? while? how? how much? how many? how long? how often? how manifested? This manipulation is useful when you are trying to remember the nature of a complicated event or information — such as from work. Rarely can people remember all of the necessary details without a multi-question approach.
- *Reinstate mood.* Imagine the mood you experienced when the memory was registered. Then, try to recapture that mood.
- *Tip-of-the-Tongue.* Guess the length, first letter, unusual letters, doubled letters, or other unusual features of the word or words to be remembered.

Retrieval Based on Associations

These manipulations access the memory through associations between the trace and other information. The secondary information may have been present during registration, or it may be conceptually associated with the content of that trace (Kolodner, 1984; Schank, 1982). An associative manipulation is usually most useful when you recall very little or none of the trace and, therefore, cannot attempt to access the trace by using attributes. Additionally, this manipulation is often used when attribute manipulations have been tried and failed.

– *Causation.* Recall the circumstances or agent that produced, or was produced by, the memory you wish to remember.
– *Reinstate situation.* Imagine the surroundings you experienced when the memory was registered, and ask yourself what you were doing, saying, or thinking.
– *Retrace.* Remember chronologically the memories that preceded or followed the one you wish to remember.
– *Return to the Scene.* Go to the surroundings where the memory was registered, and try to spot features of the room or site that pertain to the trace.
– *Recall registration manipulation.* Recall any registration manipulations that you may have used when you acquired the memory.

Retrieval Based on Retrieval Structures

You can also attempt to gain access to the trace by first retrieving any retrieval structure you may have used during registration. If the retrieval structure has been retained well, it will almost always generate the desired memory. If the retrieval structure is only partially remembered, it will function like any other association with the trace and, therefore, will be about as effective as any of the other associative manipulations.

Choosing Retrieval Manipulations

The retrieval manipulations presented here are intuitively obvious, yet many people employ just a few of them. Although we may recognize these manipulations, they probably do not come readily to mind when memory requires them. You can easily increase your use of these manipulations by copying them on a three-by-five card and keeping the card in your wallet or purse. The next time you are stumped, pull the card out and run through the manipulations. There is no guarantee that you will succeed in retrieving a given memory trace, but your success rate over a series of different attempts will increase.

Potential Use of Learning and Retrieval Manipulations

As we have seen, mental manipulations are numerous. Indeed, there are so many learning and retrieval manipulations that it would take tremendous ambition and a great deal of time to memorize them all. Few people are likely to ever try. This surplus can be put to your advantage, however, if you take time to comb the wide range of manipulations and carefully choose the ones that suit you. Even the most suitable mental manipulations will still clearly require a great deal of time, knowledge, and effort to produce new memories and retrieve old ones.

The manipulations discussed here are definitely useful in many situations. One practical limitation of these methods is time. They require you to diagnose situations before deciding which manipulation is appropriate. Often, there is not sufficient time, or you are unprepared or unwilling to undergo the diagnosis and selection process. In Chapter 7, we will discuss ways of preparing more direct manipulations for specific tasks (Herrmann, 1990b; Weinstein & Mayer, 1986). Even if you choose to concentrate on mental manipulations for memory improvement, applying them with a task-specific repertoire in mind will make your use more timely and appropriate.

Summary

- Mental manipulations have been used for centuries. They take a lot of practice and discipline to work effectively.
- Different kinds of manipulations are used for learning, retention, and retrieval tasks.
- There are four basic kinds of learning manipulations: building strength, attributes, associations, and retrieval structures.
- Forgetting renders traces unavailable, due to decay, distortion, intentional revision, and unlearning; or less accessible, due to willful inattention, suppression, repression, interference, and retrieval failures.
- Retention manipulations keep a trace available or increase trace accessibility through periodic review. They make unpleasant memories unforgettable, protect the memory from interference with new memories, and anticipate situations in which you will have to remember.
- Retrieval manipulations make the desired memory trace emerge into consciousness by searching for the trace with the appropriate strength; attending to potential attributes of the unretrieved trace; attending to associations of the unretrieved trace; and making use of a retrieval structure.
- Different kinds of mental manipulations will work for different people and for different memory tasks.

• When a person has an
important job to be done,
he will not ask someone with a
reputation for a bad memory.

Chapter 6
Scientific Background

It has long been known that external aids, such as notes, can enhance memory performance. Scientific research began investigating the effects of external aids in the 1970s by asking people what kinds of external aids they used, and whether these aids did indeed help more than mental manipulations.

This research has examined a wide variety of issues, such as the differences in reported use of aids as a function of type, for example paper notepads versus pocket electronic notepads, and subject characteristics, such as age or gender. Most of the research into the effects of external aids on memory has continued to rely on simple reports, because observation and experimentation on the use of external aids faces certain practical problems. Observational research can usually be expected to take a great deal of time because a subject might go for hours or days before using a note to remember something. Experimental research on the effects of notetaking is similarly more tedious than that with mental manipulations.

Thus far, experimentation has largely been restricted to the use of notetaking among students and in the use of electromechanical devices in people with neurological impairments, such as those due to head injury.

Eternal Aids

6

Fortunately, many memory tasks need not be solved solely in your head. A sight, a sound, a touch, or a movement often will register a more vivid trace — or will stimulate a memory to emerge more rapidly — than will a verbal description of the same sight, sound, touch, or movement.

Physical stimuli have a powerful effect on memory because they capture attention more effectively than most ideas. Indeed, the external effect of physical stimuli on your memory is often greater than the internal effect of mental manipulations (Harris, 1984). Great detectives, such as Sherlock Holmes, often have witnesses return to the scene of the crime because the physical environment can be expected to awaken memories far better than mental. Newscasters and performers on TV often have cue cards to prompt them in case they forget what to say.

Because physical stimuli may aid memory so well, many external aids have been developed both informally and commercially. You are using an informal external aid when you put an object near your front door to remind you to take it away the next time you leave. You are using a commercial external aid when you set an alarm to remind you to make a call, go to a meeting, or put an ingredient into something you are cooking.

External aids are used often by all of us. Several surveys have shown that both young adults and elderly people use external aids to cope with memory problems substantially more than they use mental manipulations (Cavanaugh, Grady, & Perlmutter, 1978). Even memory experts admit that they too use external aids much more than mental manipulations (Parks, Cavanaugh, & Smith, 1986).

Because external aids can assist your memory so powerfully, a more complete knowledge of them is essential to improving memory (see Figure 14). This chapter reviews how to take good advantage of external aids to facilitate your memory performance and, in some cases, even to relieve you of the burden of having to perform some memory tasks.

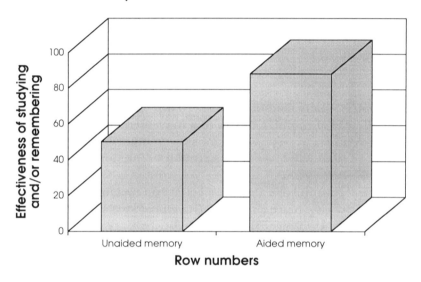

Figure 14.
The effectiveness of a person's studying and/or remembering according to whether or not memory was aided by some external object, prompt, or device (hypothetical data based on the research literature).

Possible Side Effects from Memory Aid Use

Although there are many reasons to be enthusiastic about external aids, you may want to consider an ancient question about their effects on memory ability. It has been argued that external aids reduce a person's reliance on memory per se, and that this reduced use may decrease a person's memory abilities. For example, a person might use external aids for each and every memory task and, thereby, never use his or her own memory.

It is true that the use of an external aid for certain kinds of memory tasks, especially over a prolonged period, can diminish one's memory ability for this task. However, ability for other tasks will not lessen. For example, suppose you purchase a telephone that stores the numbers of your friends and dials them at the push of a button. This may reduce your facility at memorizing phone numbers. But reliance on the phone will not affect your ability to remember the rules of games or past events of your life.

If you cherish a certain kind of memory ability, then you may not want to use an external aid for the tasks served by that ability. Alternatively, external aids can relieve you of the mental burden of performing certain tasks. They also allow you to choose which tasks you want to relegate to an aid and which tasks you prefer to manage with your own memory system.

Choosing and Using External Aids

Your choice of an external aid should depend on its purpose, its effectiveness, and whether the aid suits your tastes.

The purpose of an external aid is paramount in your choice because external aids differ greatly in how they assist memory. They are designed to assist registration, retention, and/or retrieval for a certain memory task that arises in a particular situation of everyday life (Herrmann & Petro, 1991; Intons-Peterson & Fournier, 1986; Intons-Peterson & Newsome, 1992; Petro, Herrmann, Burrows & Moore, 1991). One aid will assist a memory task concerned with an activity at home, such as timing the baking of bread; another an activity at work, such as keeping appointments; another some form of recreation, such as remembering the rules of a game.

Some aids have broader applications than others, but all apply best to a restricted range of memory tasks. Thus, you should not hope to find an external aid that will improve your memory in general. Instead, you should seek external aids that assist memory for the specific memory tasks you find important.

Your choice of an external aid should be based on a careful consideration of how well it might apply to the memory task of interest to you. Often an aid that appears on initial examination to be effective turns out not to be.

For example, a piece of string tied around one's finger is often touted as a way to remember to do things. Nevertheless, a piece of string on your finger is rarely effective because it does not tell you what you have to remember. Because of its ineffectiveness, the piece-of-string aid is hardly ever used despite its being a universal symbol of memory use.

Another example of an ineffective aid is the current "findable" keychains which help you locate them by beeping when you whistle or clap. Unfortunately, these keychains beep to any random noise, interrupting conversations and other activities. In the end, they are not very useful.

Finally, your choice of an external aid should rest on a realistic appraisal of whether it suits your tastes. Some people will advise you to make reminders of appointments by writing on your hand. This might work for you, but not if you dislike being seen with hands covered with ink.

Similarly, many state-of-the-art commercial aids, such as memory watches, are not very popular because they require too much time and effort to use properly. If you sense that you will not put in the effort to learn to use them, or if you are easily intimidated by gadgets, hi-tech memory aids might not be for you.

If you are a "gadget freak," several mail order companies sell various kinds of memory aids. Contact: The Sharper Image (P. O. Box 26823, San Francisco, CA 94126–6823), Markline (14 Jewel Drive, Dept. W, Wilmington, MA 01887–9988), Sporting Edge (22121 Crystal Creek Blvd., Bothell, WA 98021) and Exeters (6 Hughes, Suite 100, Irvine, CA 92718–1901).

External Aid Use

The remainder of this chapter presents a thorough review of external aid use. Each section discusses external aids as they apply to four broad categories of memory tasks in everyday life: physical memory for actions, studying, memory tasks at work, and personal memory tasks. Some external aids address registration, others retention, or retrieval, or a combination of these memory phases. There are many memory tasks for which no external aid has been developed yet.

If you are satisfied with your memory performance in one or more of the broad task categories, skip ahead to a category that you find more challenging. For categories of interest, skim through until you find tasks on which you would like to improve. For many tasks, several external aids are discussed. Identify the external aids that you feel will be most useful to you, and write them down as you read so that you will later remember which ones you want to obtain and use.

An effective use of these aids requires effort in planning, rather than in executing, the manipulations of external aids. Many memory tasks arise unexpectedly and end quickly, such as introductions. There is often no time to go in search of an external aid, if one is not already at hand. If you don't have an external aid such as a notepad or an alarm handy, you will have to make the effort to use a mental manipulation, or not try at all.

Physical Memory

In the memory terminology of this book, "actions" refer only to physical movements. Successful remembering of an action entails remembering the parts of the action and the precise sequence in which the parts are put together. Improved ability to remember actions has long been known to depend greatly on how much you practice them.

Nevertheless, there are many actions that we perform infrequently, making it difficult to develop expertise at executing them. We sometimes have to fix something, such as a toaster or a lawn mower, and then do not have to repeat the actions involved for years. Such situations preclude becoming practiced at the task.

In lieu of practice, you can create external aids that you can later call upon when you have to attempt the action again. One manipulation is to take notes that break a task — such as a home repair — into steps. You might also create a checklist for the several parts of the action. If the action is a common one, you can obtain instruction manuals. They often include diagrams that illustrate actions you might otherwise forget.

Most movements in sports occur in the context of a playing field. If you are attempting to acquire an athletic movement, make sketches of the movement on the playing field, court, alley, or rink showing the standard lines or markers. Later, when you are confronted by the real memory task, these lines and markers will externally aid your recall of the movement.

Studying

Throughout life, you have to study information for work, responsibilities at home, and leisure activities. Studying is, of course, crucial in school or training situations (Flippo & Caverly, 1991). In work situations, where we generally have less time for studying, it can be especially important to learn information quickly in order to cope with a question or problem. At home we must learn many things, from using our appliances to filing our income tax. It is even necessary to learn just to have fun. When playing a new card or board game, we have to know the rules.

External aids help studying in two ways: by facilitating learning and by providing external sources should one fail to remember something learned previously.

- *Notes.* Everyone uses notes sometimes when they study. Notes taken in class, meetings or from a book serve to focus your attention and facilitate your registration of key material. Crib sheets facilitate last minute preparation for exams. Notes do not replace the need for mental manipulations. Rather they ensure that you mentally manipulate the right information and force you to better organize your mental records (Anderson & Ambruster, 1991; Intons-Peterson & Newsome, 1992).
- *"Teaching Machines."* Machines that teach have been around since at least the 1930s (Benjamin, 1989). Today, microcomputer stores stock shelf after shelf with instructional schemes and programs on a wide variety of topics that facilitate learning — including learning how to use microcomputers. Many of these programs can accelerate your learning over your normal rate.
- *Memory Art.* An old learning device, not so well known today, is art. Paintings, drawings, and sketches have been designed by

artists specifically to help people use the mental manipulation — the method of loci — discussed in the previous chapter. This method involves learning a list of items by mentally placing each item in different rooms of a familiar building.

For example, if you have an interest in England, you might hang a map of it on the wall of the room where you study. When you have a small list of items to remember, mentally "place" each item in one distinct region of the map. Repeat the placements several times to yourself. When you need to "retrieve" the list, travel the map mentally from region to region, "picking up" the items as you go.

In the 14th, 15th, and 16th centuries, artists drew or painted floor plans of houses, cathedrals, amphitheaters, and other buildings so people could similarly "locate" and memorize information in this way (Yates, 1966). The use of art to aid memory today is uncommon, but you might find it a personally intriguing and effective way to learn a list of items.

- *Superstitious Memory Aids*. Sometimes people use an object to aid memory on the basis of an unfounded belief that the object has a power to influence memory. Usually, they justify this belief on the grounds that the object brought good luck to past memory tasks. Some students wear a special article of clothing, like a "thinking cap," to exams because they did especially well while wearing it in the past. Other students will use a "lucky" pen or bring their books even to closed-book exams.

The use of lucky memory objects is particularly common among college students, but it is not unusual among other professions, where a certain suit, briefcase, or pointer might be linked superstitiously to good performance. If you are inclined to use such an aid, go ahead. It won't hurt, and it may help by putting you in a mental state conducive to good memory performance.

- *Knowledge Sources*. For most subjects, we do not expect ourselves to remember every single detail. To back your memory up on topics you are likely to forget, you should use external knowledge sources. Some knowledge sources you develop on your own, such as notes from meetings, readings, and lectures. Other source materials are books and manuals. Many general sources — dictionaries, encyclopedias, thesauri, Guinness Book of Records, and Farmer's Almanac — are useful in any office. The more knowledge sources you have at your fingertips, the less time you spend going back and forth to the library.

Other books serve more personal needs, like skill improvement, travel, product supplies, or conference proceedings. All these sources keep facts readily on hand that might otherwise fail to come immediately or accurately to mind. Of course, they also provide you with information that you never knew in the first place.

A knowledge source that is valuable to most people is a spelling aid. Either because we have forgotten a spelling or because we have forgotten the rules that govern its spelling, we are uncertain of how to spell certain words. There are now excellent devices that address spelling difficulties.

– *Instant Speller.* The 6,000 most commonly misspelled words are found at the touch of a button in a portable speller.
– *Spelling Ace.* Type in the phonetic spelling of a word, and the "Ace" will find and display the correct spelling.

Obligations

Success in college often hinges on your ability to access information and communicate with others. These demands necessitate performing a stream of memory tasks each and every workday. You must remember the responsibilities of the moment, and also have pertinent information and the facts of past events at your fingertips.

– *Obligations.* School requires you to be — and appear to be — aware of many schedules, assignments and events. To be in touch, it is necessary to know your obligations, both day by day and well into the future. One common factor of your obligations is that they must be performed by a certain deadline. Another common factor is that obligations entail the remembering of details.

One valuable way to deal with memory burdens imposed by obligations is to use a record system that will manage those details for you. For many people, the primary record system is an appointment book or some form of notes, such as a to do list.

The thought that we have an impending obligation often occurs to us at odd moments. If we forget to record this thought, we usually forget to meet the obligation. Some use the note itself as a reminder. Others copy the note onto a chore list or appointment book they consult regularly throughout the day. Keeping memo pads in key places where one lives facilitates getting a new obligation on the list before the intention to do the chore is forgotten. Some people carry this practice so far that they put a memo pad at their bedside in case chores occur to them in the middle of the night.

– *Nitewriter*. A pen with a tip that lights up to record ideas and intentions that occur at night.

Since all obligations involve a deadline, they require you to be aware of the time. Some people can rely on memory alone to recall deadlines or dates, but many use aids such as notes or calendars. Accessibility is the key. Some need a calendar in one or more rooms of the home or office.

– *Appointments*. Research indicates that people forget appointments or project deadlines infrequently. Such a failure is to be avoided, if possible, because it is commonly taken as indicating a lack of interest in the person to be met or in the project to be done. Nevertheless, we do forget appointments or deadlines at times. Because appointment failures are so disturbing, people have developed a variety of external-aid manipulations to insure that such failures rarely occur.

The first thing to do to minimize your forgetting of appointments is to keep a daily record of your obligations — a to-do list. The act of keeping a daily record forces you to review the events of the day and fosters prompt realization of appointments. A daily schedule can be written on any scrap of paper, but you may wish to use any of a variety of appointment books that have been designed to organize your schedule and trigger the remembering of appointments.

Appointment books, record books, address books, wallets, card holders, systems for monitoring projects, and idea files.

A second way to minimize your forgetting of appointments is to keep multiple records of your forthcoming obligations and assignments: in appointment books, lists of chores, diaries, and calendars. If you do this, you give yourself added mental rehearsal of the details of these obligations.

- *Timing Devices.* You may be reminded of your obligations by more sophisticated devices. Instead of hoping that your obligations will spontaneously emerge and tell you what you are to do, you can use devices that take over most of the mental work. These devices can register the times of an appointment and the information about who is to be met, and later signal you with a light or sound at the time of your obligation.
- *Timer.* These wireless remote control systems turn office or household machines on and off at preset times. Timer Center controls up to eight devices; Control Center handles up to 16 devices. Radio Shack.
- *Electronic Memo Pad.* A portable multi-purpose desk-top computer. Comes with calculator, tape recorder, phone terminal, and memo pad. Computer reminds you of appointments, errands, phone messages, birthdays, and holidays. Creative Peripherals.

Other devices also actively remind you, but are more portable.

- *Electronic Memo Pad Memory Improver.* Pocket-sized, can do calculations, hold data, as well as give you reminders.
- *Memo Watch.* Memorizes several numbers with abbreviated, six-letter names; at the correct time, an alarm sounds, and the message appears on display screen. Phoenix. Casio. Seiko.
- *Memo Watch with Computer Memory.* Can be connected to a microcomputer to call up files concerning phone numbers, flight schedules, and other information.

You can also equip exits with active memory aids.

- *Message Display.* An electric lettered display to present reminders. Moving Sign.
- *Message Teller.* A pre-recorded reminder plays aloud whenever a person comes within a pre-set range of 3 to 10 feet away; records how many times the recorder has been triggered. Markline.

Figure 15.
A short-term, practical, attachable timer (from 1 to 60 minutes).

— *Simple timers that buzz or ring can give effective cues to short-term appointments or chores.*
— *Timers.* Mechanical, wind up timers often used when cooking.
— *Timers.* Pocket-size digital timers, for example, see Figure 15
— *Radio Alarm Clock.* Compact clock wakes you up to "beep" alarm and radio. Most include a "snooze" button that lets your radio play up to an hour before automatically shutting off. The alarm or shut-off may be used as a cue.
— *Simple timers that buzz or ring can give effective cues to short-term appointments or chores.* Plain old wind-up timers often used for cooking can come in handy for all sort of memory tasks. Also, pocket-size digital timers are useful.
— *Symbolic Reminding.* When you are in a hurry or do not have the time to make a note, you can create an external aid of your obligation by changing some aspect of your immediate physical environment. The unusual placement of an object increases the likelihood that a person will remember an appointment, because the sight of the object "out of place" provides an obvious symbol to remind you. For example, a person calls while you are hurrying out of the office and asks you to drop by later in the day. Because you don't have time to make a note, you turn your wristwatch over or switch it from one wrist to another.

This manipulation, called "symbolic reminding," is often criticized as an inadequate method of remembering because the unusual change in the environment may not later suggest the precise obligation you intended to meet. Despite this shortcoming, symbolic reminding remains one of the most popular memory aids.

You may also find symbolic reminding useful when you want to have a backup to an alarmwatch or clock. Here are several examples of symbolic reminding (Herrmann, 1990c) that many people find beneficial for at least some tasks:

Examples of Symbolic Reminding

- Carry an object (Pick up some small object and carry it until you have done whatever you did not want to forget to do.)
- Clothespin or paper clip in a buttonhole or pocket of a shirt or blouse.
- Connect a cord from your wrist to your belt (Moderate or large gestures will simultaneously pull on your wrist and belt.)
- Knot in handkerchief
- Position furniture oddly
- Rubber band around a wrist
- Scotch tape on a finger
- String on the bridge of your glasses
- String on your finger
- Switch the pocket of your wallet
- Switch the shoulder on which you normally carry something, such as a purse or golf bag
- Switch your watch from the usual wrist to the other wrist
- Turn your ring over
- Turn your watch face down
- Wear your belt two or three notches tighter
- Wear your clothes in an unaccustomed manner (If you normally wear a certain article of clothing, like a vest or a sweater, don't; or wear an article of clothing you normally would not, like an ascot or a scarf.)
- Wear "memory" jewelry (For example, you can wear a "memory" bracelet, necklace, or tie that you reserve for reminding you to do important tasks. To be most effective, jewelry should

be ostentatious in some way — unusually heavy, noisy, glittery, or cumbersome.)
- Wear "memory" clothing (To be most effective, it should be unusual in design, pattern, or color. If you are especially bold, it should be distasteful — a loud tie or a "shocking" scarf. Distasteful clothing has the advantage of attracting comments, and thereby eliciting additional reminders.)
- Similarly, you can position or "dress" notes and other papers symbolically with Memo Clips that call attention to them.
- *Super-Grip Magnetic Clip.* Used to keep grocery lists, recipes, phone numbers and memos close at hand on the refrigerator. You can also buy a Huge Paper clip bearing the words "Don't Forget," which can be clipped to high-priority paperwork in an obvious place.

Some people find appointment books difficult to keep or easy to neglect. Even if you have recorded an appointment, you may need to post further notices that are explicit reminders. One option is to stick your reminder where you will be sure to "run into" it.

The convenient (and ubiquitous) Scotch "Post It" self-sticking notes work well for this manipulation. They can be placed on the front door, a frequently-used mirror, the lid to the toilet, or any other spot you know you will pass regularly. Another option is to put up a message board, file, or cabinet that provides a constant reminder of things you have to do.

- *Remembrance File.* Card file box with an opening in the front to allow reading the card — which has spaces to record the date and what is to be done on that day.
- *Take-Aways.* Work routinely requires us to remember to take things away to another destination when we leave. In order to remember to do so, many people reserve a spot in their office or home for routinely putting things they intend to take away. To be maximally effective, the spot should be convenient and near a major exit, like a table or stairs near the front door. It should be checked habitually whenever one leaves.

Similarly, a shirt pocket, a fold in your wallet, or section in your purse can be set aside as a portable spot for putting things you do not wish to forget. Tickets for a plane or play, checks and personal letters are some of the "easy-to-lose" items that could be put in a special pocket. A portable memory spot will save you the time and worry of searching through all of your clothing to find important material.

When it is especially important that you remember to bring an object or papers somewhere at a certain time, you may need a more dramatic reminder. Rather than using your routine memory spot, you should put the "take-away" item in a conspicuous spot. The conspicuous placement manipulation is a common practice that experts regard as very effective (Winograd & Soloway, 1985). You can hardly ignore an object left against the front door or on the hood of your car. If the object to be taken is too large to be put in the doorway, then tape a reminder to the front door or on the steering wheel of your car.

- *Phone.* Whether you use phones heavily at work or casually at home, your use relies on several memory tasks that you could avoid. Perhaps because of the telephone's importance, the business world has produced aids of varying sophistication to assist with these memory tasks. From little black books to computers, you can find devices for every level of phone use.
- *Phone numbers.* You can attempt to memorize frequently called numbers, or you can let one of several available indexes retain this information for you. You may also use these systems to record the names, and numbers, of business contacts generally.
- *Telephone Index.* Holds up to 420 names and numbers, and automatically rotates the correct name/number panel into view.

If your phone use is heavy, and you can afford it, you may prefer an automatic dialing device. These dialers retain numbers that you key into the device along with the name of the person corresponding to the number. When you are ready to call someone, you push the button on your dialer alongside the name of the person you want to call and the dialer dials the person's number. Some dialers are portable. These devices work the same as the nonportable ones except that a push of the button activates the tones corresponding to numbers. You simply hold the device against the telephone receiver and it dials the appropriate number.

- *What was said.* It often becomes important to remember what someone said in a previous phone conversation, especially if you study with someone over the phone. Recall of prior conversations is typically inaccurate.

If you anticipate needing to remember phone conversations precisely, you may want to install equipment that will record calls. However, if you decide to obtain a recorder, bear in mind the pitfalls of using one. Etiquette dictates that you inform the people you talk to that the call is being recorded. The goodwill of friends and acquaintances can be lost in an instant if it becomes known after the fact that a phone call, especially a sensitive one, has been "tapped."

Legally, if you do not inform someone that a call is recorded and this person discloses information that you would like to use in a legal action against them, your failure to inform them renders their disclosure inadmissible evidence.

Turn on your answering machine. Many people who use an answering machine frequently forget to turn the machine on. This memory failure can cause you to miss important calls. Some machines allow you to activate them from a remote location.

- *Foreign Language Study.* Learning the language of another country can be a formidable task. Nowadays, there are translation calculators that can help you in your studies.
- *Keeping Your Possessions.* College life is a transient communal existence. You share your room with people you never knew before and visitors are not uncommon. To avoid having people inadvertently walking off with your possessions, mark them in a conspicuous manner. There are many ways to mark possessions for identification. Use Luggage Tags. Attach a bright ribbon or yarn. Attach Personalized Straps to cameras, musical instruments, and other objects you carry separately. Use a Passport Protector to keep your most important personal papers. Get a Credit Card case, which has an alarm that goes off if you close the case without returning the card.
- *Meetings and Classes.* Often we take part in meetings, informal or formal, that we later remember less precisely than we wish. We forget critical statements, sometimes important decisions. You can avoid these memory failures by either writing down careful notes or by tape recording those meetings you expect to have to recall later.

- *Copying.* As a student, you often encounter documents that you may later need to know about. You can, of course, get copies made. If you can afford it, you might want to get a portable copier. However, it might justifiably be argued that the "Xerox Revolution" has created even more memory problems in giving us so much more information to file and retrieve. Thus, many have offered this sensible suggestion: copy only those documents you will genuinely need and use.
- *Inventory.* Some school assignments and extracurricular activities require the counting of inventory or of events. One way to deal with such counting tasks is to have automatic recording devices in operation. However, many counting tasks are relatively inconsequential and do not warrant a costly automatic system. Mechanical counters are not costly and can count without using your memory at all.
- *The "Memory-Friendly" Desk.* When we work under high pressure, timing is essential. Often there is no time to be wasted in trying to remember the forgotten location of a misplaced folder, contract, or some other piece of information. Thus, it is important that your desk be arranged so that it is "memory friendly," allowing you to easily remember and find what you need.

Keep the top of your desk in an order that facilitates finding what you need (Hertel, 1988; Malone, 1988). The order you impose need not be neat, but it should be predictable by you. Office supply stores sell a variety of products that help keep, and find, materials routinely in their place: for example, Desk Organizers, Pen Holders, Eyeglass Holders. Similarly, you can use drawer organizers, which keep envelopes, letterhead sheets, etc. readily accessible. A good set of knowledge sources, such as technical manuals and other communications, should also be kept within arm's reach.

- *Intention to take supplies.* When studying away from where you live, we frequently need to bring general office materials such as note pads, folders, a stapler, forms, or certain tools. One way to avoid the inconvenience of forgetting these items is to prepare a "portable office." By keeping a fully stocked package, you will have only one take-away to recall as you leave, instead of several.

Personal Memory

Personal Finances

Keeping up with (and within) a budget involves several different memory tasks. For many people, successful budgeting demands more memory effort than they are willing to put out. Each kind of budget — household, gift, travel — has its own pattern of expenditures and overall balance. Central to any budget is the paying of bills.

- *Paying bills.* Probably the most important financial task we face is paying our monthly bills. If you are disciplined, you can combine all your bill-paying obligations by setting aside a day each week or month to handle this chore. The date itself may be chosen for its memorableness, such as the 1st, 15th, or 30th.

You need not rely on your memory to record payment dates and schedules. Calendars are one place you can record the due-dates for recurring bills. Gathering or labeling the bills in a conspicuous fashion is another helpful manipulation. They can be marked or clipped as they arrive to show which bills remain unpaid.

Some people do not trust themselves to follow a routine or to notice a conspicuous reminder to pay bills. Others simply prefer to avoid the burden of remembering. For them, more active reminders are available. Many people find such a device too expensive and prefer disciplined use of a calendar to remind them of when bills must be paid.

A variety of businesses and institutions will now carry out financial transactions for you. These automatic financial services can reduce your financial memory load considerably.

For example you need not remember to deposit your paycheck. Banks now customarily provide "direct deposit" by arrangement with many employers. You also need not remember to pay many of your bills. Most banks will pay certain bills by deducting, with your permission, money from your checking account.

Your checkbook balance. People often put off balancing their check book. Since the advent of credit cards, knowing how much money you have in your account has become even more difficult to determine. No one who uses credit cards more than in-frequently can expect to reliably remember all of their purchases and the amounts.

Fortunately, new devices exist that facilitate your recording of checks and credit card expenditures, enabling you to keep track of all your accounts. There are calculators that let you key in deposits and expenditures by check or credit card, and give you a balance for the checking account, two credit card accounts, and overall.

Personal Health

When we were children, our parents remembered what we were supposed to do to take care of our health. As adults, however, we must remember to take care of ourselves on our own. We must remember to eat right, get exercise, see doctors as needed, and to take medications when appropriate. Self-care requires that we perform a variety of memory tasks.

– *Cooking*. The good cook is a bit like an orchestra conductor. To begin with, it is necessary to take frozen foods out so they can thaw. Since this is a task that many people forget, it is often useful to own a microwave that will allow you to thaw in minutes.

Furthermore, you must either remember how to cook a dish or remember where the recipe for the dish is kept. Obviously a recipe file is essential to the latter task. Prior to cooking, ingredients must be taken out of the refrigerator or cabinets. By dating foods, you can make sure to use older items before newer ones and avoid spoilage.

As for the meal itself, there are a variety of products that can automatically start and stop one or more dishes on the stove that are not automatically timed.

Exercise

Exercise improves your cognitive functioning, so you will be better off intellectually if you exercise. If you are disciplined, you may find it easy to remember to exercise. But many people find that their schedule is so hectic that they simply forget to do so. If this applies to you, it is advisable to plan ahead and arrange times in your schedule to exercise. If you arrange to exercise with someone else, that person will serve as an added external memory aid — besides giving you extra incentive to follow through.

Taking Medication

Some people make notes to remind them to take pills. Others lay out the full daily number of pills in a dish each morning, then check the number left at each medication time. Others make use of devices that remind them to take their medication.

Two kinds of devices are sold to assist remembering medications: passive devices remind you when you happen to look at them; active devices signal you with a light or a buzzer. Passive reminders, a refinement of the dish manipulation just described, provide a systematic scheme for sorting out the pills to be taken, such as pocket-sized plastic boxes that organize daily doses in four separately-opened compartments. Active reminders are more useful for those who tend to forget or "skip" medication times.

Possessions

The simplest way to keep track of your possessions is to be organized. Everyone misplaces or mislays things from time to time (Winograd and Soloway, 1985). Indeed, misplacing things is one of the most common and annoying memory failures. Placing of things is usually so mundane an act that we often pay too little attention at the time, and the lack of attention leads us to fail to register the experience properly.

One simple way to avoid this recurring annoyance is to organize the locations of your possessions using drawers, cabinet shelves, closets, shoe boxes, cardboard cartons, egg cartons, etc. "Organizing" does not necessarily mean becoming overly neat and tidy. The fundamental principle is to consistently place your various possessions in the same spot. By following a consistent pattern for placing objects, you avoid the problem of remembering where each object was last put: the organizational scheme does the remembering for you.

Dime stores, department stores, and many other retailers sell devices that are intended to introduce order into your life: e.g., File Boxes, Parts Cabinet, Pattern-keeper notebook, Sewing Box, Tackle Box.

– *Location of possessions in drawers and cabinets.* A sophisticated way to organize your possessions is to label containers, including drawers, cabinets, shelves, boxes, and filing cabinets.

Labeling facilitates memory in two ways. First, labels on closed containers tell you at a glance what's inside. When boxes, files, or other containers are not labeled, the search for a particular object can be frustrating, if not fruitless. Second, labeling possessions can aid in their recovery if they are lost. Especially for items like clothing, which are often left in public places unintentionally, labels help others return your gloves, jackets, or hats to you.

But labeling can be applied to other common tasks as well. By getting in the habit of labeling containers and other possessions, you can relieve your memory of many frustrations and conflicts over issues of location and ownership. Labeling requires only a pen or some paint, but you may prefer to purchase products that come pre-labeled with your initials or first name.

– *Locations of valuable or personally important possessions.* Organization and labeling are not foolproof aids to remembering where your things are. In the case of valuables, it may not be sufficient to have a general idea of their whereabouts. For greater security, you will want to record the location of such possessions (see Figure 16). Many people use either a plain notebook or a book sold explicitly for this purpose. Unfortunately, when people are asked to recall what they own, they typically forget many items, because the sheer number of our possessions is beyond the capacity of our memory. And insurance companies will only cover what we "know" we own.

One possession you definitely do not want to lose track of is your personal papers (insurance, wills, and other records). Although you may keep such papers in a safety deposit box, you are likely to forget them when you need to consult them. Thus, you can find

Figure 16.
An example of a memory aid for keeping track of possessions and their locations. The book sketched here was sold in the mid-19th century in England (one is on display at the Styal Mill museum, Styal, England), but similar books are easily purchased today. The title of this book straight-forwardly indicates its purpose and, at the same time, the frustration that comes when a possession cannot be located.

the papers you need faster if you have them stored in an organized fashion.

– *Locations of Frequently Use Items.* Certain objects seem to get misplaced more often than others. Keys, purses, wallets, and jackets are frequently misplaced. "Lost and found" notices often testify to such errors on public bulletin boards (see Figure 17). When we accidentally leave something in a public place, our only hope is that we will remember doing so soon enough to retrieve it, or that a lost-and-found office will call us. But at home, chronic misplacers may find a fancy homing device useful, such as Electronic Search-and-Find System, a sonic detector system that helps you locate frequently misplaced items.

Other objects are prone to being carried off absentmindedly. For example, people often walk off with borrowed keys, pens, or flashlights. By changing the appearance of objects in an obvious way, you can make them easier to find or more difficult to forget to return. Painting them with iridescent colors, tying colorful yarn to them, or attaching them to large objects are among the many things that can be done to make possessions more noticeable.

– *Addresses*. Although you "know" where you live, remembering your address takes a little effort and a little time (more effort and time if you have moved often). Considering how often you must address letters, the accumulated time over a lifetime probably amounts to several months.

Where you put your keys. For many of us, the most common, recurring, vexing, annoying, and frustrating memory problem is to try to remember where we put our keys. The easiest way to minimize this problem is to have a special place for them. By routinely putting the keys in a certain shirt, pants, or purse pocket, you can eliminate frequent searches through all of your clothing.

If you are more inclined to put your keys down, do so in a pre-established spot, such as your dresser top or a hook by the door. It is wise to keep a set of duplicate keys available in your home or car. If you are inclined to use these extra keys often, give another set to a trusted neighbor. If you start going to your neighbor often, because you've lost several sets of keys, you may need to re-examine your "memory condition," as discussed in Chapter 2.

You may want to make your keys conspicuous by attaching them to something large and visible. Many hotels have caught on to this external aid. To keep guests from departing with their room keys, hotels attach unforgettable objects, such as a large heavy disk, a wooden pear, or a piece of leather about as long as one's forearm. At home, this manipulation can work well for special keys that you use infrequently.

A variety of products are sold to help you remember your keys. Many keychains can be attached directly to you by one of various means. Other keychains are designed with messages or iridescent paint to make you unlikely to forget them. If all else fails, you can purchase a small hide-a-key metal box that attaches under your car or stays in an obscure spot near your front door.

Chores

An apartment or a house asks a lot of the tenant or owner. The costs of heat and electricity can skyrocket if memory fails to turn them off when they are not needed. Likewise, maintenance of house plants and a yard can become a financial loss if one forgets to water as necessary.

Similarly, every apartment or house contains many appliances. Misuse of these can increase the cost of utility charges and may pose a threat to safety. Many of the timing devices discussed earlier can also be hooked up to regulate the turning on and off of appliances. Additionally, there are many more appliances which "remember" to turn themselves on or off. If you are going to buy a major appliance, car, house, boat, or any other very expensive product, inquire into what memory functions the product possesses. After all, why not try to buy the product that does what you want it to do and also facilitates memory?

Shopping

Shopping combines several memory tasks: the items to be purchased, the comparative prices at different stores, and the "running tab" of groceries in a shopping cart. A pad of paper and a pencil is obviously helpful for all of these tasks, but here are more specific aids as well.

Figure 17.
A checklist for shopping.

Baby Food		Fresh Fruit	
Cereal	❑	Apples	❑
Fruit	❑	Grapefruit	❑
Meat	❑	Lemons	❑
Vegetable	❑	Oranges	❑
Baked Food		**Fresh Vegetables**	
Bread	❑	Beans	❑
Cake	❑	Carrots	❑
Cookies	❑	Lettuce	❑
Pie	❑	Peas	❑
Baking Needs		Potatoes	❑
Baking Powder	❑	Tomatoes	❑
Flour	❑	**Frozen Food**	
Mixes	❑	Fruit	❑
Shortening	❑	Ice Cream	❑
Sugar	❑	Juices	❑
Yeast	❑	Meat	❑
Beverages		Vegetables	❑
Coffee	❑	**Household Goods**	
Fruit Juice	❑	Bleach	❑
Soft Drinks	❑	Paper Napkins	❑
Tea	❑	Paper Towels	❑
Canned Food		Pot Cleaner	❑
Evaporated Milk	❑	Soap	❑
Fruit	❑	Stationery	❑
Fruit Juice	❑	Toilet Tissue	❑
Soup	❑	Wax	❑
Vegetable	❑	Wax Paper	❑
Condiments		**Meats**	
Catsup	❑	Bacon	❑
Mayonnaise	❑	Beef	❑
Mustard	❑	Hamburger	❑
Relish	❑	Pork	❑
Salt	❑	Weiners	❑
Spices	❑	**Poultry, Sea Food**	
Dairy Food		Chicken	❑
Butter	❑	Turkey	❑
Cheese	❑	Fish	❑
Cream	❑	**Miscellaneous**	
Eggs	❑	Cereal	❑
Milk	❑	Gelatin	❑
Dried Foods		Macaroni	❑
Prunes	❑	Pet Food	❑
Raisins	❑	Rice	❑
Drugs & Sundries		_____	
Beauty Aids	❑	_____	
Cigarettes	❑	_____	
Drugs	❑	_____	
Toothpaste	❑	_____	

– *Your shopping list*. When your college allows, you may avoid eating in the dining hall in order to cook in your room or apartment. While being free to prepare your own food is a perk, especially after eating the food at most college dining halls, it is also a chore.

The standard grocery list is one of the simplest and most effective external memory aids. Many people use photocopies for each week's shopping. A checklist cues you to items you might otherwise forget, is quicker to fill out than a written list, and spares

Figure 18.
Christmas shopping list.

Remember the important people in your life with a card!

❑ Husband	❑ Secretary
❑ Wife	❑ Minister
❑ Mother	❑ Rabbi
❑ Father	❑ Godparents
❑ Daughter	❑ Godchild
❑ Son	❑ Neighbors
❑ Sister	❑ Boss
❑ Brother	❑ Hairdresser
❑ Grandmother	❑ Lawyer
❑ Grandfather	❑ Doctor
❑ Aunt	❑ Priest
❑ Uncle	❑ Mail Carrier
❑ Niece	❑ Teacher
❑ Nephew	❑ Babysitter
❑ Great Grandmother	❑ Secret Pal
❑ Great Grandfather	❑ Nun
❑ Nana	❑ Nurse
❑ Pop-pop	❑ Office Workers
❑ Special Friend	❑ Student
❑ Baby's First	❑ Christmas Birthday

you the effort of dredging up potential needs from memory (see Figures 17 and 18). Posting a blank list in the kitchen will allow you to mark items as you run out. Grocery stores sometimes sell checklists in convenient pads.

Finally, you can avoid having to constantly remember to buy staple items by buying in bulk. When you have the habit of buying certain products in large quantities a few times a year, the presence of the products at home tends to remind you not to worry about purchasing them. And you'll save money, too.

– *Prices*. When planning a shopping trip, you may need to determine how much you are likely to spend. Depending on your budget or cash-on-hand, this estimate can be important to your buying decisions. In making such a determination, your memory for the prices of different brands or stores may be unreliable. Books concerning product price and quality, such as those put out by Consumer Reports, can serve as a worthwhile memory aid.

– *Your "running tab"*. Getting "caught short" at the checkout counter can be embarrassing. Many grocery stores sell a shopping counter that keeps track of the total cost of items in your cart. Hand calculators can do the same chore.

- *How much you've spent.* Obviously, you can do this task by writing down what you spent or by keeping and totalling receipts. Nevertheless, some people find it faster and more efficient to record purchases using a device such as a Checkbook Calculator, a large, easy-to-use calculator with checkbook holder and pen).
- *Coupons.* Part of being a good shopper is taking advantage of bargains. To do so requires keeping track of the sales opportunities and being able to put your hands on coupons and sales information when they can be used. A device to organize sales information facilitates your remembering to make use of this information and save money, a typical example is a Budget Planner, a divider used to organize coupons before and during shopping and to maintain accurate budget records.
- *Party Supplies.* A party, especially if it involves many people and elaborate plans, requires you to perform several memory tasks: remembering who should be invited, remembering to send the invitations, and remembering to buy food, drink, and gifts. There are aids that will facilitate your remembering the things you have to do when planning a party.

Special Days and Dates

With different degrees of elaborateness, people traditionally give cards, notes, or calls to friends and relatives on special days. For some people, passive reminders are sufficient for recalling dates. Such devices tell you "whom and when" to honor only when you happen to look at them. The timing devices discussed for appointments can also be used to actively remind you of special days. Long-term timing devices will signal when a special day has arrived.

Personal History

- *Records of your Past.* Your college days are very important now and will remain so all of your life. If you keep records of your experiences, you will be grateful later in your life. But all records take some planning. We must either anticipate that an experience will be one we will later wish to remember or take action immediately following it. For example, when we take a camera to an event, we are obviously anticipating the event is worth recording. If we don't bring a camera, we might jot down our reminiscences after the event is over.

Some people keep a daily record in the form of a diary or log. The act of keeping a daily record facilitates memory in three ways. It relieves memory of having to retain all of the details of an event. But it also fosters a better memory for the event, because the process of making a record provides a prompt additional review of what happened. Finally, at a later point in time, the personal notes will enhance retrieval processes better than any other form of questioning or material.

Mementos can also be useful. You may never have occasion to think of certain personal events again unless a cue reminds you of them. Souvenirs, programs, tickets, and other objects serve more than sentimental purposes. They provide the clues necessary for us to remain as close as possible to the positive aspects of our pasts (Graumann, 1985). Some people complain that mementos just create a lot of clutter, but what appears to be clutter to you now may bring back vivid memories years from today.

– *Reminiscing.* Of course, photo albums, films, and mementos are helpful to this end. However, you may also want to look back on an important time or event for which you have no photos or mementos. On such occasions, try to find sensory cues from the relevant period. Appropriate sensory cues can often help the desired memory to emerge. You can, for example, play music that you have associated with this period. A collection of old records or tapes is rich with memory cues. Aromas from perfumes, prepared foods, fruits, or other sources can also provide potent cues to moments otherwise lost to time. Some products are specifically intended to link experiences and past memories with fragrances. The Aromance 2100 is a diffuser for generating environmental fragrances that awaken memories through the playing of a "fragrance" record.

Visual art may similarly suggest a past period or event. For example, you might hang maps or paintings of places you do not wish to forget posters of a certain era pertaining to old movies, rock groups, or political campaigns; or sculptures that suggest a certain event or clothing because they recall the past. Beyond decorating your office or home, art can keep a cue to memory always available in your environment (Yates, 1966).

Summary

- A sight, sound, touch, or movement captures attention so well that the best way to improve memory is often through the use of an external memory aid. Consequently:
- A knowledge of a variety of external aids, and how to make the best use of them, is essential to improving memory.
- External aids exist to help task-categories concerned with physical memory, studying, work memory, and personal memory.
- Learning and remembering may be facilitated by a checklist, manuals, diagrams, sketches, notes, "teaching machines," memory art, superstitious objects, knowledge sources, a "memory-friendly" desk. There are hundreds of devices that assist personal finances, cooking, maintaining one's health, keeping track of one's possessions, carrying out routine chores, having fun, staying in touch with your past, and other personal memory tasks. The more you simplify your day-to-day existence, the easier it will be to concentrate when you do study.

Chapter 7
Scientific Background

As discussed in the chapter on assessment, memory performance tends to be task specific. Between the performance on one memory task and on another, there is only a slight correlation. In addition, experimental research has also shown that memory performance for the same task will differ if the instructions given to one group of people are different that the instruction given to another group. For example, one set of subjects might be told to pay attention to the sounds of words on a list, while others are told to pay attention to the meanings of the words.

To complicate matters further, other research has shown that the instructions for how to remember information — emphasize the sounds of words versus emphasize the meaning — also affected how much information was accurately remembered.

Finally, a number of studies have investigated the effects of extensive training of particular memory tasks, and paid particular attention to whether improvements in a person's processes were general or, like other research, also task specific. Thus, a variety of different research projects have found that most, if not all, memory processes are specific and acquired.

T ask-Specific Manipulations

Applicability of a Manipulation

A manipulation involves one or more steps that are intended to achieve an end. In this book, all manipulations are intended to improve memory. Manipulations vary in how applicable they are to different memory tasks (Baddeley, 1982). General manipulations apply to many memory tasks. Specific manipulations apply to one or a few memory tasks.

Manipulations vary in applicability because of the number and kind of steps they involve. Those involving one step will apply to more tasks than manipulations involving several steps. Additionally, manipulations that use simple steps, requiring little prior learning, will apply to more tasks than manipulations involving complex steps, requiring considerable prior learning.

Simple rehearsal, for example, involves the repetition of one step: saying to yourself repeatedly the information to be learned. This can be applied to many, although not all, memory tasks, including learning pairs, lists, sentences, stories, words, numbers, or melodies. In contrast, the first letter mnemonic requires five steps: identifying the first letter of words to be remembered, organizing the letters into the skeleton of another word, filling in the vowels of the scheme-word, rehearsing the letters to be learned, and rehearsing the words to be learned. The first letter manipulation is widely regarded as most applicable to learning relatively short lists of words. It can be used for longer lists or other material, such as sentences or passages, but not as easily as it can be applied to short lists. It might be adapted to learn numbers and melodies, but the adaptation would probably require more effort than the task deserves. Thus, the generality of a manipulation is a function of its intrinsic properties.

The degree of generality or specificity of a manipulation has straightforward effects on memory performance. Many have supposed that the general manipulation, applicable to many or all memory tasks, is preferable to the specific manipulation. A general manipulation has the advantage of versatility. A specific manipulation is obviously restricted in usefulness. However, certain aspects of manipulation usage often render task-specific manipulations more effective than a general manipulation applied to the same task (Herrmann & Searleman, 1990b).

A manipulation is executed sequentially in four stages, shown in Figure 19. The utility of a manipulation depends on how easy

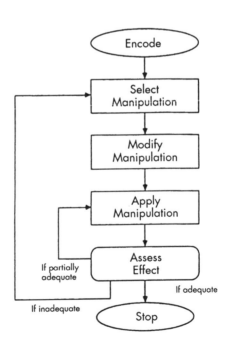

Figure 19.
A flowchart depicting the stages of implementing a mental manipulation.

it is to execute, how much time is necessary to execute it, and how effectively each stage is executed (Miller, Galanter, & Pribram, 1960).

Advantages in the Selection Stage

General and specific manipulations function differently at each stage. In order to use a manipulation, you must think of it before or while a task confronts you.

The probability of a manipulation being elicited, or brought to consciousness, by a situation is directly related to the manipulation's specificity. A general manipulation, which is associated equally with all tasks, will not be strongly associated with any given task. Conversely, a specific manipulation will be most strongly associated with the task to which it applies and unassociated with other tasks. Thus, specific manipulations are more readily elicited than general manipulations by a task or by a situation that foretells a task.

For an example, consider the task of remembering to water your plants. A specific manipulation will be more likely to elicit the intention than a general one. A mental manipulation in which the intention to water a plant at a certain time is rehearsed by imagining or physically acting out the watering will be more effective than rehearsal in which the intention is repeated only verbally to oneself.

In addition, when a task may be handled by two or more manipulations, you may want to choose among them (Garfunkel & Landau, 1981). Preferably, you would select the manipulation that is more appropriate for the task.

Such choices are invariably easier with specific manipulations than with general manipulations. Whether or not a specific manipulation is applicable is readily seen; for example, noting the features of a face is clearly useful to registering faces, but not names. However, general manipulations are less readily seen as applicable because of their vagueness. Suppose, for example, you choose to apply a verbal rehearsal manipulation. What steps would you take to rehearse a face or the fragrance of someone's perfume or aftershave?

Advantages in the Modification Stage

Although it may not be readily apparent, every manipulation must be modified or adjusted to the particular task. The amount of mental effort and time expended in such modification depends on the generality of the manipulation.

For example, suppose you need to learn someone's name — say Armandstring. Even if you already planned to learn the name by association, you must decide which type of association will be most appropriate for "Armandstring." Unless you have modified the manipulation and are prepared to associate the name with certain key kinds of information — such as the names of other people "Armandstring" reminds you of, his occupation or his regional background — you will probably spend too much time thinking of proper associations. Modifying a general manipulation on the spot requires more time during the execution phase than using a planned specific manipulation.

Advantages in the Application Stage

Finally, the manipulation must be applied to the task. The effectiveness of this application also appears to depend on whether the manipulation is general or specific. Since general manipulations involve fewer steps than specific manipulations, it might seem that general manipulations are easier to execute.

If the issue were solely the number of steps, this would be true. However, the ease of application depends on the appropriateness of the general manipulation for the task. A great deal of research now indicates that each manipulation has its greatest benefit for certain tasks. Many manipulations, including most of the mental manipulations presented in Chapter 6, are less general than they have been touted to be.

For example, the technical mnemonics are often promoted as useful for any and all tasks, as described in Chapter 1. But they in fact are most useful for only certain tasks (Herrmann, 1987). If the general manipulation does not lend itself readily for the task at hand, as in the example of applying rehearsal to remembering the fragrance of a perfume or aftershave, the specific manipulation may be considerably easier to apply than a general manipulation.

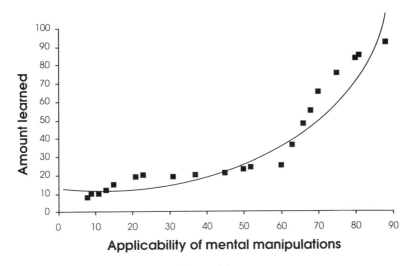

Figure 20.
The amount learned from the use of mental manipulation according to the applicability of the manipulation to the material to be learned or remembered (hypothetical data based on the research literature).

Thus, as the applicability of manipulations increase, the amount you will learn will increase (see Figure 20).

As people become proficient at performing memory tasks, their abilities increase specifically rather than generally (James, 1890; Herrmann, Rea, & Andrzejewski, 1987; Herrmann, 1990b; Schacter & Gilsky, 1986). A person who gains proficiency at a certain task is usually no more expert than the average person at a different task. Experiments have shown this result when the task used to test transfer of ability is only slightly different from the original task. Studies have found a similar failure of advanced memory ability to transfer to other tasks with a variety of skills.

Chess experts, some of whom have spent over 10,000 hours developing their expertise, reproduce with great accuracy — after just a glance — the positions of pieces on a partially played-out chess board. Given the same task, novice chess players reproduce the board with considerable inaccuracy. Nevertheless, the same chess experts recall the board positions no better than the novice players when the pieces are randomly ordered on the board (Simon & Gilmarten, 1973). Thus, the dramatic short-term memory ability of chess experts applies only when pieces are positioned according to the rules of the game.

Similarly, when most people are presented with a series of digits and asked to recall them in the order presented, they can usually recall no more than seven consecutive digits correctly. With strenuous practice over several months, their recall at the task increases substantially. Some people have been found to increase the number of digits they can recall by ten times! Interviews with these people indicate that practice allows the person to develop retrieval-structure manipulations from their background and interests. For example, one person developed a scheme to remember digits by identifying sequences as a series of winning times in running events.

However, the most interesting aspect of the results concern the generality of the memory skills acquired. If these same trained individuals are then asked to recall a series of letters, their recall drops from about 80 digits back to 6 or 7 letters (Baltes & Kligel, 1985; Chase & Ericsson, 1982; Ericsson, 1985; Rybash, Hoyer, & Rodin, 1986). Thus, despite the apparent similarity of the two tasks, the dramatic improvement applies only to the practice task.

This finding also seems to apply to retrieval of facts and knowledge. People who practice recalling examples of categories, such as animals — even without consulting books or other resources during practice — increase the number of examples that they can recall by threefold, from an average of 40 to 120 animals (Herrmann, Buschke, & Gall, 1986). Like the subjects who practiced learning digit series, these subjects reported that they developed schemes to guide their recall, such as thinking of animals at the zoo, in the wild on different continents, or in certain books. However, the increase in recall for the practice category fails to transfer to recall from other categories, such as for furniture.

It is accordingly not surprising that educational experience yields abilities that are specific to the discipline studied (Glaser, 1984; Lave, 1988). Similarly, it is also not surprising that occupational experience usually yields advanced memory abilities specific to the occupation. Bartenders have good memory for remembering what drinks they made. Waitresses are skilled at remembering what patrons have ordered, what they have been served, and where they are seated. Professors are adept at remembering books and articles applicable to their specialty. Indeed, the evidence now available indicates that memory skills acquired through practice are so specific that a bartender who can memorize new recipes for drinks quickly will be no quicker than the typical professor or car mechanic at remembering appointments.

Finally, even interests or hobbies you actively pursue develop memory skills pertinent to them. What may be surprising is that, again, the skill involved remains specific to the hobby. For example, baseball fans can learn and remember the box scores of a particular game with amazing speed and accuracy. However, when they turn the page to the stock listings, their skill with numbers fades quickly back normal. There is no evidence that memory skills acquired in pursuit of a hobby endows a person with superior memory skills for any and all tasks.

Advantages in the Assessment Stage

After a manipulation has been applied, its effectiveness can be assessed. Oftentimes, this evaluation is carried out periodically while a memory task is being attempted. The assessment should determine whether more manipulative processing is needed for the task, whether the manipulations were effective, and whether modifications or new manipulations should be added.

Even in this assessment phase, specific manipulations have an edge over general ones. If a specific manipulation is ineffective, the reason can be identified in a relatively straightforward manner: most likely, the manipulation was inappropriate for the information. If a general manipulation is ineffective, however, many reasons must be considered. The manipulation may have been inappropriate; it may not have been properly modified to apply to the task; or its execution may have been flawed — particularly if interfered with by other memory traces from tasks to which it had previously been applied.

Thus, it takes longer to assess the effectiveness of the general manipulation. Increased time and lowered accuracy in assessment diminishes the overall efficiency and effectiveness of performance.

At each stage of manipulation execution, specific manipulations are more effective than general manipulations. Before execution, however, task-specific manipulations require more preparation and forethought to remain useful. This is because there are hundreds of specific memory tasks encountered in daily life (discussed in Cohen, 1989; Gruneberg & Morris, 1979, 1992; Gruneberg, Morris, & Sykes, 1978, 1988; Harris & Morris, 1983; Howe, 1977; Neisser, 1982). It simply is not possible to learn task-specific manipulations to anticipate or prepare for all, or even most, tasks. Thus, for incidental tasks, which you executed without being aware you were performing a memory task, or for unanticipated but intentional tasks, a general manipulation is necessary. Nonetheless, when a task allows or merits your most effective effort, you should prepare specific manipulations.

The Advantages of Repertoires of Manipulations

Preparing a repertoire of two or more manipulations is better than preparing just one manipulation, because a particular, task-specific manipulation may not suit every instance of a certain task. The extent of the match between them affects the efficiency and effectiveness of the manipulation for the task.

Manipulations emphasize different attributes of task information and instances of the same task manifest certain attributes more than other instances. If just one manipulation is used, it may not match the task maximally. In contrast, the use of two manipulations increases the quantity and quality of registration and remembering, thereby making up for any lacking in effectiveness that might come with the use of just one manipulation.

Consider the example of learning names. One manipulation for learning a person's name involves its ethnic roots. Another manipulation involves analyzing peculiar aspects of its spelling or graphic form, such as unusual length, double letters, or unusual combinations of letters. These two different manipulations clearly emphasize different aspects of the same task.

Similarly, names differ in the attributes they present for manipulation. To many Americans, "Jones" is a neutral name, because its ethnic roots are obscure and its spelling is typical. "Maloy" is more identifiable for its Irish ethnic roots, but its spelling is equally typical. "Armstrong" is also ethnically neutral to many Americans, but the name combines two common words in a distinct, fairly unusual way. "Andrzejewski" is more ethnically interesting and identifiable for its Polish roots, and its spelling is unusual in both length and letter combinations.

The manipulations of ethnic and graphic analysis may be applied to all these names, but not with equal effect. The amount of interest and attention generated by an ethnic analysis would increase from Jones and Armstrong to Maloy and Andrzejewski. The amount of interest and attention generated by a graphic analysis would increase across Jones and Maloy to Armstrong and Andrzejewski. Only Andrzejewski draws a maximum reaction from both manipulations. A repertoire that includes both will allow you to match the given name to the most effective manipulation

Thus, using a repertoire of manipulations allows each manipulation to make up for any loss in effectiveness possessed by the other. Additionally, the use of two or more manipulations ensures that you pay extra attention to what you want to register or remember, thereby making success more likely (Anderson, 1983; Bransford & Stein, 1984; Gagne & Paradise, 1961; Geiselman, Fisher, MacKinnon, & Holland, 1986; Harlow, 1949; Kolodner, 1984; Morris, Bransford, & Franks, 1977; Schank, 1980). Finally, in designing repertoires, you can strategically chose manipulations to enhance your performance in a maximally efficient fashion. Rather than using manipulations that overlap in their effect, as in the name example above, manipulations may be used that overlap little or not at all.

There are clearly many ways that manipulations might be selected that facilitate memory in very different ways. For example, you might choose mental manipulations of strength and retrieval structures which have clearly different effects; a mental manipulation and an environmental manipulation; a mental manipulation and a social manipulation; or an environmental manipulation and a condition manipulation.

In summary, manipulations that facilitate memory in different ways, if judiciously selected, will lead you to respond flexibly to memory tasks and to have a greater chance of success. Figure 21 summarizes the effects of different kinds of manipulations on the efficiency of a person's studying.

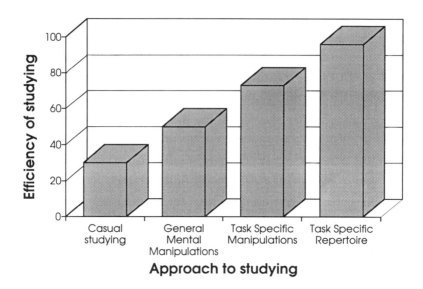

Figure 21.
The efficiency of a person's studying as a function of the kind of mental manipulation used (hypothetical data based on the research literature).

Method for Acquiring Task-Specific Repertoires

You already apply repertoires of manipulations to memory tasks. For tasks that you are not well prepared for, you fall back on natural manipulations that you have known since adolescence or childhood. Some of your natural manipulations are probably general ones, which you apply to many memory tasks. Others are probably specific, such as ones that you developed when in school for studying material or taking exams. After reading the previous chapters, you should now know many more general manipulations. This chapter will expand your knowledge of specific manipulations.

Selection of Manipulations to Make up a Repertoire

Before you expand your use of task-specific manipulations for a particular task, you should decide whether your existing repertoire for this task may be adequate after all.

Task Description: _____

Registration: (Chapter)

Condition Manipulations:_____
_____ 2

Attitude Manipulations:_____
_____ 3

Mental Manipulations: _____
_____ 5

Environmental Manipulations: _____
_____ 6

Social Manipulations: _____
_____ 4

Study-Specific Manipulations: _____
_____ 8

Retention Maintenance: _____
_____ 5

Remembering:

Condition Manipulations:_____
_____ 2

Attitude Manipulations:_____
_____ 3

Mental Manipulations: _____
_____ 5

Environmental Manipulations: _____
_____ 6

Social Manipulations: _____
_____ 4

Study-Specific Manipulations: _____
_____ 8

Figure 22.
A repertoire Generation Form. First, write in the manipulations you now
use in whatever space seems appropriate. Second, write in other manipulations that, on reflection, you feel you could use.

Figure 22 presents a form to guide you in analyzing your repertoire for a given task. Use this form in the following manner. First, recall the manipulations that you usually use for the task. The manipulation categories and chapter references are provided on the form to help you think of the manipulations you use; it is not necessary for you to classify each manipulation you recall.

After you have exhausted the list of manipulations you have previously applied to the task, consider whether these manipulations are sufficient. It is possible that the manipulations you now know would be sufficient if you made an effort to use them when you encounter the task. However, it is also possible that you may judge your natural repertoire as not up to the task.

If you feel that the manipulations that make up your current repertoire are insufficient, then you should develop new manipulations to supplement them. In many cases, some potentially useful manipulations will occur to you after you analyze your performance of a task.

You may also discover some useful manipulations in any of the many books that have been published on memory improvement. However, all previous books on memory improvement have stressed a limited number of so-called general procedures and, hence, provide only a little task-specific information. Since no previous book on memory improvement provides much information about them, this chapter presents an inventory of task-specific manipulations to help you in constructing repertoires for the tasks of interest to you.

The inventory below provides many manipulations for everyday memory tasks. For each task in the inventory, a menu of feasible manipulations is listed. The form of the inventory is similar to a dictionary, with telegraphic descriptions giving you the gist of multiple manipulations. From these telegraphic descriptions, you should be able to select and implement particular manipulations to suit your task and preferences.

Fortunately, the nature of most task-specific manipulations is evident on reading a brief description. The inventory is not intended to be read like a text. You should simply consult it for potentially relevant manipulations when you have particular tasks in mind.

Although the everyday memory tasks included will be familiar to you, the inventory does not include all possible tasks. If the task you have in mind is not included in the inventory, look for similar tasks; they will usually contain some manipulations relevant to the task of interest to you.

The menu for each task likewise includes more manipulations than any previous book, but the menus are not exhaustive. If they do not provide a manipulation that satisfies you, the menus will still probably guide your thinking and help you devise a suitable manipulation.

The manipulations you choose to include in a repertoire should meet certain criteria if that repertoire is to be truly useful to you. The manipulation should seem natural to you. It should be possible for you to imagine yourself using it comfortably and consistently. Any given manipulation will suit some people but not others. Where one person will favor visual manipulations, another will favor auditory manipulations. People who enjoy and collect gadgetry may prefer environmental manipulations, while outgoing types will be more drawn to social manipulations.

Many of the manipulations that you have learned in this book or from other sources are bound to strike you as implausible or foolish. You should dismiss them. At least some manipulations will strike you as plausible and prove effective for you.

Once you have decided to add a manipulation to a repertoire, add it to the manipulations you listed on the Repertoire Generation Form. When you add new manipulations, indicate in some way, such as by using a different color pen, that these are untried manipulations. This marking is useful when you select the manipulations that you should study in your preparation of a functional repertoire. Many people forget which manipulations they knew originally and which were obtained from the inventory. The origin is important to bear in mind because new manipulations need extra study if they are to become useful; a false belief that one know the manipulation all along will not guarantee it will be used.

Once you have selected one or more manipulations to add to your repertoire, you can begin to implement them. From the manipulations that you have chosen, you should identify one or two appropriate manipulations you do not currently use in the task. Research has shown that prior study of a repertoire can facilitate subsequent memory performance for the relevant task when the number of manipulations is small and manageable. Attempting to acquire many manipulations will lead to worse performance than memorization of a manageable few.

Obviously, the apparent difficulty level of a manipulation will bear on your decision to use or dismiss it. Generally, the more difficult registration manipulations produce a better trace, because these manipulations usually require more attention. But if your time for a task is limited, you will obviously want to pick an easier manipulation. Finally, if the manipulation seems familiar because it is the same as, or similar to, one that you use in other contexts, you will be more likely to succeed at incorporating it into your task repertoire.

After you decide to add a manipulation to a repertoire, you must do some work to make it work for you. It is not sufficient to identify a manipulation and decide to use it.

1. First, make a list of the kinds of situations in which you expect the task to recur — for instance, home, work, or shopping. If possible, specify the particular situations — for instance, with certain people, or dealing with certain information.

2. Second, establish a strong association between the manipulation and the task. Simply rehearsing the association will usually not be enough.

3. Finally, you should engage in extended self-association training. This training involves the following steps. Write the name of the task on one side of a card and the manipulation you intend to use on the other side. Then leave the card in a prominent spot, such as next to your bed, on your kitchen table, or on your desk at work. Each time you pass the card, try to recall the manipulations as quickly as possible. At first, you will notice a brief lapse before you recall the manipulation. With practice, it will come to mind immediately.

Once you are confident that you have associated the manipulation with the task, you need to take two more steps to incorporate the manipulation into your repertoire. First, use the manipulation whenever you can. If circumstances limit your opportunities to do so, imagine yourself using the manipulation.

Second, keep a record for two to four weeks, indicating how often you encountered the task, whether you used the manipulation, and how successful each use was. After you have kept this record long enough to establish a "track record" of performance, analyze the effectiveness of the manipulation. Does it really work for you? If it doesn't work so well, is it because you are not yet skilled at it, or is it because the manipulation does not suit you after all? If you decide the problem lay with the manipulations and not your own efforts, re-evaluate whether you really need a manipulation for this task. If you do, find another manipulation that might prove more effective.

Note that the repertoires addressed here are those that are most important to studying and college life. For a wider array of repertoires pertaining to everyday life in general, see Herrmann (1990c).

An Example of Developing a Task-Specific Repertoire

To make the foregoing discussion clearer, consider the task of learning and remembering combinations for a lock.

Just suppose that you had a job or were in a school where you had to learn a combination from time to time, and forgetting it would get you in hot water. To identify a manipulation for learning combinations, you would first recall for yourself the manipulations that you would naturally apply to this task. Then, you would consult the menu of possible manipulations listed in the inventory, under "combinations to a lock." This menu is reproduced in Figure 23. Suppose that the manipulation for visualizing the numbers in position on the lock seems the most plausible choice to you. Your next step would be to identify situations in which you are likely to be given a new combination lock to use. After identifying them, associate the visualization manipulation with these situations, such as by the card method described above. Once the manipulation is well associated with task situations, practice imagining yourself using the manipulation. Finally, keep track of how often you use the visualization manipulation, and evaluate how effective it is.

Registration:
- visualize the numbers in position;
- rehearse opening it;
- associate the numbers with certain ages of your life and a significant event that occurred at each of these ages;
- notice mathematical properties of the numbers — what they are divisible by, and how the numbers relate mathematically to each other, such as one being about twice the other;
- write the numbers down and save it;
- write the numbers in an inconspicuous spot near the lock.

Remembering:
- try to recall the feel of turning the tumbler;
- consult notes.

Figure 23.
A menu of manipulations appropriate for registering and remembering combinations for combination locks.

Obviously, the development of a task-specific repertoire requires a good deal of effort. For that reason alone, there is a limit to the number of such repertoires that you could — or even would want — to learn. Thus, you will want to begin with just one or two tasks that seriously annoy you or that you consider especially important. Once you have improved on those tasks, you may wish to work on a further tasks. Yet even if you only improve your performance on just those few tasks that most trouble you, you will have achieved the memory improvement that most genuinely matters to you.

An Inventory of Task-Specific Manipulations

The inventory that follows presents menus of manipulations relevant to over 40 memory tasks pertinent to studying and college life. The menus have been developed by us along with the students who took courses with me concerning memory and/or memory training.

Information in the Task Menus

Each entry in the inventory is unique, although similar tasks will contain some similar manipulations. Two kinds of information may be included in a task menu. First, menus include manipulations from the previous chapters that are especially suitable for a particular task or appropriate modifications of those manipulations. Second, the menus may include manipulations that have been designed specifically for the task. Most of the menus do not mention manipulations concerning condition, attitude, and general manipulations of social context. Condition manipulations tend to be applicable to all tasks and, therefore, specific to none. Attitude manipulations tend to be specific to individuals rather than to tasks. And general manipulations of social context, like those for condition, apply to essentially all tasks.

Nevertheless, you may need — and should feel free to add — condition, attitude, or social context manipulations to your repertoire for a particular task. By reviewing the assessment procedures and manipulations presented in Chapters 2, 3, and 4, you will be the best judge of which, if any, of these areas need improvement.

Menus change systematically with task demands. Some tasks require more manipulations than others. Some tasks exclusively involve remembering, such as when we try to remember the name of someone whom we met a long time ago. Other tasks involve only registration, as most intention tasks, in which we register an act we intend to carry out and hope the intention will emerge into consciousness when needed.

Occasionally, remembering tasks are based on information acquired in an incidental memory task. For such remembering tasks, registration is past and cannot be altered. However, the remembering in such cases can still be aided by engaging in preparation. Obviously, the inventory will be useful to you to the extent that you have properly identified your task and can match it to the correct task description in the inventory.

Organization of the Inventory

The inventory is divided into four sections, each devoted to one of the four general kinds of memory tasks: everyday knowledge, events, intentions, and actions. (Knowledge relating directly to study skills will be taken up in the next chapter.) Under every category, a table of contents precedes a series of menus for the specific tasks.

I. Everyday-Knowledge Task Menus

Table of Contents

- **Answer to a question** — Remembering an answer to a question that you are sure you know but cannot presently answer.
- **Conversation ill-prepared for** — Remembering information to offer in conversation for a topic you once knew but have since forgotten.
- **Combination to a lock** — Learning and remembering the numbers of a combination.
- **Current events** — Remembering what is in the news.
- **Dates of events** — Learning and remembering dates.
- **Lyrics** — Learning and remembering lyrics of songs (see also "Poetry").
- **Melody** — Learning and remembering the melody line of music you play or fancy.
- **Phone numbers** — Learning and remembering.
- **Rules of games** — Learning and remembering the rules of sports, board games, or parlor games.
- **Script** — Learning and remembering a script for a film or play (see "Poetry" if learning verbatim; see "Speeches" if learning the gist first).
- **Special numbers** — Learning and remembering special numbers (Social Security; service; license; own address).

Knowledge Task Menus

- **Answer to a question that you are sure you know, but cannot presently answer**
  Remembering: reflect on key terms; use the tip-of-the- tongue formula, make notes about related ideas to see if they trigger the answer; ask for a paraphrase of the question — the person's

paraphrase will often trigger, if not contain, the answer; stall — the answer may come in time.

- **Conversation, ill-prepared for — remembering information to offer in conversation for a topic you know little about**
  Registration: study up on possible topics of discussion prior to getting together with people; keep abreast of events and be well-read; consult newsmagazines, encyclopedias; ask an informed friend to prime you on the topic.
  Remembering: say nothing if nothing can be recalled; if you remember too little, you may seem naive or foolish; don't jump into the conversation right away, let the conversation elicit what you know; admit lack of knowledge or information before saying anything.

- **Combination to a lock**
  Registration: visualize the numbers in position; rehearse opening it; associate the numbers with ages of your life and a significant event of each of these ages; notice mathematical properties of the numbers — what they are divisible by, and how the numbers relate mathematically to each other, such as one being about twice the other; write it down and save it; write it in an inconspicuous spot near the lock.
  Remembering: try to recall the feel of turning the tumbler; consult notes.

- **Current events in the news or in local goings-on**
  Registration: during reading or listening to the news, note a half-dozen key events; test your recall of these events; read news magazines regularly; discuss events with a certain person or persons regularly; associate current news to related previous events.
  Remembering: reflect on key events; skim through a news magazine if it is available; ask others for their impression of a certain event or of current events generally — their answer will trigger your own ideas.

- **Dates of events**
  Registration: note the century and associate the last two numbers with an age of someone you know; keep a notebook on dates you would like to remember; refresh yourself before situations in which remembering dates will be useful.
  Remembering: try to recall how you learned the date; notes.

- **Lyrics of songs (See also "Poetry" in Chapter 8.)**

Registration: get the message of the lyrics in mind; learn each phrase one at a time; note how rhyming fixes — that is, requires — certain words to be said; sing the lyrics, e. g. associate the lyrics with the music; sheet music; recordings; tapes.

Remembering: remember the message of the song; recall which sounds were the basis of rhyming and reconstruct which words contained this sound; consult sheet music.

– Melody-lines of music

Registration: play each phrase and attempt to recall from memory vocally or on an instrument; play successive phrases and identify which ones have similar or recurring structure; imagine the notes on sheet music; associate with the lyrics or, if no lyrics exist, make them up; sheet music; review and practice.

Remembering: recall the structure of the song, its recurring or distinctive phases; sheet music.

– Phone numbers

Registration: examine the number for mathematical relationships; translate the number into letters according to the dial and then form these letters into a word or phrase; attend to the tones of the numbers while dialing; note the number; record the number in a dialing device.

Remembering: try to recall how you learned the number — for example, using math patterns or letter associations; notes, dialing device, phone book.

– Rules of games (sports, board games, parlor games)

Registration: identify the winning conditions and the conditions that thwart winning; play with others or with simulator machines; when you are surprised about a ruling, take note; keep notes on rulings that surprised you; buy a book on game rules, such as Hoyle's (see References); review rules before playing the game.

Remembering: think of the logic of the game and then reconstruct (remembering that rules are often illogical); notes or a rule book.

– Script for a play or film (See "Poetry" if learning verbatim; see speeches if learning the gist first; both are covered in Chapter 8.)

– Special numbers (Social Security; your own address)

Registration: note mathematical patterns; translate the number into (a) historical dates of interest to you, (b) your current or previous weight, (c) letters according to a number code and then into a word; record it.

Remembering: recall how you learned it; reinstate the context of prior use; records.

II. Event Menus

Table of Contents

- **Location of misplaced object** — that was misplaced a longer time ago.
- **Location of keys** — Remembering where you put your keys.
- **Long sentence, question or request** — Remembering all of what was said to you in a long utterance (so you can answer it).
- **Message given on awakening** — Remembering what was said to you on awakening before arising or before going back to sleep.
- **Name acquisition** — learning someone's name during an introduction so you will call them properly by name when you see them.
- **Photos** — Remembering when and where was it taken, who is in the photo, and sometimes who took the photo.
- **Prior statements in conversation** — Remembering the point of view on an issue that you expressed previously, so you avoid appearing inconsistent, absentminded, or hypocritical.
- **Prior statement in correspondence** — Remembering what you wrote to someone previously.
- **What one was saying** — Remembering what one was talking about after a momentary distraction.

Event-Task Menus

- **Actions just performed or recently performed** — remembering whether you did something minutes or hours before, such as brushing your teeth or putting something away
  Remembering: think of possible consequences of action or of events that would have been contingent on the action; seek physical evidence of the action if this is possible (for example, to determine if you brushed your teeth, feel your toothbrush).
- **Birthday** — remembering the date of someone's birthday, as distinguished from realizing you must do something about it, which is covered under III. Intention Repertoires
  Registration: is it close to someone else's birthday? Keep records on birthdays; calendar/diary, a reminder's service, appointment books; steer conversation to birthdays/horoscopes; find association between person and the date; cluster birthdays.
  Remembering: try to recall when this person last celebrated his or her birthday, scan a calendar; try to narrow down to season,

then to month, etc.; ask a friend; ask the person what their sign is; say "your birthday is coming up?"

- **Conversation, current** — what you said just before you were interrupted in the middle of the sentence
  Preparation: anticipate before the conversation what is to be discussed, thereby fostering better encoding; develop an interest for what is discussed — in other words, evaluate the conversation: is it interesting, trivial, seditious, salacious, etc.; summarize the conversation to yourself; in some professional situations it is acceptable to record what is happening so that, if a tape is being made, it is easy to ask for a replay; resist being interrupted; keep focused on the conversation, and treat the interruption as peripheral.
  Remembering: pause, sometimes it will come back; reconstruct the conversation and guess what was probably said; cue eliciting act: say — "Oh heck, I don't want to say anything more"; people will usually ask you to finish and mention a key word or two that will trigger your memory; or inquire, "What do you think?"

- **Conversation, past** — on a previous occasion
  Remembering: recall position where conversation took place; look at paper notes are written on; rehearse some of the topics of conversation; ask the person.

- **Date of a past event** (see entry for "Events")

- **Dates of future events** — on one's schedule
  Registration: associate the date with the event; associate one event with another on the same date; imagine a calendar with key dates marked; associate the date with past historic events; record on your calendar and on your appointment book.
  Remembering: imagine your calendar; calendar; appointment book.

- **Directions to perform a particular act as given to you by someone else, such as your teacher or roommate**
  Registration: make sure that you have the directions right in the first place — have the person repeat the directions (even if you already do have them right, going over them gives you a second rehearsal); notes; if there is another person with you, ask if he or she understood it — the discussion will provide extra review for you and also establish an alternate source should you forget part or all of what is to be done; look back on the directions in the interim.

Remembering: imagine yourself in the situation where instructions were given; consult notes; consult someone who was present when instructions were given; find someone who knows what to do from experience or knowledge.
- Events — such as individual incidents, the sequence of incidents, who attended, when it occurred
Registration: describe for yourself the gist of the event just afterwards — select a few key words that capture the event and rehearse these words; self referencing; anticipate the likely way the episode will unfold its script; prioritize, decide ahead of time what things will be worth attending to and remembering; make mental or physical notes about salient aspects of the event; discuss with others right away; discuss with friends immediately afterwards; reflect on the event as soon as you can.
Remembering: recall the theme and key descriptors and then reconstruct; check for sensory detail — real memories tend to have more sensory details than imagined ones; check for verbosity — real memories lend themselves to less equivocation than imagined memories; recreate the scene in your mind; recall major landmarks at the event; imagine yourself at different spots in the location of the event, looking upon the event from different perspectives; reconstruct the temporal order of the sub-parts of the event (Adams, 1985); question yourself about particular attributes of the event — recall of particular attributes will often trigger other attributes; decide which kind of error is least objectionable in the situation — omission or commission — and guess accordingly; recall everything that might be correct to yourself and then pick and choose; recall from different points in the sequence of the event; recall in different orders — start to finish, then finish to start; consult notes; find old souvenirs, mementos, photos, or any material associated with the event (Graumann, 1985); consult someone else who was present; make a cue gathering statement to someone else who was present; let someone interview you about the event, that is, to guide you through the retrieval process — sometimes a guided recall by someone else is better than interrogating yourself.
- Face recognition
Remembering: reinstate a context in which you may have met; imagine people you know who have similar faces; don't be pre-

occupied with studying their facial features, but instead make judgments about them: who do they remind you of; do they seem honest, sensitive, interesting, and so on with whatever characteristics are of value to you (Bahrick, 1984; Winograd, 1976); sometimes an album or a yearbook will help; take cues from others; if you fail to recognize the person, admit it but be apologetic.

– **Finding a file**

  Registration: pay attention to the labels on the file; if files are out of order, do not file the new folder until the order is corrected; label files properly; keep a directory — a list of labels to files.

  Remembering: take everything out and go through each folder.

– **Finding something in a file**

  Registration: pay attention to the organization of the filing system; periodically go over the file and reorganize; label files properly; keep a directory — a list of labels to files; keep notes about reorganization of files.

  Remembering: take everything out and go through each folder.

– **Loans** — remembering your borrowers

  Registration: imagine yourself handing the person the money or object you loaned; associate the loan with other events of the day and with whom else might have been present, associate the loan with the date it is to be paid back; keep records, note on your calendar and appointment book when the loan is due or when you should ask for its return; when you make the loan, ask the person when the money or object loaned will be returned.

  Remembering: calendar; appointment book.

– **Location of keys**

  Registration: put keys in a regular spot, on a key rack, in a special pocket; re-check lock to see key was not left when you entered or left; keep keys on a string attached to clothing; check to see if you know where your keys are; pat your pockets if you keep your keys on your person or check where you normally carry them.

  Remembering: retrace your steps; ask someone else; use a key chain that attaches to your belt or other part of clothing; large key rings; glow-in-the-dark key chain; keep extra keys accessible somewhere, although this practice may dispose you to be careless and to lose your keys.

- **Location of misplaced object, recent**

  Registration: be methodical, go step by step; have a routine for the way you lay out things in chores — it may seem boring but use of consistent placement habits makes it easier to find things later; use object organizers at every opportunity; assign standard places to put things; be aware of who is around as you do a task in which things might be misplaced, so you can ask later if necessary; before you have a chance to lose things, make an object check, that is, check that everything is where you had intended it to be; take objects with you on your person if feasible.

  Remembering: reinstate what you were doing just before you misplaced it; retrace your steps; develop a search plan; (1) check object organizers and standard places; (2) clear the area in which the object disappeared; (3) turn the place upside down in searching for it; (4) if that fails, pick up the area and put everything back where it is supposed to be and develop a new plan; ask anyone who was around where they think you may have misplaced the object; if you are desperate, ask a friend to help you look for it.

- **Location of misplaced object, some time ago**

  Registration: rehearse name of object with location; imagine the object in the location; imagine returning and finding the object in the future; put objects in an expected place; be orderly, give everything its place; keep a place for priority items — in marked storage closets, cabinets; periodically check that things are where they are supposed to be, remembering that things can be in their places even in a messy-looking house.

  Remembering: recall last use of item; recall probable last use of item; walk to places of possible last use; if all else fails, go through all of your possessions (you may be lucky and as as a bonus find something else that was missing); remember ways you found the object before; go out and buy a new one — it will reappear; make sure you have not loaned the object to someone; make sure that someone else did not move the object or put it back in an unfamiliar place; ask a friend; blame someone else and they will help you find it.

- **Long sentence, question, or request** — remembering all of what was said to you, so you can answer it

Registration: pay attention to key words and remember them instead of the whole question or request; pay extra attention to people given to making long utterances or to situations where long questions often occur as in court or class; ignore everything else; note pad where possible; you may, if you like, restate the question or request and confirm it, or ask the questioner to paraphrase the utterance; you may politely ask the questioner to be brief; pick out key terms and rehearse them.

Remembering: recall your key terms; consult note pad if possible; as you recall the answer, watch faces of others to determine if you missed a point; after reply, ask if you covered everything satisfactorily, rather than ask if you remembered everything, acknowledge that the statement, question, or request was long and say that you don't have time to deal with all that was mentioned but that you will address the most important points, and then respond to whatever you recall.

– **Message given to you while not fully awake** — such as just before falling asleep, when awakened from sleep, or on awakening

Registration: prioritize this situation so that when it occurs you will be more likely to take note of the message; make a note on a pad by the bed; ask the person giving you the message to leave a note for you.

Remembering: reinstate the context, retrieve key words or gist and reconstruct; notes if you made them.

– **Name acquisition** — during an introduction

Registration: if possible, prime yourself ahead of time by asking someone the names of people you might meet at a social function — if you know the name before being introduced, half the battle is won; if possible arrive before most of the people — this will prevent you from having to meet everyone at once and will give you more time to study the people you are meeting; use the face-name imagery technique, which has three steps: (1) think of a "substitute" word that represents some object that sounds like the person's last name and for which you can form a mental image — such as "duck" for Donald; (2) select the most outstanding feature of the person's face; (3) form an image of your substitute word on the person's face; use distributed rehearsal; use the SALT method: (1) say the name out loud; (2) ask the person a question while using the name; (3) say the name at least once in conversation; and (4) terminate the conversation by using the name again; think of a rhyme for the name; decide who the person looks like — for example, a celebrity or someone else you know; translate the name, with some distortion, into another language; note the person's eccentricities; analyze the national or ethnic origins of the name; take an interest in the person; as you leave the situation, look back and see if you can recall the name or names of people met — if you can't recall, ask someone with you; jotting down their name at the earliest opportunity, such as in an address book; this practice is especially helpful when encountering several introductions in a row on a receiving line; discuss whom you met with others; it is considered socially acceptable to ask someone their name after just being introduced when the introduction situation is hurried and hectic — it is even regarded as a compliment under such conditions that you considered them worth the trouble of asking; reflect on who was met as soon as possible after leaving a social function, including what they looked like and pronouncing their name aloud; review a list you made or which was available for the social function; imagine settings in which you might encounter them in the future and then imagine meeting them and saying their names in this setting; if you cannot recall someone's name after a good effort to recall, ask someone who might know it.

Remembering: reinstate the context of when and where you first met (see also, "First meeting with someone") and how you felt at the time; use the tip-of-the-tongue method; go through the alphabet and ask yourself if the name began with each letter; use notes, address book, programs to social or professional functions; take note of rosters of office locations in companies or buildings; ask the person whose name you want to remember cue-gathering questions; ask someone nearby who is out of earshot of this person; ask the person how to pronounce their name, leading them to tell it without your having to admit you forgot it (however, if their name is Jones, this can make you look silly); avoid having to refer to them by name.

- **Photos** — when and where it was taken, who is in it, or who took it

Registration: look at your photos when they come back from the developer and attempt to remember right away who and what is in them; write on back the photo what, where, when as soon as you get it; periodically look over and remind yourself about old photos.

Remembering: check the photos for notes.

- **Prior statements in conversation** — remembering the point of view you expressed previously on an issue

  Registration: pay attention to expressed points of view, especially on controversial issues; keep track of positions of others and self after conversations that are likely to recur; in formal situation, use notes, recording devices; try to give only points of view that you really believe in.

  Remembering: try to remember your previous positions; use conversation retrieval skills; recreate previous occasion; reconstruct likely position; think before speaking; let the other party begin first; elicit cues from others.

- Prior statements in correspondence — made by you or by someone else

  Registration: keep track of your correspondence, especially important letters; keep notes on correspondence or copies.

  Remembering: recall purpose of the last letter; reconstruct what you might have said; look at previously received letters if you have them.

III. Intention Menus

Table of Contents

- **Appointments and meetings** — Realizing you have an appointment.
- **Birthday** — Realizing you must honor someone with a card or gift on his or her birthday.
- **Chores** — Realizing you have to do chores, as determined by yourself or by your spouse, parent, or roommate: such as cleaning up after a meal, taking out the garbage, feeding a pet, or leaving the toilet seat down.
- **Conversation** — Remembering what you were saying after a distraction.
- **Correspondence** — Realizing when to send correspondence properly, on time, and with the relevant information, including thank you notes, or business letters.

- **Deadlines** — Realizing that you must meet deadlines or due dates, such as license renewals or sending in forms.
- **Errands** — Realizing that you have errands to do.
- **Errands, the nature of** — Remembering which errands you intended to do or why you came to a room.
- **Hurried message** — Remembering something you were told in a hectic situation which you were supposed to pass on to a particular person (for example, relaying necessary information or conveying hot gossip) and delivering the message.
- **Packing for a trip** — Remembering to pack all the necessary items to take on a trip.
- **Paying bills** — Realizing that you must pay bills by a deadline.
- **Phone calls** — Realizing that you must call someone at a certain time.
- **Proper behavior or etiquette** — Realizing that certain statements or actions are taboo in certain circumstances before committing them.
- **Return library books** — Realizing that you must return library books before they are overdue.
- **Set clocks when time changes** — Realize that you should reset your clocks and watch when seasonal time changes occur.
- **Spontaneous idea** — Realizing that you must write down or act on an idea that came to you spontaneously when you were busy (for instance, when you were engaged in conversation).
- **Spontaneous idea while asleep** — Realizing later an act you wanted to do or an idea you wanted to use that came to you spontaneously while you were asleep.
- **Starting something on time** — Realizing when you have to start something on time, such as when you are timing several items in cooking.
- **Stopping something** — Realizing that you must terminate something, such as stopping a sporting event, taking a roast out of the oven, or turning off lights when you leave a room.
- **Take-aways, routine** — Realizing that you should take routine carry-items with you, such as wallet, purse, comb, handkerchief, and keys.
- **Take aways, special** — Realizing that you must take a certain or unusual item with you when you leave home.
- **Wake-up** — Remembering to get up early or on time for a particular purpose.

Intention Tasks Repertoires

- **Appointments and meetings**
  Registration: imagine yourself going to the place of the appointment at the appropriate time; imagine what you will be doing just before the appointment and associate that activity with the appointment to follow; imagine the face of your watch set to the time of the appointment alongside of a symbolic image of the action that the appointment involves (such as a piggy bank to represent a trip to the bank, a shopping cart for the grocer's, or a hammer for the hardware store); sketch or diagram what you are to do; imagine the consequences of doing the act and imagine the consequences of failing to do the act.
  Reminding: make a note about the appointment or meeting as soon as you can after arranging it; habitually keep a record of the things you have to do, in an appointment book, calendar, diary, or bulletin board; transfer notes about new appointments into your appointment book as soon as possible; keep track of your intentions with a two-tier system of recording intentions — a calendar that keeps all long- and short-range intentions and an appointment book with the same information as well as any last-minute appointments; review your schedule at least twice a day — once at night to make sure that your plans are workable, and once in the morning to energize them in your mind; use alarms clocks or an alarm watch; you can ask another to remind you; routinely change the environment when you cannot jot down an intention — such as tipping a lampshade, switching your watch to the other wrist, putting something on the floor in a conspicuous place.
- **Birthday** — giving someone a card or gift
  Registration: memorize the date and associate it with some other event that precedes it; record birthdays in address book as soon as you find out about them; transfer the date onto a calendar; keep the calendar in a conspicuous spot; post memos to yourself to send the card; at the beginning of the year, purchase cards for everyone you send cards to, address and sign the cards, and file them in appropriate slots of an object organizer divided into 12 months.
- **Chores** — you have to do
  Registration: leave out tools for what is to be done, such as a

vacuum cleaner; avoid being deflected from the chores; use notes, calendars, memo board; ask someone to remind you, such as the person who required or assigned the chores.

- **Conversation** — remembering what you were saying after a distraction

  Remembering: retrace your thoughts; ask people you are talking to what they think about what you were saying — their answer will usually cue you to the topic; in a work situation, jot down your last thought as the distraction occurs.

- **Correspondence** — sending correspondence on time and with the relevant information, especially thank-you notes and business letters

  Registration: write a note to yourself indicating the gift or topic; as soon after you decide that correspondence should be sent, make notes regarding its possible or necessary content; note on calendar and in appointment book when correspondence should be written and sent; there is software for intention management and year-round clocks with alarms for pre-set dates on which to do things (see Chapter 5).

  Remembering: check calendar, appointment book, or other external aids; you can depend on others to remind you at your own risk, except for secretaries whose job responsibilities often include "reminder services."

- **Deadlines** — due dates for license renewals or sending in forms

  Registration: imagine doing something that immediately precedes the deadline and associate it with the deadline — when you perform this associated act, it will then tend to evoke the deadline in your mind; the nature of the manipulations will vary with the kind of deadline involved — exact deadline tasks must be performed on or before a specific time; interval deadline tasks must be performed on or about a specific time; recurring deadlines must be met at routine times; optional intentions may or may not be performed on or about vague deadlines; obligatory deadlines require more preparation than the optional deadlines; exact deadlines invite more use of external memory aids like alarm watches than other kinds of intentions; (1) appointment book, calendar, diary, bulletin board, notes in obvious places; (2) alarms; ask a friend to remind you — risky; review schedule daily.

- **Errands** — which errands you intended to do or why you came into a room

Registration: carry one of your tools, utensils, or materials with you — it will remind you.

Remembering: consult list and cross off items as you get them; return to the place where the intention was formed; reconstruct; look around for clues as to what you might have been doing; if list is not available, wander through the store glancing at products.

– **Hurried message** — something you were told in a hectic situation; delivering message on time

Registration: prioritize — note value of source and recipient (you may decide to forget the message); rehearse distributively; make up images for the content of message; rehearse aloud; repeat message to source; write message down at first opportunity; turn your watch over on your wrist or switch the watch to the other wrist to remind you to write the message down later; set an alarm watch to remind you to write it down later; ask source to repeat ("No! Really? How is that again?"); ask source to remind you later to convey message — although this may not apply often; ask someone else to remind you; refresh often until you record the message on a reliable memory aid.

– **Packing for a trip**

Remembering: imagine parts of the body and clothes for those parts; imagine what you will need for every day of the trip; keep a checklist for trips; unpack only those things necessary; keep dirty clothes in a bag near your suitcase.

Remembering: imagine parts of the body and clothes for those parts; make a checklist before you leave; systematically go through every drawer and closet, and repeat this process after you have packed the suitcases and have placed them outside your room; ask someone to interview you about which things you may have left behind. However, if you forget toiletry items and you are staying at a hotel, call the front desk and they may help you (see Figure 24).

– **Paying bills** — realizing that you must pay bills by a deadline

Registration: note the due dates of bills on your calendar; review your calendar at least once daily; keep the bill in a visible place to serve as a reminder that it needs to be paid.

– **Phone calls** — calling someone at a certain time

Registration: imagine yourself standing by a phone next to a

FORGET IT?

If you forgot
- Toothbrush
- Toothpaste
- Shampoo
- Iron
- Razor
- Hairbrush
- or almost
  anything

Call Guest
Request

HYATT
Thinking of you.™

FORGOT
SOMETHING?

We want to make sure you're comfortable.
If you've forgotten or are in need
of any essential toiletry items,
check with our front desk
for the items you need.
Dial 503

Holiday Inn®

Figure 24.
Examples of reminders provided by hotels to travelers.

clock with the hands set to the time the call is to be made; put call in your appointment book; set an alarm; some automatic dialing systems have ability to alert you to when a call is to be made; regular review of your appointment book; leave a note in a visible place to serve as a reminder.

- **Proper behavior or etiquette** — realizing taboos before transgressing
  Registration: be sensitive to situations in which you might say or do the wrong thing; note your faux pas, and those of others, so you don't repeat them.
- **Return library books**
  Preparation: prioritize; consider consequences of failure; write return dates on your calendar a few days before the books are due; place the books by your front door.
- **Routine take-aways** — wallet, purse, comb, handkerchief, keys, etc.
  Registration: check you pockets or purse before leaving home; use the same pockets consistently for particular items; keep a checklist; connect a chain to your wallet; get in the habit of checking for wallet after transactions; leave keys in the car so you won't forget to bring them with you — risky, but some people do this.
- **Set clocks when time changes** — when seasonal time changes occur
  Registration: mark on your calendar the Sunday in the spring and fall when the time is to changed; remember the saying, "spring forward, fall back."
- **Special take aways** — certain or unusual items that are necessary
  Registration: prioritize what you must take; imagine leaving with the take-away item; placing take aways in a regular spot, such as in front of door; periodic check of obligations; review take aways before you leave; make a note; alarms.
- **Spontaneous idea, during conversation** — remembering to later write down an idea that came during a conversation
  Registration: during the conversation associate the idea with something you will do later; say little or nothing until you write it down; continuously rehearse the idea; associate the idea with your prior activity; set wrist alarm to remind you later to make a note of the idea; ask a friend to remind you; place a note in a

conspicuous place; if you have to do it shortly, put a memo in your hand; rehearse when you can.

Remembering: if there is a feeling of knowing, think of first letter, syllables, images of the task; brainstorm periodically to recall ideas you forgot; keep pads of paper or 3-by-5 cards, with a pencil, in a room; change the physical environment in some way (turn a ring, switch the wrists for your wristwatch; position something oddly on your desk; write a memo as soon as possible.

– **Spontaneous idea, while asleep** — acting on or using an idea that occurred while you were asleep

Registration: dwell on the idea before going back to sleep; change the physical environment in some unusual way — for example, position something oddly on your night table, put your watch on the bedpost; keep a notepad at your bedside.

– **Starting something on time**

Registration: prioritize task; associate the task with events that immediately precede it; imagine a large clock with the hands on the starting time as you picture yourself about to begin the action; set alarms and timers; remind yourself with increasing frequency as the starting time approaches.

– **Stopping something** — a sporting event, taking a roast out of the oven, turning off lights when you leave a room

Registration: prioritize the task; imagine the things you will do during the interval and determine which thing is likely to precede the time for stopping; make up an image of a large clock with the hands placed at the time for stopping, and picture yourself alongside about to stop things; avoid leaving the scene of the event — for example, don't leave the kitchen; use alarms and timers.

– **Wake-up** — getting up at a specific time to do something

Registration: prioritize the next day's responsibilities; rehearse the intention ("I must get up at ___ o'clock to go to the dentist"); think of the consequences of failure; set the alarm clock; set two clocks, or a clock and a wristwatch alarm if possible; place clocks in an unusual place, such as under the bed; leave the blinds up; put shoes, briefcase, or some other relevant object next to the bed; if at a hotel, ask for a wake-up call; arrange for a friend to check on you.

Remembering: make yourself jump out of bed the instant you remember what you have to do that day; buy an extra clock.

IV. Action Menus

Table of Contents

Action Repertoires

- **Actions** — remembering what you were just doing, (removing a key from a lock; turning off stove)
  Preparation: associate the place you are in with what you have to do; attend to what you are doing; mentally repeat the name of the action and "done" on completing the action; realize what you are doing is important and concentrate on it throughout the day; imagine yourself performing task, rehearse, keep repeating your intention to do so; link the task to some aspect of where you are — thus, the context will serve to remind you of your task; write it down on a piece of paper and put it in a special place; do tasks on certain days; watch others and imitate them; when you stop, go over in your mind what you still have to do.
  Remembering: look at your surroundings, sometimes they will trigger what you were doing; retrace steps; jot down ahead of time what you are doing and then later refer to this note; use a checklist for common situations.
- **Drive to the right place** — while en route
  Registration: imagine the destination and the route to the destination before you start out; remember what you are to do there.
- **Gas cap** — putting it back on after getting gas
  Remembering: always put the cap in the same conspicuous

place, such as on top of the car or on the driver's seat; buy a car that connects the gas cap by wire cord to the car or have such a cord connected to your gas cap; position a memo on the dash reminding you to replace the cap; buy an extra gas cap and carry it with you in the trunk; go to a full-service gas station.

- **Polite acts** — performing expected acts of courtesy
  Preparation: prioritize and make politeness habitual except for those who do not deserve it; review details of etiquette before events; anticipate the beginnings and endings to events where etiquette is critical; an opened door, someone handing you something, someone holding your coat, someone bumping into you, pauses in conversation; take your lead from others; discuss local customs with a native.
  Remembering: remind yourself of the level of etiquette called for by a situation; prepare by examining an etiquette book.
- **Step in a sequence** — in an action with several steps
  Remembering: always finish a step and remember that you have done so; review what you have done; notice which steps are already done; observe those participating around you, ask.
- **Utterances** — avoiding slips of the tongue
  Remembering: be aware of past slips involving words to be used; in the case of word order problems, get some rest; once your patient has made a slip, be aware of it and the related content so as to monitor his or her speech when the topic recurs.
- **Word choice** — avoiding Freudian slips
  Remembering: once you have made a Freudian slip, be aware of it and the related content so as to monitor your speech when the topic recurs.

Summary

- Because there are so many manipulations that may be applied to a memory task, it may be too time-consuming to consider which manipulation is most appropriate.
- Therefore, before certain annoying tasks arise, prepare a repertoire of manipulations that are most suited to these tasks.

- Remembering to perform a
  chore or do a favor for a
  friend is often regarded
  as a genuine sign of affection.
  But the converse is also true.

Chapter 8
Scientific Background

Educational theory also has roots in antiquity, and theorists have long hoped to develop general principles of teaching, learning, and remembering that cut across disciplines. They have developed certain general results, for example, that distributed studying is more effective than cramming, but, like basic memory investigators, educational research also reveals study processes unique to a particular discipline. Several investigations have illustrated this uniqueness by focusing on learning in a particular discipline, math or history, and then by demonstrating that certain kinds of thinking were peculiar to the discipline, such as creating visual representations of a problem or identifying common themes over time. Other research has attempted to teach students certain mental manipulations unique to a discipline, and to determine whether learning becomes more effective the more specific the learning process becomes. For example, laboratory studies have found that verbal and imaginal learning strategies differ in effectiveness, with verbal strategies more appropriate for abstract tasks, and imaginal strategies better for concrete tasks.

Similarly, research examined whether study formulas, such as the well-known SQ3R (Survey, Question, Read, Recite, and Review), apply equally well to all courses, finding that they do not facilitate learning as well as previously thought, unless they are adapted to address a particular discipline. Thus, educational research suggests, like memory research, that skill development requires adaptations to the specific task demands of different disciplines to be most effective.

Study-Specific Manipulations and Study Skills

We appreciate that you purchased this book to help improve your memory for matters relating to academic work. This chapter emphasizes study-specific manipulations and study skills. However, to fully benefit from its contents, you should review information in prior chapters, especially Chapter 7.

Keep in mind that the best advice is of little assistance if it is not heeded. Doing better academically often involves changing your study habits, and it always involves a willingness to work and to apply yourself. There are better and worse means to improve study skills, but there are no easy means to do so. Your success with the following techniques and strategies should be directly related to the amount of effort you are willing to invest in this enterprise.

An Inventory of Study-Specific Manipulations

Table of Study Tasks

- **Author** — Remembering the author of a story, book or poem.
- **Geography** — Learning and remembering the locations of countries or states.
- **Grammar** — Learning and remembering the rules of grammar.
- **History** — Learning and remembering historical facts.
- **Information read previously** — Remembering something that you read.
- **Languages** — Learning a new language.
- **Lecture** — Learning and remembering what was said in a lecture.
- **Mathematics** — Learning and remembering solutions to problems.
- **Poetry** — Learning and remembering poetry you wish to recite or quote.
- **Prose** — Learning and remembering a passage, either according to its gist or verbatim.
- **Speeches** — Learning and remembering the gist of a talk you must give (see also "Prose").
- **Spelling** — Learning and remembering how to spell difficult words correctly.
- **Vocabulary** — Learning and remembering unfamiliar words.

Study Task Menus

- **Author** — remembering the author of a story, book or poem
  Registration: when you first read the items, associate your reactions to it with the name; note to yourself what other works have been written by the author, if any; analyze the name for unusual characteristics — rare letter combinations, the name's ethnic origins; keep a notebook of works that are of special interest to you; form some "literary" friendships with people who like to discuss reading material of the kind you like.

Remembering: if you have a feeling of knowing, try to recall when and where you read this particular work; try to remember exactly with whom you have discussed it; also refer to the entry on learning "names" of people you have met in the Events section.

- Geography

Registration: get a visual image of the outline of the geographical unit; verbally describe the shape to yourself (for example, V-shaped on the bottom, left, and right sides, flat and rectangular protrusion up on the top side=Texas); liken the shape of the unit to something you know (Italy, the boot); make sketches of the geographical unit in relation to other units, and check for accuracy; refresh occasionally.

Remembering: recall how you learned about the piece of geography; look at a globe or atlas.

- Grammar

Registration: study a book on grammar; test yourself for ability to state key rules; assess the logical impact of grammar rules; test your ability to articulate the grammatical deficiencies of poorly formed sentences, using the drills that most grammar books make available with such sentences); test yourself and restudy when you notice yourself forgetting what you learned.

Remembering: recall how you learned the grammatical point in question and its logic; a grammar book; consult someone who knows grammar.

- History

Registration: state the fact; paraphrase the fact; associate the fact with its precedents and consequents; imagine the event; relate past facts to current events; keep a notebook of important historical facts; get books on the historical era you are interested in and read them; find someone with similar historical interests and discuss them; review notebook periodically; make flash cards; highlight texts.

Remembering: reconstruct, retrace, conjure up associated image; if feasible, consult your notes or books.

- Information you read previously

Registration: analyze the author's purpose — is it an expression of fact, opinion, analysis of a problem, or an advancement of a new idea or argument; concentrate; try and remember important points in diagrammatic or pictorial form; try to predict what the author will say as you read it or re-read it; try and summarize mentally each paragraph or section after reading; take notes; read in a quiet place, without distractions; occasionally glance at notes.

Remembering: imagine the place where you did the reading; reconstruct; look at notes.

- **Languages** — learning a new language
  Registration: simple rehearsal, repetition in the case of vocabulary words; reviewing rules in the case of grammar; use flash cards; notes; associate or link unfamiliar English words to words or roots of foreign language; consistently practice reading silently and aloud, and speaking alone and with others; listen to tapes, including songe, in the language.
  Remembering: use what you know as often as possible; use two-way dictionaries and grammar books.

- **Lecture** — learn and remember what was said in a lecture (see also a study skills book, as listed in the References)
  Registration: predict what the speaker is going to say next; attend to summary statements and statements pointing out importance; take notes — but not too many. That will deprive you of the chance to learn during the lecture. Take just enough notes to remind you later; review.
  Remembering: reinstate the context; recall the summary statements.

- **Mathematics** — learning and remembering solutions to math problems
  Registration: rehearse; practice; solve forwards and backwards; flash cards; explain problem to someone else; review.
  Remembering: think of problems you have solved that are similar to the one you are trying to solve.

- **Poetry**
  Registration: learn line by line — pick out key words; note patterns of phrase structure that are similar and different across lines; characterize its meter; say the lines with emphasis; rhythmic rehearsal, in which you say the lines with a singsong or tonal variation; get the beat of each line and associate it with the beat of the last line; notes; books; recite to a friend with similar interests in poetry and discuss the reading.
  Remembering: recall the poem's structure and rhythm; notes or book if permissible.

- **Prose**
  Registration: if learning the gist of a passage — (1) reduce paragraphs to about six key terms; (2) diagram the paragraph or draw a network of the passage's ideas; (3) note the signposts to content: title, headings, topic sentences of paragraphs, illustrations, or summary; (4) analyze the relations between the key terms, generate synonym substitutes for the key terms, associate the key terms with a memory manipulation; (5) read aloud with emphasis; (6) picture the scene depicted; (7) paraphrase and simplify; (8) write a summary. In addition, you may wish to follow a prose study formula that prescribes the steps of studying prose. For example, the SQ3R (Survey, Question, Read, Recite, and Review) method has long been recommended to assist one in focusing study efforts. However, recent research indicates that study formulas are usually not effective unless the formula prepares one for a certain kind of prose, such as scientific writing. If learning a passage verbatim, follow the learning repertoire for poetry.
  Remembering: if for gist, reinstate in your mind the paraphrases, the analyses, the images you used in learning; notes if permitted.
- **Speeches** — the gist of a talk you must give (see also "Prose")
  Registration: identify key terms in the speech and associate them in sequence with the Method of Loci; make notes; go over and over the substance; rehearse as many times as you can.
  Remembering: recall the key terms; consult notes.
- **Spelling**
  Registration: memorize rules of spelling in grammar or spelling books; practice spelling and checking the spelling of others; check books on how to improve your spelling.
  Remembering: remember rules; think of a similar sounding word that you know how to spell; use a pocket speller; use a computerized spelling checker.
- **Vocabulary**
  Registration: any of those in Chapter 5; if you know something about the meaning of stems and roots of words, it helps to analyze how the word suggests its meaning; attend to the syllables of the word; routinely attempt vocabulary quizzes in magazines; bookstores carry several books on vocabulary acquisition; also, the VisEd Company makes a set of flash cards of useful English

words; make your own flash cards of words you want to be sure of knowing; form friendships with people who value words, especially crossword puzzle enthusiasts; review from time to time; buy a new vocabulary book and see what you still know.

Remembering: (1) think of length, (2) think of the first letter, (3) think of related words; browse through dictionary under suspected letter; browse through a thesaurus under a related word; ask.

A Discussion of Specific Study Skills

The preceding study-specific manipulations should help you to learn and recall various types of academically related information. In an academic setting, these manipulations are most effective when combined with appropriate strategies for study. Below are a series of study strategies that we have developed over more than 40 years of college teaching. We have exposed our students to these strategies in the past, and those who have mastered them have displayed a marked improvement in their academic performances.

As in the case of study manipulations, mastery of these skills will require some attention and effort on your part, but the dividends should be significant and immediate. Accompanying the following text are a series of study guides to which you may refer for a quick refresher on some of the more important skills. Since your academic work involves disparate courses, we have organized the following material to be independent of, yet appropriate to, any particular subject matter.

Study Blueprint

In studying, as in many other endeavors, it helps to be organized and to have a broad perspective on what is expected of you. The purpose of our study blueprint is to remind you of activities that can improve your study performance. We will elaborate on these activities in subsequent study guides (see Figure 25).

- *Strategy:* Keep in mind that any course you are taking has been carefully planned by the instructor. Try to develop an understanding of the instructor's objectives. Your biggest asset in this task will be the course syllabus. Do not regard it simply as a compilation of assignments. Instead, view it as a road map that displays an intellectual journey on which the instructor wishes to take you.

Try to ascertain the instructor's destination. To the extent that you can do this, you will find that classes make more sense, that you can anticipate developments, and that you may even discover shortcuts, arriving at the journey's end ahead of most and without strain or fatigue.

A good sense of the direction the course is taking will enable you to determine better which portions of the terrain are most interesting and important. Do not become so immersed in detail that you miss the general direction of the course. Quite simply, without a sense of direction you can become lost.

- *Indepth Reading Procedures:* As many students have discovered, often painfully, when an instructor makes a reading assignment, simply turning the pages and reading the words is seldom sufficient for good understanding of the material.

Reading is best viewed as an active undertaking in which you contribute to the outcome, rather than simply passively receiving wisdom. One of the most difficult things for students to realize is that books and articles not infrequently contain errors of reasoning that can be perceived by nearly anyone who is alert to them. Indeed, some of your instructors are likely to choose certain readings that contain weaknesses just to give your critical abilities some exercise.

Shortly, we will supply you with some specific techniques to promote your understanding, retention, and ability to deal critically with material you read.

- *Meaning Extraction Techniques:* As a student, you will experience a large number of assignments from widely differing

Students generally know how to study but because of boredom, fatigue, or anxiety, they often forget to engage in all of the study activites that would be desirable. The **Study Blueprint** will remind you to do all of the activites you should.

Strategy: find your unique challenges of a course the first week of class.
Indepth Reading Procedures:
Pre-Read -- (your first reading may be your last so make it effective.)
Read headings, the summary, identify key words, identify examples, examine figures and tables, read questions at end of chapter, if there are problems - analyze the givens and what is asked of all problems.
Read -- generate questions that appropriately ask about what is in the text.
Post-Read -- skim, generate questions about the gist.
Meaning-Extraction Techniques:
Outline, hierarchy, key word list, relations table (table shows how one set of elements relates to another, e.g. countries by characteristics, species by attributes, etc.), flowchart, graph, pictograph, historical time line.
Note Taking: after class, generate questions that address each paragraph or cluster of notes; continue to condense -- take notes on notes, and notes on notes on notes...
Exam Preparation:
Plan your preparation -- how much to study and when; overview of time, part time; study time; self-test time.
Gather questions from notes and texts; identify kinds of questions; design the exam as you predict it.
Test yourself repeatedly and/or do problems over; decide what you don't know.
Study and memorization
Rehearse - silent/aloud; act out; cumulative; rhythmic.
Associate - with something in your past, with other knowledge, with words or concepts.
Make relevant - identify ideas which are similar, different, and in the same class.
Make an alternative mental record - transform (paraphrase, restate), reduce (acronym - e.g. NOW = National Organization for Women), elaborate (as on a story).
Test again - review material before going to sleep, program self to be relaxed.
Take care of yourself - get enough sleep, eat well, relax before the exam, and do **not** review material immediately before the exam.
Exam Strategies: read test, take 1 minute to plan use of time
Multiple choice -- answer what you know first, eliminate wrong alternatives.
Essay -- jot down a few key terms or ideas first, then write.
Problem -- seek a pattern to the solution, mentally compare with homework assignments.
Post exam -- paper, lab, practicum, analysis.

(Remember to take an active, not a passive attitude toward your studying. Don't become so involved in details that you lose the general overview -- that is often the source of essay questions. Good Luck!)

Figure 25.
Study blueprint.

courses. In the process of completing these responsibilities, you will encounter a formidable amount of information. Accept that you cannot memorize everything you encounter, nor should you. Instead, you should utilize means to identify and extract important information that relates both to the specific assignment and to the more general objectives of the course.

There are a variety of techniques we will discuss below that can be employed to extract meaning from readings, lectures, and other formats. However, all of these techniques require you to actively process the information to which you are exposed. Again, an active approach not only helps you to understand material better, it also aids in your retention of that material.

– *Note Taking*: Unless you are skilled at shorthand or write remarkably fast, it is unlikely that you can write down everything an instructor says. Indeed, even if you could, you shouldn't. Most instructors will try to make two to three major points in a single class. Everything else is amplification, example, bridging concepts, and context.

You will want to develop the ability to recognize the major points of a lecture and to make sure that you have them properly related to one another (Anderson & Ambruster, 1991). You will also need to include sufficient context, so you can reconstruct the important elements of the class later. Unfortunately, most students do not reexamine their lecture notes until immediately before an examination. They frequently discover that their notes are insufficient and vague, because the information that was in their heads during the lecture has since disappeared.

Until you have developed good note-taking skills, try spending ten minutes immediately after a class reviewing your notes, while asking yourself whether a stranger would understand their importance and the context. At this point, you will still retain the context of the class and you can easily fill in whatever information may be necessary to establish interrelationships. Remember, the next time you look at your notes, you will be the stranger you imagined.

– *Exam Preparation:* Most students, often with considerable justification, dread examinations. Having taken an exam, many are surprised to discover that they were not as familiar with the course material as they had thought themselves to be. Others find that preparing for an exam takes a great deal of time without yielding appropriate benefits. Howver, if you have been following the four study guides listed above, you should find that you have less trouble preparing for exams than others, and your performance should reflect your prior organization and active approach to the materials.

Examinations are usually designed to test your understanding as well as your recall of course material. Many instructors will assume that you remember the material to which they exposed you, and they will want to see what you can do with it.

Can you manipulate information in meaningful ways to construct answers to questions that you may not have encountered before? As with other study skills, preparing to take an examination benefits from both an active approach and a continuing attempt to maintain an overview on the objectives of the instructor. Additionally, examinations place considerable emphasis on your ability to accurately recall information. To augment the suggestions concerning exam preparation below, we have included a condensed list of four memory strategies that should help you to focus on and retain useful information.

– *Exam Strategies:* Many students who spend considerable time and energy preparing for an examination still fare poorly. The difficulty may be due in large part to the dreaded "white-out," a state of mind — or, perhaps better, a state of non-mind — where all facts disappear from consciousness and the brain refuses to focus on anything more than its inability to achieve focus. Physiology often contributes to this condition in the form of elevated adrenalin levels, which can interfere with concentration and cause such undesirable phenomena as "butterflies," indigestion, headaches, etc.

Higher adrenalin levels can easily stem from worry about the exam situation and they directly relate to perceived stress. In particular, students who are aware they are not properly prepared for an exam are more prone to experience a level of stress that can interfere with effective exam taking. Fortunately, this is a problem you are less likely to encounter if you follow the advice we present in this chapter. However, it is perfectly natural to be somewhat tense before a testing situation. One means to reduce the likelihood of stress-related problems is to take a brisk walk a half-hour before the exam. Your system is prepared for physical activity and the walk will help to reestablish normal adrenalin levels.

The approach for dealing with multiple choice questions is quite different from that for treating essay questions. We supply some particular advice on taking each type of exam below, but throughout both experiences there are two consistencies. We urge you to take an active approach to the questions, and encourage you to stay in control of your answers rather than letting the questions push you around.

In Depth Reading Procedures

Virtually every instructor will suggest that students read assigned material before the class in which it will be discussed. Perhaps one in two students will heed this advice. Postponing the reading does not make it easier to do. In contrast, coming to class prepared will help you derive more from each session. Doing so also increases the likelihood that you will participate in class discussion, something many instructors reward (see Figure 26).

- *Pre-Read:* The Study Guide on In-depth Reading Procedures contains directions for pre-reading. Despite your probable desire to complete the assignment in a timely fashion, this is worth the time and effort it takes (Anderson, 1985; Nist & Mealy, 1991; Pearson, 1984). It will orient you to the material, give you a clearer understanding of the objective of the reading, and help you appreciate where the material fits into the general course format (Meyer, Young, & Bartlett, 1989). In short, it saves you time in the long run, and increases the likelihood that you will benefit from the reading.
- *Read:* If you take an active approach to the material you read, you will seek not only the meaning of the work, but also the purpose and plan of the author (Mandl & Trabasso, 1984; McWhorter, 1986; Postman, Keckler, & Schneckner, 1985). Be sensitive to the possibility of errors and shortcomings in the as-

Examinations often occur long after an assignment has been read. Developing good reading habits can save both time and effort when facing an examination. Such habits will also make classes more interesting.

Pre-Read:

Seek the major obejctive of the reading -- the task is to identify the central topic, argument, or idea of reading and assess how the author supports the position. Keep in mind that any reading assignment usually has only one major objective, though there may be important supporting material.

Strategies for pre-reading -- read headings, summary questions at end of chapters, etc. Identify key words and examples; examine figures and tables. Try to discover the major objective of the author, how it is arrived at and how supported. The objective is to be ready to begin reading with a good sense of where the author is heading and how he or she will get there.

Read:

Starting to read -- the first two pages of most articles will reveal the goal of the author. Assess this and also try to recognize the premises or propositions on which the article or chapteris based. Identifying unstated assumptions is often an excellent start toward critiquing an author's position.

Taking notes while reading -- do not become immersed in detail. Note major issues, how they relate to each other, and how they are supported. Reduce your outline notes to a two or three line summary including key words. This is what you will commit to memory for examinations and it will serve to access the broader context of the chapter or article. Remember that the next time you review these notes you will probably be preparing for an examination.

Post-Read:

Generate questions -- appropriately ask about what is in the text. What important principles are illustrated by the reading? Are there words, tables, charts, concepts, or statistics that you didn't adequately understand? (If so, it may be well worth the effort to seek clarification on these points.)

Develop a sense of context -- how does the reading concern other readings you have done for this course? Does it support or disagree with other readings you have been assigned? (If so, it may suggest an essay question that your teacher may employ) How does the reading relate to the class for which it was assigned - does it integrate with or conflict with material presented by your teacher?

Assess the importance of this reading -- you will want to devote more study time to those readings that are of greatest significance. Are there other readings that cite or are based on this one? Was the reading discussed in class? Was it the focus of a paper assignment? If any of the preceding are the case, the reading is likely to be useful in your examination.

Figure 26.
Indepth reading procedures.

signment. Pay particular attention to what are termed "unstated assumptions." Few authors clearly state the premises on which their work rests, yet these are frequently necessary for a full appreciation of their position. Identifying premises is equally important for developing critiques of an author's position. If you can demonstrate the falseness or inappropriateness of the premises of a work, you can discredit the entire effort.

For instance, we have assumed, without stating it, that many students are interested in improving their memories and study skills. If this assumption can be called into question, the entire rationale for this book is jeopardized. Often your best critiques of readings will employ similar fundamentals, rather than becoming bogged down in concerns about petty details.

Your task is to ascertain what is important about the work and how that relates to the course. Resist the temptation to skip over portions of the book that involve tables, charts, or points that are difficult to follow. It is frequently in such areas that authors synthesize major evidence and/or arguments.

When reading, remember that, unless stated otherwise, the instructor probably does not intend you to memorize the entire content of the assignment. Identify the one, two or three major arguments of the assignment, and the best evidence for these arguments. Then make a few clear notes that contain sufficient context for you to reconstruct their significance when you review them for an exam. Do not become mired in detail. Continually strive to identify the major points in a work and view the remainder as secondary. Doing this will not only facilitate an active understanding of the reading, it will also greatly ease your preparation for exams in the future. Finally, it will reduce the volume of material you have to retain.

– *Post-Read:* Having read the assignment, you are in a good position to assess its importance in terms of course objectives. Did the assignment contain pivotal information, or did it supplement and amplify points made by other authors and/or by the instructor in class? There is often considerable value in perceiving such interrelationships. First, at the abstract academic level, it will help tie information together into a more meaningful bundle. Second, at the practical level, instructors are aware of such interrelationships — indeed, they usually work hard to set them up — and these are therefore fruitful areas for examination questions.

Meaning Extraction Techniques

The amount of information you will encounter in courses requires selective organization. You do not wish to record and to recall all the information you are exposed to, but you will need means to extract and organize that which is most salient (Caverly & Orlando, 1991). There are various techniques that you may employ to accomplish this, and all carry the same benefit. They require you to actively transform the information. Doing so helps you to perceive interrelationships and encourages you to assess the relative importance of information. Furthermore, as we noted in earlier chapters, active processing markedly improves recall (see Figure 27).

The ability to extract and organize important concepts and propositions from class notes and reading assignments is one of the most important skills a student can possess. This study aid will familiarize you with some of the more effective techniques for extracting meaningful content from your readings and lectures.

Visual Techniques:

Flowchart - emphasizes dynamics of interrelationships, displays processes:

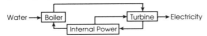

Graph - furnishes an excellent means of presenting complex relationships between two or more variables:

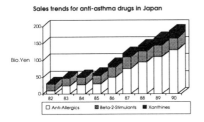

Historical Time Line - provides a convenient means of representing multiple events:

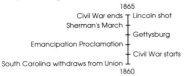

Verbal Techniques:

Outline - one of the most popular and reliable techniques for organizing and abstracting information:

  I. Sociological Theories
    A. Functionalism
      1. basic assumptions
      2. criticisms
    B. Conflict Theory....

Hierarchy - a means of organizing information into progressively more inclusive (and often more important) structures

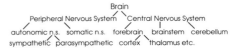

Relations Table - shows how one set of elements relates to another and allows a quick comparison across the elements comprising the table. Thus:

Figure 27.
Meaning extraction techniques.

Verbal Techniques

– *Outline:* This is a common means for abstracting and organizing information. Properly done, outlines provide a view of a body of information that is organized in terms of more inclusive categories. Outlines encourage you to recognize the major points of a work and upon which they are based. Also, organizing the material in outline form provides you with a mental flag that you can use to access more specific information. In the Study Guide example, the term sociological theory can help you to recall functionalism and conflict theory, the background to these theories.

Remember that outlines need not be detailed. After all, that's why they're called outlines. But they must be logically constructed. If you discover that you are having difficulty organizing material in outline form, it probably means you are having problems with comprehension and/or overview. It is much better to work at these issues now and solve them, than to re-encounter them when you are trying to prepare for an examination.

- *Hierarchy:* This is a particular type of outline that places even more emphasis on the development of inclusive structures. Hierarchical representations are not appropriate for all forms of information, but they are particularly useful in the sciences, and for those aspects of other disciplines that emphasize vertically structured and logical relationships.

  As the example on the accompanying Study Guide demonstrates, hierarchies generally present less informational context than standard outlines, but they graphically represent structured relationships in a manner that is easy to assimilate and recall. As in the case of more general outlines, creating a hierarchy is a learning process that will help you to better understand the information you encounter.

- *Key Word List:* This is a meaning extraction technique that can be used for virtually all types of information, but its utility is limited. Key word lists provide you with an inventory of terms to which you have been exposed, but they do not ask you for any organization or overview of the material. Thus, key word lists do little to improve your perception of interrelationships. They have little utility in preparing for essay examinations, but are somewhat useful for multiple choice examinations. They provide a means of assessing your general familiarity with course concepts and, unlike some of the techniques discussed here, you can construct them easily and quickly. Flash cards can improve the rate at which you will learn key words, but they do nothing to promote your appreciation of the framework embracing the terms you study.

- *Relations Table:* A table of relations usually represents interrelationships across a range of items. It differs from a hierarchy in emphasizing vertical relations less, while making horizontal relations much clearer. You can employ relations tables to integrate information on a rather wide variety of topics, and doing so yields a significant study benefit.

Creating such a table forces you to seek relations across elements you have encountered in a course. This gives you an excellent sense of the interrelationships among the elements of the course, and it promotes the development of the broad overview we are recommending. Not incidentally, a well-prepared relations table is an excellent study device. It provides you with an easily assimilated representation of the information in the course that can be reviewed and recalled in less time than you would need for other techniques (Raybeck, 1992b). The catch (you were expecting one, weren't you?) is that constructing such tables can be time consuming and difficult. However, if you are willing to invest the time as the course progresses, you will soon discover that examinations cease to be causes for great concern. Indeed, you should shortly find yourself spending much less time in exam preparation, yet performing significantly better. It is a bit like preparing food ahead of time for the freezer. The preparation can be laborious, but at mealtime all you need do is throw it in the oven.

Visual Techniques

There are a variety of visual techniques that can be utilized to represent information and interrelations among elements. The success of these techniques depends to some degree on their appropriateness for the material, and also on the user. Humans rely on vision for the majority of the information they process. However, we differ in our ability to develop and retain visual images. For some, this is a difficult undertaking. For others, it is both easy to do and easy to recall. You will need to assess your own strengths and weaknesses in deciding the degree to which you will adopt the visual techniques described below.

- *Flowchart:* As the name suggests, flowcharts are particularly good for dealing with process and for displaying the way a system operates and changes over time. They are quite useful for developing an overview of a system and an appreciation of cause-effect relations within a system.
  You may find it helpful to color-code some of the elements in

the flow chart to reflect membership in a similar class or category. Thus, in the Meaning Extraction Techniques Study Guide, the arrows linking water to boiler, and boiler to turbine might be in blue representing water. The arrows from turbine to electricity, and from internal power to other parts of the system might be in yellow. This will help you to perceive and recall that these relations are electrical. Similarly, a colored representation of the physiology flow chart might depict the heart and lungs as the same color and different from the body, which is a more inclusive system.

– *Graph:* For certain kinds of information, graphs can not only usefully represent interrelationships, they may be a necessary means of doing so. For example, in the sciences and social sciences, you are often asked to perceive and understand interrelationships between two or more variables. These disciplines rely heavily on graphs to display such relationships. Constructing a graph provides a comparatively simple image of what may be a very complex set of relations. You will also come to better understand the function of graphs, and you will be able to read them more readily. This has a practical value, since many science and social science examinations employ graphs in the construction of questions.

– *Historical Time Line:* As the name suggests, this technique is used principally to represent a sequence of historical events. It condenses a good deal of information into a visual format that can represent not only the order of events, but also the intervals between them. Nor is this technique restricted to historical materials. Indeed, it can be used with virtually any sequence of events, ranging from the steps in developing film to those involved in studying for an examination.

Exam Preparation

If you use the techniques described above, you will find that you have been preparing for your examinations all along. Nonetheless, you will probably wish to spend time preparing for a specific exam shortly before you have to take it (see Figure 28).

Preparing for any given exam requires some forethought, organization and memory (Wark & Flippo, 1991). Given your prior

Preparing for an examination should be an active enterprise in order to be effective. You generally have two major tasks: to recall information and to manipulate it in response to questions. The techniques described below with help you to master both these objectives and will, if practiced responsibly, increase your confidence in exam taking situations.

Plan your Preparation:

Time management -- decide how much you are to study, what times of the day and where. Break down what is to be learned into parts and study these as well as the entirety.

Try to develop an overview -- remember that your instructor will be interested in your ability to remember, to understand, and to deal actively with the course material. While details are important, take time to devleop an appreciation of concepts and of how things fit together.

Review your reading assignments and lectures -- examine where and how they integrate. Areas where readings and lectures cross-relate, or where two or more lectures focus on a given concept or particular material are likely to be the subject of considerable attention, including essay questions.

Anticipate -- devise possible essay and multiple choice questions from your notes and from the readings, again paying attention to points of intersection. Design an exam as you think it will be and try it. Even if your choices are mistaken, you will be forced to interrelate the materials for which you are responsible.

Test yourself -- answer questions and/or do problems over and over again. Periodically decide what you do not know, focus on it, and repeat the study cycle.

Study and Memorization: Four Strategies

Increase the strength of a memory

Take a mental snapshot -- scan it systematically, close your eyes and question yourself.

Register multimodally -- with as many senses as you can.

Act out -- imagine key events and overtly act them out.

Rehearse simply -- repeat items over and over.

Rehearse cumulatively -- repeat successively larger groupings of items.

Make the memory relevant

Analyze visually -- break down the visual characteristics into meaningful patterns.

Identify attributes -- verbally describe what is to be learned.

Analyze the meaning -- examine all of the implications of the information.

Prioritize -- judge the importance of the knowledge to be learned.

Personalize -- relate information to you or to part of your past.

Associate

Connect present with past events.

Identify meaningful relationships -- such as synonyms, contrasts or category commonality.

Cluster by meaning -- group items with similar meanings and, if possible, group the resulting groups.

Sequence -- arrange items in their natural sequence.

Diagram -- sketch the relationship of items to be learned.

Create frameworks for retrieval

Elaborate numbers and dates -- state in the form of years, phone numbers, moneyminutes, etc.

State principles -- describe a pattern or regularity that is apparent in the material to be learned.

Abbreviate -- form a smaller word by using a few letters from a larger word or words.

Sentence or story generation -- form a sentence or story that contains the items to be learned.

Imagine items linked -- form an image linking the first and second terms, than the second and third, etc.

Figure 28.
Exam preparation.

preparation, you should be able to follow the suggestions below easily — and with less investment of time — than your peers.

One seldom-discussed aspect of preparing for an examination involves assessing the instructor. Good instructors will be interested in your ability to actively manipulate course concepts and information, while poor instructors may simply want you to tell them what they have told you.

Regrettably, what prepares you well for the exams of poor instructors won't work for good ones. However, what works well for the exams of good instructors also tends to work for the exams of poor ones. If in doubt about the intent and style of your instructor, it is safer to assume that he or she is good, and is intent on developing your ability to synthesize and criticize.

Plan Your Preparation: Do not postpone preparing for an exam. Delaying your start doesn't make your work any easier. Instead, it encourages you to see the preparation process as complex and daunting.

Rather than viewing the whole task as one great mountain of information to be clambered over and laboriously mapped, you will find it very helpful to break your preparation into segments. Allocate a given amount of time for each segment and set up a place and time where you can study well. Finally, leave time for integrating the segments prior to the exam.

The process of integration involves developing an overview of the general objectives of the course and how things fit together. Again, relating your specifics back to the syllabus is often a useful means of synchronizing your efforts and perceptions with those promoted by the course.

When you review your readings and lecture notes, do so as an integrated packet, and be alert for interrelationships. Remember that your instructor consciously chose your readings to coincide with specific material being presented in class. Once you have covered each class, seek out connections across classes and between their respective readings. A good instructor will often incorporate such interrelations in the plan of a course.

You will develop a good sense of possible essay questions if you can anticipate those aspects of the course that the instructor deems most important. One means of sharpening your ability to forecast exam content is to develop your own questions. In the case of essay questions, strive for those which involve a synthesis of course materials — questions that require you to put things together. Do not waste time on essay questions that simply call for a recapitulation of information. Even if you are confident that this is the nature of the task you will be facing, you will get a great deal more out of the material if you prepare it actively.

In contrast, when preparing for multiple choice questions, be sensitive to areas of the readings or lectures where there may be conceptual confusion. Do not avoid such problem areas; instead, seek them out. They often produce questions that can be quite difficult to manage, unless you have spotted the problem in advance and prepared for it.

Study and Memorization: No matter what kinds of intellectual tasks you will be required to perform, you must first recall the information before you can act upon it. Examinations, even the best and most active, always place a premium on being able to recall information. No doubt this helped motivate you to purchase this book.

In preceding chapters, we have presented, often with considerable detail, information and a series of mental manipulations that should help you to develop a better, more accurate memory. The accompanying Study Guide incorporates a reference list of the four memory strategies that are apt to be most appropriate for your needs and specific suggestions for exam preparation (Anderson, 1980; Annis, 1983; Nist & Diehl, 1985; Pauk, 1984; Shepherd, 1987; Weinstein, Goetz, & Alexander,1989; Weinstein & Mayer, 1986). These include directions for increasing the strength of a memory by employing a variety of techniques to focus on and manipulate the information you wish to recall. We also include suggestions for making particular memories relevant to particular tasks and to the general objectives of the course. We list manipulations for associating memories with one another and for clarifying sequential and structural relationships. Finally, we suggest means you can employ to create meaningful frameworks to organize more specific memories, so that these may be retrieved in an orderly fashion. Each specific suggestion has been fully explained earlier in this book. These explanations can usually be found in Chapters 5 and 7, or by using the index.

Exam Strategies

The work you have done to this point will have helped you understand and recall the course material. However, in terms of your academic performance, all your previous work may mean little if you cannot effectively perform in an examination setting. Every teacher has encountered exam performances that do not seem to accurately reflect a student's understanding. In the worst of situations, a good student may "clutch" and be unable to recall, organize, and convey information appropriately (see Figure 29).

Common exam catastrophes include answering an insufficient number of questions, overlooking an exam page completely, misreading a question and providing an excellent answer for a question that wasn't asked, and the notorious "white out" in which the student is unable to produce a coherent response to questions and sometimes even returns a blank test.

Even more common problems involve exam performances that display poor organization, that miss major connections between the elements of a course, and that fail to reflect an adequate familiarity with course material. For obvious reasons, you will want to avoid these difficulties (Flippo, 1985).

The advice contained in this chapter and earlier ones can greatly increase the likelihood that your exam performance will accurately reflect your familiarity with and understanding of course information. Of course, if you fail to pursue the ideas contained in this book and to work on your studies, that accurate reflection may not be a flattering one.

– *Preliminaries:* A degree of reasoned confidence is one of your best defenses against "white out." If you have followed much of the advice contained in these chapters, you can rightfully expect to be well prepared for any examination.

As you approach an exam, remember that your instructor expects it to be both an opportunity for you to exhibit your understanding of the course's contents, and a learning experience. Recall the overview you have developed on the course, as it may prove very useful in dealing with specific questions. Remember that accuracy is much more important that verbosity.

Most students are nervous about the limited time available for

Students who have studied faithfully and prepared well for examinations may still encounter significant problems when they actually take an exam. While examinations are probably the most stressful aspect of the student experience, the strategies below should enable you to make the most of your preparation.

Preliminaries:

Keep your confidence. Remember that you are better rested and better prepared than most.

Don't be afraid to spend some initial time becoming familiar with the exam.

Read the exam through quickly. Be sure you understand the instructions and the questions. Don't panic if some of the questions initially seem somewhat obscure.....remember you haven't applied yourself yet.

Plan realistically how you will use your time and note the way examination points are distributed (e.g. if two essay questions are worth half of the exam points, you should spend approximately half of your time on them).

Multiple Choice Questions:

Remember, these questions are usually written very carefully and may be somewhat tricky. Read quickly, but carefully.

Treat each question as if it seeks a precise response (it usually does).

Answer the questions you know first, then return and answer those questions for which you can eliminate at least one wrong alternative.

Eliminate alternatives by comparing one with the others. Don't assume that the first alternative which seems familiar is the correct one. Read them all and watch out for absolutes such as always, all, everyone, etc. These frequently invalidate an alternative.

Essay questions:

Read questions carefully and take time for thought. Try to identify the central issue(s). Generally, an essay requires synthesis or seeks the application of a major concept or method that is prominent in the course. The teacher with normally use essay questions to test your general comprehension and ability to deal actively with the course.

Make a brief outline or at least some notes on your major points. Stay in charge of your answer. Don't succumb to the concept that more words make a better essay. Shorter more accurate answers are preferable to lengthy displays of poorly organized information.

If you include much detail, make sure it is pertinent to the question. You may get marked down for factual errors on information which you never needed to include.

Problem Solving:

Read carefully and identify the nature or class of the problem you are facing. Once you have identified the class of problem, translating it into a familiar formula or structure is much simpler.

Seek for a familiar pattern. If it is a word problem, try to find an underlying structure that you have dealt with in homework assignments, etc.

At the End:

Re-read the instructions. Have you answered all the questions you were supposed to? (A significant number of students lose points because they fail to follow instructions.)

Re-read the major essay questions. Have you interpeted the questions accurately?

(Later, when your exam is returned to you, study it carefully. Try to identify the types of mistakes you may have made so that you can improve your performance next time. Remember -- exam taking is a skill and continued effort and practice will make you better at it. Good Luck!)

Figure 29.
Exam strategies.

examinations. Consequently, they often begin answering questions as soon as they open an exam book. The idea seems to be, if they are writing, they are performing as they should.

Resist this temptation. Spend a few minutes familiarizing yourself with the exam and how it is structured. This will save time later, and will help prevent misinterpretation of the instructions or the questions.

An overview of the exam can greatly assist you in planning how you will apportion your time and effort on specific questions.

Some students take a cursory look and then save the biggest parts of the exam for last. This is frequently a bad idea, especially, if the student is left with insufficient time for the section. Obviously, more time should be devoted to those portions of the exam that carry more weight in grading. Your instructor should have weighted portions of the exam to reflect their importance and/or their difficulty. Consequently, such areas need and deserve extra time.

– *Multiple Choice Questions:* Strategies involved in answering multiple choice questions differ from those which are most appropriate for essay questions. Multiple choice questions place a premium on your ability to selectively access information and to make fine-grained comparisons between alternatives that often seem rather similar.

You are usually confronted with four or five alternate choices. Good multiple choice questions are very carefully phrased and, properly interpreted, permit only one correct response. A careful reading of the question and the choices can help you to eliminate obvious poor choices. You can then concentrate your attention and memory on those remaining.

Do not be disturbed if some of the questions are hard to understand. Rather than spend time ineffectively trying to "force" an answer that won't come, move on to other questions. You may well find that the other questions suggest connections that may help you with your earlier difficulties. Even if this is not the case, it is better to concentrate on unanswered questions and to improve the likelihood of correct choices than to spend your time trying to get one question correct.

– *Essay Questions:* Essay questions are the heart of most social science and humanities examinations. They require students not only to recall specific information, but to construct syntheses as well. A good essay question will actively engage your understanding as well as your memory. The instructor will expect you not only to remember the material, but to be able to manipulate it in meaningful ways. Doing well on essay questions requires recall, understanding, and organization.

Some students approach an essay question as though it is a large distant target. They blast away at the question in hopes that some of their facts will hit the target and impress the instructor.

We do not recommend this strategy. No instructor finds pleasure in an essay answer that lists reams of poorly-related and/or irrelevant facts, even if they comprise tables and lists the instructor has introduced in class. Instructors are much more favorably impressed by succinct, well organized answers that reflect an ability to select and emphasize important material that is pertinent to the question asked. They also appreciate the parallel ability to omit the peripheral and irrelevant.

In general, fewer words are preferable to many, especially if they are carefully chosen and well organized. Please try to believe this. Overly wordy answers are among the most common shortcomings, even of top students.

A good means of dealing with an essay question is to shape the answer before committing it to paper. It is worth your time to make a brief outline of your answer in which you identify your principal argument and organize your support for it. Outlines help you avoid going off on tangents. They promote good organization and brevity, both desirable qualities.

One final — and somewhat subtle — tip concerning essay questions. A good instructor may use an essay question as part of a learning experience that promotes a new insight into the material on the part of students. In such circumstances you may be able to gain confidence in your ability to deal effectively with the question by looking for a major connection between elements of a course that are suggested by the question.

When you perceive an intended association, you will likely experience an "aha!" sensation, a feeling of certainty that you understand the instructor's objective and are on target. These feelings are usually trustworthy and enable you to begin to construct your answer immediately.

– *Problem Solving:* Examinations in the sciences, economics, mathematics and philosophy frequently require students to apply general principles they have learned to solve classes of problems with which they are familiar (Segal, Chipman, & Glaser, 1985). While the class of a problem should be familiar, the specific problem will not be. However, learning to recognize the class that a particular problem represents greatly facilitates deriving a correct answer. You then know which tools are most appropriate.

You will be better able to deal with specific problems, if you have emphasized the nature of problem-classes in your exam preparation. By learning to recognize distinguishing characteristics of problem-classes, you increase the likelihood both that you will choose appropriate methods to solve a problem and that you will save time while doing so.

Thus, while problem solving is a very specific activity, it benefits from the same sort of active overview that we have recommended in preparing for any examination situation.

– *At the End:* If you have followed the preceding advice, including writing succinct answers, you will likely find that you have some time left at the end of an examination. Use this time to ensure that you have not inadvertently misinterpreted either the instructions or the major questions.

If you still have time, review your essay answers for their clarity. You may know the material quite well but, if you fail to communicate your understanding to your instructor, you will not get credit for your knowledge. Remember, the instructor is not a mind-reader. He or she can gauge your understanding only by what you commit to paper. Answers that appear vague and ambiguous *are* vague and ambiguous. It will do you no good to explain later that "What I really meant here was ... "

Concluding Comments

It may surprise you to learn that we actually do not expect most student readers to follow all of the advice in this chapter or throughout this book. Indeed, many of you will follow only a small minority of the suggestions we have made here.

However, to return to where we started this chapter: There are better and worse means to improve study skills, but there are no easy means.

The profit you derive from this chapter relates directly to the amount of effort you are willing to expend on improving your academic performance. Of course, no one's effort is infinite. The suggestions we have made in this chapter will enable you to do as well as you can or, if you prefer, as well as you wish to do.

We especially recommend that you consult the Study Guides (Figures 26–29) when you are not sure on how to proceed with a particular study task. When students describe how they studied for a test or prepared for a term paper, they often report having used only a few of the many appropriate techniques. Even students who have been instructed in study skills often do not study any more effectively than students who have not been so instructed. The instructed students explain that they did not use more techniques because — despite their training — they simply did not think of them.

The Study Guides were developed to serve as external aids (Harris, 1984; Intons-Peterson & Fournier, 1986; Intons-Peterson & Newsome, 1992) to remind students of the study techniques that may be applicable to particular study problems — planning a program of study; indepth reading procedures; extracting meaning from lecture notes and texts; preparing for exams; and taking exams. The motivated student who wants to study properly can merely glance at the Study Guides and be reminded of techniques that otherwise they might not have tried.

Irrespective of the amount of effort you decide to invest in your studies, we remain consistent in our general recommendations. Continually strive for an interrelated overview of the tasks before you, and continue to process information actively. You will improve both your understanding and your recall of the material you treat.

Tape recorders, cameras, and video camcorders can passively register enormous amounts of information far better than you can. However, unlike these machines, you can actively manipulate information to derive new insights and arguments. This, after all, is the real goal of education.

Summary

– Doing better academically often involves changing your study habits. There are better and worse means to improve study skills, but there are no easy means to do so.
– One key to success is to discover and learn the particular techniques and strategies that apply to particular courses.
– Another key to success is to learn and master some of the more important general study skills, ones that are independent of any particular subject matter — yet are appropriate for any course. These general skills pertain to Indepth Reading Procedures, Meaning Extraction Techniques, Exam Preparation, and Exam Strategies.
– There are better and worse means to improve study skills, but there are no easy means. The benefits you will derive from learning about study study skills depend on how much effort and opportunity you have to expend on improving your academic performance.

• What people can recall
often makes them look
better than you.

Chapter 9
Scientific Background

Because so many lines of research have challenged the simple notion of generalizable memory ability, many investigators have concluded that effective memory use requires conscious application of the diverse techniques discussed in this book.

Consequently, researchers increasingly examine the effectiveness of memory strategies. In some cases, psychologists ask people what they do to perform well on memory tasks, and then try to identify the habits of studying, exam preparation, and exam-taking of the high performers. In other cases, researchers attempt to train subjects in the approach to learning, studying, and remembering that the researchers believe will lead to the most intelligent learner.

In other cases, investigators attempt to teach one or two or more differing study strategies to students already classified as good or poor students. This latter design is based on the assumption that good learners will make the best use of the most effective approach, and vice versa for the poor student. For example, experiments indicate students with higher IQ scores improve in their learning more if training involves many strategies, whereas students with lower IQ scores improve more when trained with a smaller number of strategies.

Utilizing questionnaires, other workers have examined how the better learner uses time management, external aids, self-care habits, and social skills. It is clear that the most successful students demonstrate competence in each of these aspects of study.

Study Savvy

9

Previous chapters have given you hundreds of options for improving your memory through conditioning, attitude, social, environmental, and mental techniques. Designing your own task-specific repertoires is one important way of managing these options. Repertoires can help you use manipulations suitably, quickly, and efficiently.

The final step in a complete approach to improvement is to develop and practice your skills at applying this information to your own memory performance. A person with memory "savvy" knows how to recognize memory problems, link them with appropriate manipulations, and employ these manipulations in ways most suited to memory tasks (Bellezza & Buck, 1989; Ericsson, 1985; Herrmann, 1990a). The greater your savvy, the better your chances for success, both academically and professionally (see Figure 30).

Improving the Appropriateness of Manipulation Use

In deciding whether a manipulation is appropriate for a given task, ask two key questions. First, do you find the manipulation compatible with the context involved? For some people, a shopping list is a direct product of the meals they will cook. They might

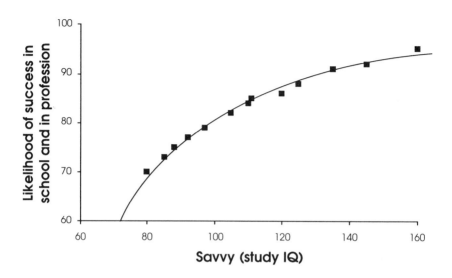

Figure 30.
The likelihood of success in school and in a profession as a result of a
person's study savvy, i. e., IQ for learning new ideas, procedures, and
technologies (hypothetical data based on the research literature).

register it more effectively in memory by attending to the meaning
of the items than by attending to their pronunciation. Those who
shop by rote, with very little notion of how the products will be
used, might find the pronunciation manipulation more appropriate.

Second, does the manipulation require more effort than you
want to give to the task? Although a manipulation may be appropriate to registering or retrieving a certain kind of information,
the effort required by the manipulation may not suit you. For a
week's shopping, using a manipulation that forms a retrieval
structure would probably be a waste of time, considering that you
could simply jot down a list more quickly and easily. For a big
exam, however, manipulations that form retrieval structures
might well be an appropriately rigorous choice.

To satisfactorily answer these two questions, you must blend
knowledge about your own skills and inclinations with a clear understanding of both your targeted memory tasks and the manipulations you could apply to them.

Self-Observation of Memory Performance

The simplest way to improve the appropriateness of your use of manipulations is to critique your performance when you have actually applied manipulations to a given memory task (Hodgson & Miller, 1982). As we discussed in Chapter 3, a key time to learn about appropriateness is when you have just failed at a memory task. On such occasions, you should note possible adjustments to the technique or the focus of your effort that might have enabled you to succeed at the task (Brennen, Winograd, Bridge, & Hiebert, 1986; Herrmann, Grub, Grueneich, Sigmundi, 1986).

For example, we sometimes fail to learn a person's name, despite having heard it clearly when introduced. If we make a note that we failed to do so, we are more likely to take steps to avoid making the same mistake in the future. Alternatively, there are certain memory tasks that we know we are good at. An awareness of the manipulations that make you skillful at these tasks may suggest ways to improve your performance of other tasks.

Self-observation can also be conducted in a more ongoing and systematic fashion. A memory diary with a checklist of tasks gives you information about your current successes and failures at memory, making it easier to target tasks that deserve more effort. Even if you don't keep formal records, you might routinely stop to mentally review your recent performance.

Interpreting Feedback about Your Memory Performance

Others can be a useful and independent source of information about our memory performance (Best, 1992). Their praise or criticism, however, must itself be interpreted and assessed. As we learned in Chapter 4, others frequently offer distorted views on our performance (Gentry & Herrmann, 1991). Accepting inaccurate praise and criticism at face value can mislead us into approaching memory tasks inappropriately.

Therefore, evaluate the feedback you get. If it does not square with your own impression of your abilities but you suspect the person may be right, monitor your performance of the task for a few weeks. Your performance during a period of self-observation will indicate whether you need to prepare specifically for the task. If the feedback does not square with your own impression, and you have good reason to believe the person is wrong, then disregard the feedback.

Comparison of Your Memory Performance with that of Others

By watching others or listening to the comments they make about their own memory performance, you can compare your performance to theirs. Perhaps they exploit specific techniques more effectively, or perhaps they "naturally" approach a task in a way that could be useful to you. If your performance compares favorably, you may confirm the appropriateness of your manipulations.

Such comparisons are only effective, however, to the extent that people allow you to witness their memory successes and failures. Just as people distort the comments they make about our performance, they may also distort the comments they make about their own performance. Research indicates that people sometimes downplay, or even deny, their superiority at memory tasks, because they feel that to do otherwise would be immodest or might make others feel inferior. As discussed in Chapter 4, people may also feign poor memory performance in order to attain other goals.

Because of this, interpret memory performances of others judiciously. The surest sources of comparisons are people you know well enough to distinguish their actual performance from their motives and capacities for controlling apparent performance. If you are fortunate enough to have a friend who shares your interest in memory, frank discussion of how you approach certain memory tasks would provide the best possible form of comparison.

Continuing Education

Your continued study of memory and study skills will keep your knowledge about manipulations growing. New trade books and magazine articles on memory improvement, tapes developed as improvement guides, and occasional TV shows on specific scientific developments in memory research may opportunely inform and inspire your interest. Courses or training programs in memory improvement can challenge and inform you even more fully. Continued study of memory will deepen your theoretical understanding, enabling you to make better use of your memory manipulations.

Bad Habit Identification and Control

In addition to learning more about the appropriateness and use of manipulations, you should periodically attempt to identify and eliminate habits that hinder your memory performance. Some bad habits are fairly general and interfere with many kinds of tasks (Breme & Rosen, 1982). Others are very specific. On the next two pages is a form which you can use to assess your bad memory habits.

This checklist resembles the ones presented in Chapter 3. It differs, however, because this checklist focuses on bad habits that apply to many memory tasks, not your expectations of success or failure at particular memory tasks. It assumes you have already put some thought and effort toward specific improvement, including an attitude assessment. In fact, its utility depends on your having sufficient experiences to recognize habitual memory patterns.

Your responses to this checklist can be evaluated in a few ways. An overall score can be accumulated by adding the values of all responses that you circle according to the following scale: "never" — 1, "sometimes" — 2, "half-the-time" — 3, "often" — 4, and "very often" — 5. The overall score will vary quite a bit depending on your age and background, but a typical answer for most items will be either "sometimes" or "half-the-time."

Checklist for bad memory habits. Directions: Indicate how often you act in the manner described.

Habits	Never	Some-times	Half the time	Often	Very Often
Memory Attitudes					
1. Holding a memory task in low regard.	x	x	x	x	x
2. Holding your memory ability in low regard.	x	x	x	x	x
Conditioning					
1. Assuming that poor physical condition won't hinder memory performance, or tolerating fatigue before an expected memory challenge.	x	x	x	x	x
2. Using adverse substances when performing or about to perform memory tasks.	x	x	x	x	x
3. Living an excessively busy lifestyle.	x	x	x	x	x
4. Living an excessively routinized lifestyle.	x	x	x	x	x
5. Not making or not referring to a daily schedule.	x	x	x	x	x
Environmental Use					
1. Keeping possessions in a disorganized state.	x	x	x	x	x
2. Memory arrogance — not using mental manipulations or environmental aids because you feel that it should be possible to perform the task without added effort or use of an aid.	x	x	x	x	x
Mental Manipulations					
Registration					
1. Half-hearted rehearsal — learning while with others, or while watching TV.	x	x	x	x	x
2. Learning indiscriminately, without selecting main points or ideas for greater concentration.	x	x	x	x	x
3. Daydreaming or letting your thoughts wander when you should be learning.	x	x	x	x	x

4. Intentional disattention — going through the motions of learning while aware your mind is elsewhere.	x	x	x	x	x
5. Cramming rather than using a series of study sessions.	x	x	x	x	x

Remembering

1. Failure to prepare — not studying prior to a known challenge to your ability to remember.	x	x	x	x	x
2. Tolerance of memory errors — accepting a memory error because correcting it seems too difficult or inconvenient.	x	x	x	x	x
3. Compulsive remembering checks repeatedly checking whether you have done or remembered something, even when you remember just making such a check.	x	x	x	x	x

A more important way to evaluate your responses involves comparing answers to different questions. Obviously, those habits you rated as most frequent may be ones that interfere with your performance. They most likely should and can be changed — with effort.

Development of Managerial Skills

Superior memory skill requires more than the learning of an array of memory manipulations. You must also be able to skillfully manage these manipulations according to the demands of different tasks and situations (Schoenfield, 1985). Whether you are registering information during learning or retrieving it during remembering, you can take steps to organize and check your efforts.

These managerial manipulations will help you use memory aids and practices as efficiently as possible.

Managerial Manipulations for Learning

1. Make sure that you are registering the correct information. Familiarize yourself with everything to be learned before you begin to register information

2. Consider whether your learning would be more efficient if you studied the material in parts or in its entirety. If you employ part learning, spend time subsequently studying the whole of the material.

3. Use more than one kind of manipulation when possible for the same material. For most tasks, you can find both an appropriate strength and attribute manipulation. For example, you might learn a list of items by first rehearsing the items, then by making attribute judgments on each item. Most experts believe that the use of different techniques leads to a more durable and accessible memory trace.

4. Distribute your studying over several occasions. Massed practice usually leads to slower learning than distributed practice. A study session of two hours is usually less effective in fostering registration than two one-hour study sessions separated in time. However, whether you mass or distribute your practice, it is a bitter truth that the amount learned is directly related to the amount of time spent in practice.

5. Repeatedly test yourself as you learn. Before a study session, first estimate how much you will recall. Be prepared for plateaus in your learning, in which continued efforts at registration are not followed by increases in recall. Plateaus will eventually give way to additional increases in recall. Overlearn the material if it is especially important or detailed: after you have learned 100% of it, study and test yourself further.

6. As you test yourself, imagine the situation in which you will be called on to remember the information you have learned. Be sensitive to whether you will be required to recall information in a forwards direction or backwards. For example, if you are learning French, study vocabulary from English-to-French as well as from French-to-English.

7. Study on a schedule, and review periodically after learning.

Managerial Manipulations for Remembering

1. During remembering, recall at a relaxed pace. Hurrying leads you to miss recalling parts of the information you remember. Hurrying is also more likely to elicit inaccuracies than a slow, deliberate recall. If possible, try to delay giving your recall when the desired information is not yet accessed.

2 Recall in an order that is optimal for the information and presentation conditions.

   a. Follow a chronological order when possible, such as when trying to recall a story or an event.

   b. When information has been presented briefly and recently, recall recent information first, then initial information, and finally the information in between.

   c. When a considerable amount of information is involved, and it is not chronologically organized, it will help to break the task down into parts. After you have done so, alternate between attempting to recall the parts and the entirety of the memory trace.

3. Question yourself in a balanced manner. Ask yourself related questions, which call for specific bits of information. Then ask yourself divergent questions, which relate indirectly to the information you want to remember. Alternate between convergent and divergent questions until recall succeeds, or until you feel that you are blocked.

4. Mentally edit what you have in mind before you recall it to others. You can check the correctness of your retrieval in several ways.

   a. Estimate the likely accuracy of your recall (Johnson & Raye, 1982; Schooler, Gerhard, & Loftus, 1986). People usually have a reasonably good idea of what they know. One way to form your estimate is to ask yourself how likely you would be to recognize the right answer. For subjects you know well, your estimate should be high. You should tend to have much lower estimates for unfamiliar subjects. You may, however, have further reasons to doubt or trust your recall for given facts, regardless of your general familiarity. Whether high or low, your estimate is likely to be right more times than not. Of course, a feeling of knowing is still not a guarantee that you remembered correctly. When you need stronger assurances, take time to perform further checks.

b. Check the content you have recalled. Is it internally consistent and plausible? If not, your retrieval may have been flawed. Try to remember again, using other manipulations if possible.

c. Be sensitive to the fact that you may err in many ways. Initially, you might misinterpret the question or query posed for remembering. You can intentionally or unintentionally leave something out (omission). A memory trace can emerge that is either not called for (a false-alarm intrusion) or related to another trace just remembered (a repeat intrusion). Correct traces might be remembered out of sequence; at the wrong time, such as remembering an appointment after it was to occur; or in the wrong place, such as recalling information that is socially inappropriate. With continued attempts to remember, erroneous retrievals can repeat their emergence (a double false alarm intrusion). Finally, after retrieving part of the desired information, you may think you have finished remembering, when you are not actually done (Reason & MyCielska, 1983). Double-checking these sources of error can be a way of cross-examining your recall process.

d. Screen your recall to be sure that you don't "blurt out" something from memory that may be offensive.

e. Give extra scrutiny to answers that come quickly and seem very familiar. Some errors are "strong habits" that intrude upon retrieval.

5. If your recall or recognition efforts fail despite conscientious attempts, avoid frantically repeating them.

a. Give the task a rest. Chances are good that the desired item will eventually emerge into consciousness.

b. Try the yoga method of recall. Lie down in a quiet spot where you won't be disturbed. Systematically relax the muscles in your body. When you are extremely relaxed, put questions to yourself about the information you would like to recall.

6. Claim an honest level of confidence in the accuracy of your memory. Express your certitude or doubt prudently.

7. For recurring memory problems, establish a routine sequence of steps to guide your recall process. Include checks for errors — such as intrusions or omissions — you have found yourself prone to commit.

Improving the Efficiency of Manipulation Use

Knowledge about how to improve memory will only go so far. Proficient memory performance requires gaining experience in the use of memory manipulations while performing memory tasks (James, 1890; Watson, 1925). However, when people have acquired considerable experience at certain memory tasks, impressive memory abilities often result.

For example, prolonged occupational experience may lead to excellent memory abilities for job-related memory tasks. Thus, if you desire a superior memory, you must be prepared to practice memory tasks over a considerable period of time. You can no more expect to improve memory skills by merely reading a book than you can your tennis or golf game by doing the same. Hard work and practice are essential.

Practice

As mentioned earlier, a good way to excel at a learning task is to practice it directly (Anderson, 1982; Colley & Beech, 1989; Payne, 1982). Research has shown that the normal maximum memory for a series of numbers — around seven — can be increased by practice over several months so a person will recall as many as 80 digits in a row. Remembering lists of digits probably is not a task at which you care to excel. But the dramatic improvement practice affords this task indicates how much you stand to gain by vigorously practicing a task of special interest to you. Acquisition practice is probably the best way to produce a dramatic and durable change in memory ability. However, it must be pointed out that practice requires a great deal of hard work (Chase & Ericsson, 1982).

Practice may also be used to develop retrieval skills for certain tasks. If you know that a particular retrieval task occurs on many occasions, a sure way to excel at this task is to engage in remembering practice (Herrmann, Buschke, & Gall, 1986).

For example, suppose you want to be facile with the different terms in a course. After you have learned to define each term, practice recalling them — without restudying. Next, practice recalling all of them — again without restudying. Then practice recalling again, and again, until you are satisfied with your improvement.

You will discover that the speed and number of items you recall will increase. Typically, a half-dozen repetitions or about 10 minutes per recall are necessary to produce substantial progress. Research has indicated that daily attempts over a few weeks may triple the number of items recalled.

Remembering practice is also very effective for enhancing retrieval of information you once knew well but now recall poorly. If you expect to be called upon at a meeting about some topic that is now hazy, practice retrieving the topic several times beforehand. Even without any relearning, you will undoubtedly recall more information and have faster access to it. By combining relearning with remembering practice, you can further improve your performance.

Contrived Practice

Daily life presents numerous opportunities to practice certain memory tasks. We frequently have occasion to remember names we know but do not readily retrieve, such as those of old movie stars or distant relatives. If you are interested in improving your performance of common tasks, you will naturally get a lot of practice.

Other tasks present far fewer opportunities. We seldom get "practice" at receiving and remembering directions to a new location. When this task does arise, it is usually important that we arrive on time, and we therefore rely on maps, written directions, or other memory aids. Few people trust their recall of verbal directions enough to engage in practice. If you are interested in improving your performance of uncommon tasks, you will need to devise ways to simulate the experience.

Computer Simulated Practice

Several software packages will now take a person through training exercises that teach the use of various memory manipulations. Most of the manipulations taught are the technical mnemonics. More diversified packages are likely to appear in the new future. The names of some of these software packages may be obtained from any computer store which stocks educational software.

Mental Practice

Even without direct or simulated practice, you can "run through" tasks in your mind. Imagine a memory situation you would like to conquer. Next, imagine yourself carrying out appropriate manipulations: you are taking good care of yourself ahead of time; adopting a positive view towards the task; making use of the environment when you perform the task; and using the mental manipulations most appropriate for the task. Athletes report that "mental practice" focuses their approach in actual competition. It can do the same for your memory (Hardy, 1984).

Role Playing

If there is a person you feel comfortable about asking, enlist that person to help you recreate the situation you want to improve. Suppose that you want to improve your ability to learn names at an introduction. (By the way, this is the single most disliked memory task by young and old alike. The sequence of introductions is often unpredictable, and we are socially expected to engage in conversation while registering the name in memory.)

In order to practice learning names at introductions, you must have similarly distracting and brief circumstances. Solitary practice is inadequate. Instead, ask your friend to assume any made-up names and introduce him-or-herself to you in a natural way. If practiced thoroughly, simulated introductions will improve your use of manipulations during actual introductions. By reversing roles in the situations you create, you can also obtain a good comparison between your own memory performance and your partner's.

Summary

− A superior memory requires a response to memory tasks that is prompt, appropriate, and proficient.
− You can work towards a superior memory by developing a knowledge of a variety of manipulations; learn how to manage these manipulations so you use them to best effect; observe your performance; eliminate bad memory habits; and practice using manipulations.

Epilogue

For a long time, memory experts have tried to improve memory by teaching a few tried and true manipulations, such as the technical mnemonics generated in ancient Greece. Perhaps they have done so because they hoped to find a single solution to memory problems. Now, however, it is abundantly clear that memory is much more complex than envisioned by the old approach to memory improvement. And it is equally clear that memory is best improved by providing a person with many methods, allowing a flexible response to diverse memory tasks. Our memory is good only to the extent that we are prepared with those manipulations that enable us to respond effectively to the specific tasks that challenge us.

The specificity of memory abilities is further demonstrated by the "superstars" of memory. Examination of these memorists reveals that some of these people were born with special memory gifts, but the abilities for which they were renowned were not the result of gifts alone. They were the result of effort and experience, methods that are available to everyone (Atkinson, 1912; Brown & Deffenbacher, 1975; Herrmann & Chaffin, 1988; Hunt & Love, 1972). We are all capable, if we desire, of achieving substantial improvement in our memory performance. Regardless of how arcane or common your ambitions are for improved memory performance, the avenue to progress is the same: development of repertoires of manipulations that can enhance memory performance, especially repertoires of task-specific manipulations.

Most of what we know about exceptional "students" comes from historical study. There are scholars who devote a large part or all of their career to examining records of people from the past. These "psychological histories" look at the personal and professional lives of individuals, to the extent that the information is available. In the case of memory, only a few investigations have done the painstaking work needed to identify what personal and intellectual characteristics make up a superior memorist or mnemonist (Atkinson, 1912; Brown & Deffenbacher, 1975; Hermann & Chaffin, 1988; Wilding & Valentine, 1988). Nevertheless, enough evidence has been amassed to indicate you can be confident with the general tenor of this epilogue: the development of truly exceptional memory skills requires intellectual gifts, an enormous amount of work, and a social situation that provides considerable reward for developing these memory skills. However, all people can significantly improve their memory skills through the practice of the techniques and strategies we have described in this book. Good luck!

Glossary

Absorption	A process by which the contents of working memory are continually being recorded as traces in long-term memory.
Accessibility of a trace	The potential of a trace to be found with sufficient cues.
Activation of a trace	The increase in the strength of a trace in long-term memory due to information represented in the trace, or related to the trace, being held in in working memory.
Applicability of manipulations	The range of tasks for which mental manipulation will be effective: generally applicable manipulations facilitate most or all memory tasks while specifically applicable manipulations facilitate just certain tasks.
Arts of memory	Paintings, posters, or maps that have been designed to aid memory either in registration of new information or in remembering of old information.
Assessment of Memory and Study Abilities	Identification of strengths and weaknesses at memory tasks in general as revealed by self-observation or by formal testing by a psychologist.
Associations of a trace	One of the four aspects of a trace that may be affected by a mental manipulation. Associations join traces to one another in either a unidirectional or bidirectional manner.

Associative Mental Manipulations	Techniques that focus attention on two or more details of information at the same time in working memory, thereby leading traces of these details to be absorbed together in long-term memory.
Attention	The orienting to and observing of the world around us and the contents of working memory.
Attention, distribution	The way in which the intensity of attention varies across details available to the senses and working memory.
Attention, level	The intensity with which attention is paid to things in general.
Attributes of a trace	One of the four aspects of a trace that may be affected by mental manipulation. An attribute is one facet of the meaning of the information in a trace.
Attribute mental manipulations	Techniques that foster deeper comprehension of aspects or qualities in the material to be learned.
Availability of a trace	Status of a trace as either in memory or not in memory (because it was never learned in the first place or because biological processes destroyed the trace over a retention interval).
Bad memory habits	Automatic ways of responding to memory tasks that impair memory performance.
Central processor	A component of the memory system that selects and implements manipulations of any type to facilitate memory performance.
Components of memory	The parts of the memory system, as viewed physiologically as parts of the brain or conceptually as parts of memory processes.
Condition for memory tasks	Emotional and physical fitness as it affects your ability to pay attention and perform memory tasks.
Conversational manipulations	Verbal techniques that delay or redirect the flow of conversation so as to gain time for memory processing.
Cue gathering	Looking or listening for things that might facilitate your registration or remembering.

Decay of a trace	The physiological erosion of a memory trace.
Distortion of a trace	An alteration of a memory trace, in which inaccuracies are usually undetected.
Efficiency of manipulation use	The speed with which you are able to execute a manipulation.
Emergence	A process in which traces in long-term memory become sufficiently active and re-enter your working memory.
Encoding	The incidental form of registration.
Environmental manipulation	A behavior that focuses on, and takes control of, objects or events around you to stimulate, or even substitute for, memory.
Feedback about memory performance	Praise or criticism from others about your performance.
Formal assessment of memory abilities	Determination of your specific memory abilities from your performance of a variety of tests, administered and interpreted by a psychologist.
General mental manipulations	Manipulations that supposedly apply to many memory tasks.
Group pressures on memory performance	The influence of the expectations or memory performance of others — people you are with, normative groups to which you belong — which may lead you to doubt or disavow your recollection.
Incidental manipulations	Behaviors of any type that raise attention level, without focusing on details, for a period after the manipulation is carried out.
Intentional forgetting	Willful forgetting due to deliberate inattention to the memory trace.
Intentional manipulations	Behaviors of any type that raise attention to a particular memory task and, in addition, consciously focus on certain details of the information encountered in the task.
Interference between traces	A source of forgetting in which the primary memory trace to be remembered is confused with one or more other memories.
Language of memory	Common words or colloquial expressions that describe memory performance.

Learning	An intentional form of registration.
Learning practice	Development of skill at learning in a particular kind of memory task through repeated attempts at the task.
Long-term memory	A component of the memory system that holds information indefinitely.
Managerial memory manipulations	Techniques that enhance memory skill through organizing your use of manipulations.
Manipulation	In the context of memory improvement, a behavior that acts on the world around you or on your mental processes to facilitate memory performance.
Memory aid	An object or device that facilitates memory performance
Memory aid, commercial	A product that facilitates memory performance or even does the memory task for you.
Memory attitude manipulation	A behavior that corrects your misimpressions of your memory performance; fosters a positive, realistic, and adaptive approach to memory tasks.
Memory attitudes that affect memory performance.	Attitudes that are negative or unrealistic toward a task, motivation to perform a particular task, your self concept about your abilities to perform the task, negative feelings about information to be registered or remembered.
Memory communication	Ways of making claims, verbally or nonverbally, about memory performance that affect another's acceptance of the claims.
Memory condition manipulation	A behavior that enhances your memory performance by improving your physiological and emotional states.
Memory contrivance	A deliberate distortion that portrays someone else's memory performance as better or worse than it actually was in order to achieve certain social goals.
Memory etiquette	Rules of behavior concerning how one should react when someone else fails at a memory task.

Memory reputation	The beliefs that others commonly hold regarding the likelihood you will succeed or fail at different memory tasks.
Memory savvy	Knowledge about how to recognize memory problems, link them with appropriate manipulations, and adjust your performance to fit the memory tasks that arise.
Memory stereotypes	Beliefs people hold about the memory performance of others, based on group characteristics, such as gender, race, physical appearance, or occupation.
Memory tasks imposed by others	Situations in which you are expected to perform certain memory tasks, as dictated by social norms and events, or by personal relationships.
Memory tasks	At the most general level, there are four categories of memory tasks: knowledge, events, intentions, actions.
Mental conditions that impair memory performance	Lack of concentration, excessive emotions, anxiety, mood difficulties.
Mental manipulation	A behavior that orders and organizes thoughts to assist registration, retention, and remembering.
New approach to improving memory abilities	The improvement of memory ability with scientifically-validated manipulations that affect memory directly or indirectly through other psychological functions, such as physical and mental condition, memory attitudes, perception and use of the physical environment, social interaction.
Old approaches to improving memory abilities	Methods of memory improvement developed prior to this century, some as many as 2000 years ago, which are being repackaged and promoted to this day.
Phases of memory processes	Registration, retention, and remembering.
Physical conditions that impair memory performance	Sensory deficiencies, major and minor health problems, poor nutrition, use of adverse substances, stimulants, fatigue, lack of sleep.

Placement manipulations Placing objects in conspicuous locations to facilitate the realization of an intention.

Preparation manipulations Learning and retrieval manipulations that are used prior to registration and remembering tasks to facilitate the effectiveness of manipulations used at that time.

Priming The increase in trace strength that results from familiarizing yourself with the material to be learned or retrieved.

Realization The incidental form of remembering.

Repertoire In the context of memory improvement, a set of task-specific manipulations tailored to particular memory tasks.

Repertoire, natural A set of task-specific manipulations that you instinctively apply to a particular memory task.

Retrieval An intentional form of remembering.

Retrieval practice Development of skill at retrieval in a particular kind of task through repeated attempts at the task.

Retrieval structure manipulations A retrieval structure is developed by creating trace information that suggests the information in another trace.

Retrieval structure of a trace One of the four aspects of a trace that may be formed by a mental manipulation. A retrieval structure is a set of secondary information that may direct retrieval to the information that one wants to remember.

Self-observation of memory performance Taking stock of your performance in a variety of memory tasks by completing questionnaires and keeping a memory diary.

Social context manipulation A technique that identifies social factors harmful to performance or that alters social behaviors to maximize memory performance.

Social contexts that affect memory performance Social tasks that make extra demands on memory, such as cocktail parties or receiving lines and aspects of common interactions that influence performance, such as the pace of conversation.

Stages of manipulation execution	A manipulation is elicited, modified to the particular task, applied to the task, and assessed for its effectiveness.
Strength mental manipulations	Techniques that increase attention, usually through rehearsal, and thereby increase the strength of the traces absorbed.
Strength of a trace	One of the four aspects of a trace that may be affected by a mental manipulation. The stronger an item's trace, the more familiar we are with that item.
Study formulas	Sets of key words that are intended to orient you properly for studying.
Superior memorists	People reputed to have had uniformly excellent memory skills, but who in fact excelled at certain tasks.
Superstitious environmental manipulations	Objects or actions that people believe will provide good luck to their memory performance.
Symbolic memory tasks	Tasks whose performance, successful or unsuccessful, affects the state of a personal relationship between people.
Task menu	A term used in this book to refer to the set of manipulations that may be especially suitable for a particular task.
Task situations	Broad categories of daily life in which memory tasks occur: homelife, work, obligations, recreation.
Task-specific manipulation	A behavior that is especially effective for a particular kind of memory task.
Test anxiety	Fear and nervousness that inhibits memory performance, especially for a topic of particular importance to the individual.
Test wise	A knowledge of, and ability for taking, tests.
Timeliness of manipulation use	The speed with which a manipulation is elicited when needed.
Trace	A record in working memory or long-term memory of details of a percept or an idea.

Warm up   The increase in speed and proficiency at per-
                         forming a memory task that results from ini-
                         tial attempts at the task.

Working memory   A component of the memory system that
                         holds information for approximately one
                         minute.

References

Adams, L. T. (1985) Improving memory: Can retrieval strategies help? *Human Learning, 4,* 281–297.

Alzheimer, A. (1907) Uber eine eigenartige Erkranskung der Hirnrinde, *Allg. Z. Psychiatrie-Gerichtlich Med., 64,* 146–148.

Anderson, J. R. (1982) Acquisition of a cognitive skill. *Psychological Review, 89,* 396–406.

Anderson, J. R. (1983) *The Architecture of Cognition.* Cambridge, MA: Harvard University Press.

Anderson, R. C. (1985) Role of the reader's schema in comprehension, learning, and memory. In H. Singer and R. B. Ruddel (Eds.) *Theoretical Models and Processes of Reading* (third edition). Newark, Delaware: International Reading Association.

Anderson, T. H. (1980) Study strategies and learning strategies. In R. J. Spiro, B. C. Bruce, and W. F. Brewer (Eds.) *Theoretical Issues in Reading Comprehension.* Hillsdale, N. J.: Erlbaum.

Anderson, T. H. & Armbruster, B. B. (1991) The value of taking notes during lectures. In R. F. Flippo and D. C. Caverly (Eds.) *Teaching Reading & Study Strategies: At the College Level.* Newark, Delaware: International Reading Association.

Annis, L. F. (1983) *Study Techniques.* Dubuque, IA: William C. Brown.

Ash, S. E. (1956) Studies of independence and conformity: I. A minority of one against a unanimous majority. *Psychological Monographs, 70, 9* (Whole no. 416).

Atkinson, R. C. & Shiffrin, R. M. (1968) Human memory: A proposed system and its control processes. In K. W. Spence and J. T. Spence (Eds.) *The Psychology of Learning and Motivation, Vol. 2.* New York: Academic Press.

Atkinson, W. W. (1912) *Memory: How to Develop, Train and Use It.* Holyoke, MA: Elizabeth Towne.

Baddeley, A. D. (1982) Domains of recollection. *Psychological Review, 89,* 708–729.

Baddeley, A. D. (1986) *Working Memory.* New York: Basic Books.

Bahrick, H. P. (1984) Memory for people. In J. E. Harris & P. E. Morris (Eds.), *Everyday memory, actoins and absentmindedness.* London: Academic Press.

Baltes, P. B., & Kliegel, R. (1986) On the dynamics between growth and decline in the aging of intelligence and memory. In K. Poeck (Ed.) *Proceedings of the Thirteenth World Conference of Neurology.* Heidelberg: Springer Verlag.

Bellezza, F. S. (1981) Mnemonic devices: Classification, characteristics, and criteria. *Review of Educational Research, 51,* 247–275.

Bellezza, F. S. (1983) Menemonic-device instruction with adults. In M. Pressley and J. R. Levin (Eds.) *Cognitive Strategy Research.* New York.

Bellezza, F. S. & Buck, D. K. (1988) Expert knowledge as mnemonic cues. *Applied Cognitive Psychology, 2,* 147–162.

Best, D. L. (1992) The role of social interaction in memory improvement. In D. Herrmann, H. Weingartner, A. Searleman, C. McEvoy (Eds.) *Memory Improvement: Implications for Memory Theory.* New York: Springer Verlag.

Best, D. L., Hamlett, K. W., & Davis, S. W. (1992) Modification of memory complaint and memory performance in elderly adults. *Applied Cognitive Psychology.*

Birnbaum, I. & Parker, E., Eds. (1977) *Alcohol and Human Memory.* Hillsdale, N. J.: Erlbaum.

Block, R. I. & Wittenborn, J. R. (1984) Marijuana effects on semantic memory: Verification of common and uncommon category members. *Psychological Reports, 55,* 503–512.

Bower, G.H. (1981) Mood and memory. *American Psychologist, 36,* 129–148.

Bransford, J. D. & Stein, B. (1984) *The Ideal Problem Solver.* New York: W. H. Freeman.

Breme, F. J. & Rosen, D. A. (1982) How to flunk out: A paradoxical approach to study skills. *ERIC Reports*, ED 240 478.

Brennan, S., Winograd, P. N., Bridge, C. A., & Hiebert, E. H. (1986) A comparison of observer reports and self-reports of study practices used by college students. In J. A. Niles and R. V. Lalik (Eds.) *Solving Problems in Literacy: Learners, Teachers, and Researchers.* Rochester, N. Y.: National Reading Conference.

Broadbent, D. E., Cooper, P. F., Fitzgerald, P. & Parkes, K. R. (1982) The Cognitive Failures Questionnaire (CFQ) and its correlates. *British Journal of Psychology, 21,* 1–16.

Brown, E. & Deffenbacher, L. (1975) Forgotten mnemonists. *Journal of the History of the Behavioral Sciences, 11,* 342–349.

Caverly, D. C. & Orlando, V. P. (1991) Textbook study strategies. In R. F.

Flippo and D. C. Caverly (Eds.) *Teaching Reading & Study Strategies: At the College Level*. Newark, Delaware: International Reading Association.

Chase, W. G. & Ericsson, K. A. (1982) Skill and working memory. In G. H. Bower (Ed.) *The Psychology of Learning and Motivation, Vol. 16*. New York: Academic Press.

Cohen, G. (1989) *Memory in the Real World*. Hillsdale, N. J.: Erlbaum.

Cole, M. & Scribner, S. (1974) Culture and Thought. New York: Wiley.

Colley, A. M. & Beach, J. R. (Eds.) *Acquisition and Performance of Cognitive Skills*. Chichester: Wiley.

Craik, F. I. M., & Lockhart, R. S. (1972) Levels of processing: A framework for memory research. *Journal of Verbal Learning and Verbal Behavior, 11*, 671–684.

Crawford, M., Herrmann, D., Randal, E., & Holdsworth, M. & Robbins, D. (1989) Self perception of memory performance as a function of gender. *British Journal of Psychology, 80*, 391–401.

Darley, C. F., Tinklenberg, J. R., Hollister, T. E., & Atkinson, R. C. (1973) Marihuana and retrieval from short-term memory. *Psychopharmacologia, 29*, 231–238.

Davies, G. M. & Thomson, D. M. (1988) *Memory in Context: Context in Memory*. Chichester: Wiley.

Dixon, R. A., Hertzog, C., & Hultsch, D. F. (1986) The multiple relationships among metamemory in adulthood (MIA) scales and cognitive abilities in adulthood. *Human Learning, 5*, 165–178.

Druckman, D. & Swets, J. A. (1988) *Enhancing Human Performance*. Washington, D. C.: National Academy Press.

Ellis, H. C. & Hunt, R. R. (1989) *Fundamentals of Human Memory and and Cognition*. Dubuque, IA: William C. Brown.

Erdelyi, M. H. & Goldberg, B. (1979) Let's not sweep repression under the rug: Toward a cognitive psychology of repression. In J. F. Kihlstrom and F. J. Evans (Eds.) *Functional Disorders of Memory*. Hillsdale, N. J.: Erlbaum.

Ericsson, K. A. (1985) Memory skill. *Canadian Journal of Psychology, 39*, 188–231.

Estes, W. K. (1980) Is Human Memory obsolete? *American Scientist, 68*, 62–68.

Feinaigle, M. G. von (1812) *The New Art of Memory*. London: Sherwood, Neely, and Jones.

Flippo, R. F. (1988) *TestWise: Strategies for Success in Taking Tests*. Carthage, IL: Fearon Teacher Aids/Simon & Schuster.

Flippo, R. F. & D. C. Caverly (Eds.) (1991) *Teaching Reading & Study Strategies: At the College Level*. Newark, Delaware: International Reading Association.

Fodor, J. A. (1983) The Modularity of Mind. Cambridge: MIT Press.

Folkard, S. & Monk, R. (1978) Time of day effects in immediate and delayed memory. In M. Gruneberg, P. E. Morris and R. N. Sykes (Eds.) *Practical Aspects of Memory*. London: Acadimic Press.

Forrest-Pressley, D. L., MacKinnon, G. E., & Waller, T. G. (1985) *Metacogntion, Cognition, and Human Performance, Volumes 1 and 2*. New York: Academic Press.

Gagne, R.M. & Paradise, N.E. (1961) Abilities and learning sets in in knowledge acquisition. *Psychological Monographs, 75* No. 14 (Whole no. 518), 308.

Garfunkel, F. & Landau, G. (1981) *A Memory Retention Course for the Aged: Guide for Leaders*. Washington, D. C.: The National Council in Aging.

Geiselman, R. E., Fisher, R. P., MacKinnon, D. P., & Holland, H. L. (1986) Enhancement of eyewitness memory with the cognitive interview. *American Journal of Psychology, 99*, 385–401.

Gentry, M. & Herrmann, D. J. (1990) Memory contrivances in everyday life. *Personality and Social Psychology Bulletin, 18*, 241–253.

Glaser, R. (1984) Education and thinking: The role of knowledge. *American Psychologist, 39*, 93–104.

Gold, P. E. (1987) Sweet memories. *American Scientist, 75*, 151–155.

Goldsmith, L. R. & Pillemer, D. B. (1988) Memories of statements spoken in everyday context. *Applied Cognitive Psychology, 2*, 273–286.

Grafman, J. (1984) Memory assessment and remediation in brain-injured patients: From theory to practice. In B. A. Edelstein and E. T. Couture (Eds.) *Behavioral Assessment and Rehabilitation of the Traumatically Brain-Damaged*. New York: Plenum.

Graumann, C. F. (1985) Memorabilia, mementos, memoranda: Towards an ecology of memory. In F. Klix and H. Hagendorf (Eds.) *Human Memory and Cognitive Capabilities, Part A*. Amsterdam: North Holland.

Greenwald, A. G. (1980) The totalitarian ego. *American Psychologist, 35*, 603–618.

Gruneberg, M. M., Morris, P. E., & Sykes, R. N. (1978) *Practical Aspects of Memory*. London: Academic Press.

Gruneberg, M. M., Morris, P. E., & Sykes, R. N. (1988) *Practical Aspects of Memory*. Chichester: Wiley.

Gruneberg, M. M. & Morris, P. E. (1979) *Applied Problems in Memory*. New York: Academic Press.

Gruneberg, M. M. & Morris, P. E. (1992) *Aspects of Memory* (2nd ed., Vol. 1). London: Routledge.

Hardy, L. & Ringland, A. (1984) Mental training and the inner game. *Human Learning, 3*, 143–226.

Harlow, H. F. (1949) The formation of learning sets. *Psychological Review, 56*, 51–65.

Harris, J. E. & Morris, P. E. (1984) *Everyday memory: actions and absentmindedness*. New York: Academic Press.

Harris, J.E. (1984). Methods of improving memory. In B.A. Wilson and N.

Moffatt (Eds.) *Clinical Management of Memory Problems*. Croon Helm: Beckenham.

Harris, J.E. & Wilkins, A.J. (1982) Remembering to do things: A theoretical framework and an illustrative experiment. *Human Learning, 1,* 123–136.

Hasher, L. & Zacks, R. T. (1979) Automatic and effortful processes in memory. *Journal of Experimental Psychology: General, 108,* 356–388.

Hastie, R., Ostrom, T. M., Ebbesen, E. B., Wyer, R. S. Jr., Hamilton, D. L., & Carlston, D. E. (1980) *Person Memory*. Hillsdale, N.J.: Erlbaum.

Herrmann, D.J. (1982) Know thy memory: The use of questionaires to assess and study memory. *Psychological Bulletin, 92,* 434–452.

Herrmann, D.J. (1984) Questionnaires about memory. In J. Harris and P. E. Morris (Eds.) *Everyday Memory: Actions and Absent-Mindedness*. New York: Academic Press.

Herrmann, D. J. (1987) Task appropriateness of mnemonic techniques. *Perceptual and Motor Skills, 64,* 171–178.

Herrmann, D. J. (1990a) Self perceptions of memory performance. In W. K. Schaie, J. Rodin, and C. Schooler (Eds.) *Self-directedness and Efficacy: Causes and Effects Throughout the Life Course*. Hillsdale, N.J.: Erlbaum.

Herrmann, D. J. (1990b). The representational bias of acquired memory processes. *Zeitschrift für Psychologie (Centennial Edition), 198,* 265–281.

Herrmann, D. J. (1990c) *SuperMemory*. Emmaus, PA: Rodale.

Herrmann, D. J. & Chaffin, R. (1988) *Memory in Historical Perspective*. New York: Springer Verlag.

Herrmann, D. J. & Petro, S. (1991) Commercial memory aids. *Applied Cognitive Psychology, 4,* 439–450.

Herrmann, D. J. & Searleman, A. (1990) A multi-modal approach to memory improvement. In G. H. Bower (Ed.) *Advances in Learning and Motivation*. New York: Academic Press.

Herrmann, D. & Searleman, A. (1992) Memory improvement and memory theory in historical perspective. In D. Herrmann, H. Weingartner, A. Searleman, and C. McEvoy (Eds.) *Memory Improvement: Implications for Memory Theory*. New York: Springer Verlag.

Herrmann, D. J. , Crawford, M., & Holdsworth, M. (1992) Gender linked differences in everyday memory performance. *British Journal of Psychology*.

Herrmann, D., Rea, A., & Andrzejewski, S. (1988) The need for a new approach to memory training. In M. M. Gruneberg, P. E. Morris, & R. N. Sykes (Eds.) *Practical Aspects of Memory*. Chichester: Wiley.

Herrmann, D. J., Grubs, L., Sigmundi, R., & Grueneich, R. (1986) Awareness of memory ability before and after relevant memory experience. *Human Learning*.

Herrmann, D., Weingartner, H., Searleman, A., & McEvoy, C. (Eds.)

(1992) *Memory Improvement: Implications for Theory.* New York: Springer Verlag.

Hertel, P. (1988) External memory. In M. Gruneberg, P. Morris, and R. Sykes (Eds.) *Practical Aspects of Memory.* Chichester: Wiley.

Hertel, P. (1992) Mood and improving memory. In D. Herrmann, H. Weingartner, A. Searleman, and C. McEvoy (Eds.) *Memory Improvement: Implications for Memory Theory.* New York: Springer Verlag.

Hertzog, C. (1992) Improving memory: The possible roles of metamemory. In D. Herrmann, H. Weingartner, A. Searleman, and C. McEvoy (Eds.) *Memory Improvement: Implications for Memory Theory.* New York: Springer Verlag.

Higbee, K. L. (1981) *What Do College Students Get from a Memory Improvement Course.* New York: Eastern Psychological Association.

Higbee, K. L. (1988) *Your Memory* (2nd edition). Englewood Cliffs, N. J.: Prentice-Hall.

Hodgson, R. & Miller, P. (1982) *Selfwatching.* London: Century Publishing Company.

Howe, M. (Ed.) (1977) *Adult Learning: Psychological Research and Applications.* London: Wiley & Sons.

Hunt, E. & Love, T. (1972) How good can memory be? In A. W. Melton and E. Martin (Eds.) *Coding Processes in Human Memory.* Washington, DC: V. H. Winston & Sons.

Idzikowski, C. (1984) Sleep and memory. *British Journal of Psychology, 75,* 439–449.

Idzikowski, C. (1988) The effects of drugs on human memory. In M. M. Gruneberg, P. E. Morris and R. N. Sykes (Eds) *Practical Aspects of Memory.* Chichester: Wiley.

Intons-Peterson, M. J. & Fournier, J. (1986) External and internal memory aids: When and how often do we use them? *Journal of Experimental Psychology: General, 115,* 267–280.

Intons-Peterson, M. J. & Newsome, G. L. III (1992) External memory aids: Effects and effectiveness. In D. Herrmann, H. Weingartner, A. Searleman and C. McEvoy (Eds.) *Memory Improvement: Implications for Memory Theory.* New York: Springer Verlag.

James, W. (1890) *The Principles of Psychology.* New York: Holt.

Johnson, M. K. & Raye, C. L. (1981) Reality monitoring. *Psychological Review, 88,* 67–85.

Khan, A. U. (1986) *Clinical Disorders of Memory.* New York: Plenum.

Kihlstrom, J. F. & Evans, F. J. (1979) *Functional Disorders of Memory.* Hillsdale, N. J.: Erlbaum.

Klatzky, R. L. (1984) *Memory and Awareness.* New York: W. H. Freeman.

Kolodner, J. L. (1984) *Retrieval and Organizational Strategies in Conceptual Memory: A Computer Model.* Hillsdale, N. J.: Erlbaum.

Lachman, M. E., Steinberg, E. S., & Trotter, S. D. (1987) Effects of control beliefs and attributions on memory self-assessments and performance. *Psychology and Aging, 2,* 266–271.

Landauer, T. K. (1986) How much do people remember? Some estimates of the quantity of learned information in long-term memory. *Cognitive Science, 10,* 477–494.

Lapp, D. (1983) Commitment: Essential ingredient in memory training. *Clinical Gerontologist, 2,* 58–60.

Lave, J. (1988) *Cognition in Practice.* Cambridge, England: Cambridge University Press.

Loftus, E. (1980) *Memory: Surprising New Insights into How We Remember and Why We Forget.* Reading, MA: Wesley.

Loftus, E. F., Banaji, M. R., Schooler, J. W., & Foster, R. A. (1987) Who shall remember?: Gender differences in memory. *Michigan Quarterly Review.*

Loisette, A. (1896) *Assimilative Memory: Or How to Attend and Never Forget.* New York: Funk & Wagnalls.

McEvoy, C. L. (1991) Memory improvement in context: Implications for the development of memory improvement theory. In D. Herrmann, H. Weingartner, A. Searleman, and C. McEvoy (Eds.) *Memroy Improvement: Implications for Memory Theory.* New York: Springer-Verlag.

McWhorter, K. T. (1986) *College Reading and Study Skills.* (3rd ed.). Boston, MA: Little, Brown.

Malone, T. W. (1983) How do people organize their desks? Implications for the design of office information systems. *ACM Transactions on Office Information Systems, 1,* 99–112.

Mandl, H. & Trabasso, T. (Eds.) *Learning and Comprehension of Text.* Hillsdale, N. J.: Erlbaum.

Matlin, M. & Stang, D. (1978) *The Pollyanna Principle.* Cambridge, MA: Schenkman.

Mayes, A. R. (1988) *Human Organic Memory Disorders.* New York: Cambridge University Press.

Meyer, B. J. F., Young, C. J., & Bartlett, B. J. (1989) *Memory Improved: Reading and Memory Enhancement Across the Life Span Through Strategic Text Structures.* Hillsdale, N. J.: Erlbaum.

Middleton, A. E. (1888) *Memory Systems: New and Old.* New York: G. S. Fellows.

Miller, G.A., Galanter, E. & Pribram, K.H. (1960) *Plans and the Structure of Behavior.* New York: Holt.

Morris, P. (1977) Practical strategies for human learning and remembering. In M. Howe (Ed.) *Adult Learning: Psychological Research and Applications.* London: Wiley & Sons.

Morris, P. (1983) The cognitive psychology of self-reports. In J. Harris and P. Morris (Eds.) *Everyday Memory, Actions and Absentmindedness.* London: Academic Press.

Morris, C. D., Bransford, J. D., & Franks, J. J. (1977) Levels of processing versus transfer appropriate processing. *Journal of Verbal Learning and Verbal Behavior, 16,* 519–534.

Neisser, U. & Winograd, E. (1988) *Remembering Reconsidered.* New York: Cambridge University Press.

Neisser, U. (1978). Memory: What are the important questions. In Gruneberg, M. M., Morris, P. E. and Sykes, R. N. (Eds.) *Practical Aspects of Memory.* London: Academic Press.

Neisser, U. (1982) *Memory Observed: Remembering in Natural Contexts.* San Francisco: Freeman.

Nist, S. L. & Diehl, W. (1985) *Developing Textbook Thinking.* Lexington, MA: D. C.: Heath.

Nist, S. L., & Mealey, D. L. (1991) Teacher-directed comprehension strategies. In R. F. Flippo and D. C. Caverly (Eds.) *Teaching Reading & Study Strategies: At the College Level.* Newark, Delaware: International Reading Association.

Norman, D. A. (1982) Learning and Memory. New York: W. H. Freeman.

Park, D. C., Smith, A. D., & Cavanaugh, J. C. (1990) Metamemories of memory researchers. *Memory & Cognition, 18,* 321–327.

Parker, E.S. & Weingartner, H. (1985) Retrograde faulitations of human memory by drugs. In H. Weingartner and E.S. Parker (Eds.) *Memory Consolidation: Psychology of Cognition.* Hillsdale, N. J.: Erlbaum.

Pauk, W. (1984) *How to Study in College* (3rd ed.) Boston, MA: Houghton Mifflin.

Payne, D. (1992) Memory improvement and practice. In D. Herrmann, H. Weingartner, A. Searleman and C. McEvoy (Eds.) *Memory Improvement: Implications for Memory Theory.* New York: Springer Verlag.

Pearson, P. D. (Ed.) (1984) *Handbook of Reading Research.* New York: Longman.

Peeke, S. C. & Peeke, H. V. (1984) Attention, memory, and cigarette smoking. *Psychopharmacology, 84,* 205–216.

Perlmutter, M. (1988) Research on memory and its development: Past, present, and future. In F. E. Weinert and M. Perlmutter (Eds.) *Memory Development: Universal Changes and Individual Differences.* Hillsdale, N. J.: Erlbaum.

Petro, S., Herrmann, D., Burrows, D., & Moore, C. (1991) Usefulness of commercial memory aids as a function of age. *International Journal of Aging and Human Development.*

Plude, D. (1992) Memory improvement and attention training. In D. Herrmann, H. Weingartner, A. Searleman and C. McEvoy (Eds.) *Memory Improvement: Implications for Theory.* New York: Springer Verlag.

Poon, L.W. (1980) A systems approach for the assessment and treatment of memory problems. In J.M. Ferguson and C.B. Taylor (Eds.) *The Comprehensive Handbook of Behavior Medicine, Vol 1* (191–212).

Poon, L. W., Gurland, B. J., Eisdorfer, C., Crook, T., Thompson, L. W., Kaszniak, A. W., & Davis, K. L. (1986) Integration of experimental and clinical precepts in memory assessment: A tribute to George Talland. In L. W. Poon (Ed.) *Handbook for Clinical Memory Assessment of Older Adults*. Washington, DC: American Psychological Association.

Poon, L. W., Rubin, D. C. & Wilson, B. A. (Eds.) (1988) *Everyday Cognition in Adult and Late Life* (The Fifth Talland Conference). New York: Cambridge University Press.

Postman, R. D., Keckler, B., & Schneckner, P. (1985) *College Reading and Study Skills*. New York: Macmillan.

Pressley, M. & Levin, J. R. (1983) *Cognitive Strategy Research*. New York: Springer Verlag.

Pugh, E. (1970) *A Dictionary of Acronyms and Abbreviations*. Clive Bingley Ltd. and Hamden Court: Anchor Books, London.

Raybeck, D. (1981) The ideal and the real: The status of women in Kelantan Malay society. *Women and Poiltics, 1,* 7–21.

Raybeck, D. (1986) The elastic rule: Conformity and deviance in Kelantan village life. In S. Carstens (Ed.) *Cultural Identity in Northern Peninsular Malaysia*. Athens, Ohio: Ohio University Press.

Raybeck, D. (1992a) A diminished dichotomy: Kelantan Malay and traditional Chinese perspectives. In V. Kerns and J. Brown (Eds.) *In Her Prime: New Views of Middle-Aged Women*. Chicago: University of Illinois Press.

Raybeck, D. (1992b) The coconut-shell clock: Time and cultural identity. *Time and Society, 1,* 323–340.

Reason, J. & MyCielska, M. (1983) *Absentmindedness*. Hillsdale, N.J.: Prentice-Hall.

Risko, V. J., Alvarez, M. C., & Fairbanks, M. M. (1991) External factors that influence study. In R. F. Flippo and D. C. Caverly (Eds.) *Teaching Reading & Study Strategies: At the College Level*. Newark, Delaware: International Reading Association.

Rock, I. & Gutman, D. (1981) The effect of inattention on form perception. *Journal of Experimental Psychology, 7,* 275–285.

Rybash, J. M., Hoyer, W. J., & Roodin, P. A. (1986) *Adult Cognition and Aging*. New York: Pergamon.

Schacter, D. L. & Gilsky, E. L. (1986) Memory remediation: Restoration alleviation, and the acquisition of domain-specific knowledge. In *Clinical Neuropsychology of Intervention*. New York: Martibus Nijolf Publishing.

Schank, R. C. (1982) *Dynamic Memory*. Cambridge: Cambridge University Press.

Schoenfeld, A. H. (1985). *Mathematical Problem Solving*. San Diego: Academic Press.

Schneider, W. & Shiffrin, R.M. (1977). Controlled and automatic human information processing: I. Detection, search, and attention. *Psychological Review, 84,* 1–66.

Schooler, J. W., Gerhard, D., & Loftus, E. (1986) Qualities of the unreal.

Journal of Experimental Psychology: Learning, Memory, and Cognition, 12, 171–181.

Searle, J. R. (1969) *Speech Acts.* Cambridge: Cambridge University Press.

Searleman, A. & Herrmann, D. J. (1993, in press) *Memory in a Broader Perspective.* New York: McGraw Hill.

Segal, J.W., Chipman, S.F. & Glaser, R. Eds. (1985) *Thinking and Learning Skills, Volumes 1 and 2.* Hillsdale, N. J.: Erlbaum.

Shepherd, J. F. (1987) *College Study Skills* (3rd ed). Boston, MA: Houghton Mifflin.

Shiffrin, R.M. & Schneider, W. (1977) Controlled and automatic human information processing: II. Perceptual learning, automatic attending and a general theory. *Psychological Review, 84,* 127–190.

Simon, H. A. & Gilmarten, K. (1973) A simulation of memory for chess positions. *Cognitive Psychology, 5,* 29–46.

Smith, A. (1988) Effects of meals on memory and attention. In M. M. Gruneberg, P. E. Morris and R. N. Sykes (Eds.) *Practical Aspects of Memory.* Chichester: Wiley.

Spielberger, C. D., Gonzales, H. P., & Fletcher, T. (1979) Test anxiety reduction, learning strategies, and academic performance. In H. F. O'Neill and C. D. Spielberger (Eds.) *Cognitive and Affective Learning.*

Spilich, G. (1986) Cigarette smoking and memory: Good news and bad news. In G. J Spilich (Chair) *Symposium on "Cognitive and Environmental Agents: Theoretical and Pragmatic Implications."* New York City: American Psychological Association, August.

Squire, L. (1987) *Memory and Brain.* New York: Oxford University Press.

Squire, L. R. & Butters, N. (1984) *Neuropsychology of Memory.* New York: Guilford.

Sternberg, R. J. (1985) *Human Abilities.* New York: W. H. Freeman.

Talland, (1968) *Disorders of Memory.* Harmonsworth, Middlesex: Penguin.

Tulving, E. (1984) How many memory systems are there? *American Psychologist, 40,* 385–398.

Wark, D. M. & Flippo, R. F. (1991) Preparing for and taking tests. In R. F. Flippo and D. C. Caverly (Eds.) *Teaching Reading and Study Strategies: At the College Level.* Newark, Delaware: International Reading Association.

Watson, J. B. (1925) *Behaviorism.* London: Kegan Paul, Trench, Trubner.

Watts, F. N. (1988) Memory deficit in depression. In M. M. Gruneberg, P. E. Morris and R. N. Sykes (Eds.) *Practical Aspects of Memory.* Chichester: Wiley.

Wechsler, D. (1945) A standardized memory scale for clinical use. *Journal of Psychology, 19,* 87–95.

Weinstein, C. E., & Mayer, R. E. (1986) The teaching of learning strategies. In M. C. Wittrock (Ed.) *Handbook of Research on Teaching* (3rd ed.). New York: Macmillan.

Weinstein, C. E., Goetz, E. T., & Alexander, P. A. (1989) *Learning and Study Strategies: Issues in Assessment, Instruction, and Evaluation.* New York: Academic Press.

White, D.R. (1971) *A Glossary of Acronyms, Abbreviations and Symbols.* Germantown, MD: Don White Consultants.

Wilding, J. & Valentine, E. (1988) Searching for superior memories. In M. Grunebery, P. E. Morris and R. N. Sykes (Eds.) *Practical Aspects of Memory.* Chichester: Wiley.

Wilson, B. A. (1987) *The Rehabilitation of Memory.* New York: Guilford.

Wilson, B. & Moffat, N. (1984) *Clinical Management of Memory Problems.* Rockville, MD: Aspen Systems.

Winograd, E. & Soloway, R. M. (1985) Hiding things from ourselves: Objects and special places. *Journal of Experimental Psychology: General, 115,* 366–372.

Wittenborn, J. R. (1988) Assessment of the effects of drugs on memory. *Psychopharmacology, 6,* 67–78.

Wyer, R. S. & Srull, T. K. (1986) Human cognition in its social context. *Psychological Review, 93,* 322–359.

Wyer, R. S. & Srull, T. K. (1989) *Memory and Cognition: In Its Social Context.* Hillsdale, NJ: Erlbaum.

Wyon, D.P., Andersen, B., & Lundqvist, G.R. (1979) The effects of moderate heat stress on mental performance. *Scandanavian Journal of Work Environment and Health, 5,* 352–361.

Yates, F. (1966) *The Arts of Memory.* Chicago: Chicago University Press.

Yesavage, J. A., Sheikh, J. I., & Lapp, D. (1990) Mnemonics as modified for use by the elderly. In L. Poon, D. Rubin, and B. Wilson (Eds.) *Everyday Cognition in Adult and Late Life.* New York: Cambridge.

Yesavage, J.A., Rose, T.L., & Spiegel, D. (1982). Relaxation training and memory improvement in elderly normals: Correlations of anxiety ratings and recall improvement. *Experimental Aging Research.*

Young, M. N. & Gibson, W. B. (1962) *How to Develop an Exceptional Memory.* Hollywood: Wilshire Books.

Zarit, S. H., Gallagher, D., & Kramer, N. (1981) Memory training in the community aged: Effects on depression, memory complaint, and memory performance. *Educational Gerontology, 6,* 11–27.

Index